EARL OF ROCHESTER: THE CRITICAL HERITAGE

THE CRITICAL HERITAGE SERIES

General Editor: B. C. Southam

The Critical Heritage series collects together a large body of criticism on major figures in literature. Each volume presents the contemporary responses to a particular writer, enabling the student to follow the formation of critical attitudes to the writer's work and its place within a literary tradition.

The carefully selected sources range from landmark essays in the history of criticism to fragments of contemporary opinion and little published documentary material, such as letters and diaries.

Significant pieces of criticism from later periods are also included in order to demonstrate fluctuations in reputation following the writer's death.

EARL OF ROCHESTER

THE CRITICAL HERITAGE

Edited by

DAVID FARLEY-HILLS

Routledge
Taylor & Francis Group
LONDON AND NEW YORK

First Published in 1972
Reprinted in 1995 by Routledge

2 Park Square, Milton Park, Abingdon, Oxfordshire OX14 4RN
&
711 Third Avenue, New York, NY 10017

First issued in paperback 2014

Routledge is an imprint of the Taylor & Francis Group, an informa business

British Library Cataloguing in Publication Data

ISBN 13: 978-0-415-13429-3 (hbk)
ISBN 13: 978-0-415-75667-9 (pbk)

Publisher's Note

The publisher has gone to great lengths to ensure the quality of this reprint but points out that some imperfections in the original may be apparent

General Editor's Preface

The reception given to a writer by his contemporaries and near-contemporaries is evidence of considerable value to the student of literature. On one side we learn a great deal about the state of criticism at large and in particular about the development of critical attitudes towards a single writer; at the same time, through private comments in letters, journals or marginalia, we gain an insight upon the tastes and literary thought of individual readers of the period. Evidence of this kind helps us to understand the writer's historical situation, the nature of his immediate reading-public, and his response to these pressures.

The separate volumes in the *Critical Heritage Series* present a record of this early criticism. Clearly, for many of the highly productive and lengthily reviewed nineteenth- and twentieth-century writers, there exists an enormous body of material; and in these cases the volume editors have made a selection of the most important views, significant for their intrinsic critical worth or for their representative quality—perhaps even registering incomprehension!

For earlier writers, notably pre-eighteenth century, the materials are much scarcer and the historical period has been extended, sometimes far beyond the writer's lifetime, in order to show the inception and growth of critical views which were initially slow to appear.

In each volume the documents are headed by an Introduction discussing the material assembled and relating the early stages of the author's reception to what we have come to identify as the critical tradition. The volumes will make available much material which would otherwise be difficult of access and it is hoped that the modern reader will be thereby helped towards an informed understanding of the ways in which literature has been read and judged.

B.C.S.

Contents

ACKNOWLEDGMENTS

I would like to thank Dr Malcolm Errington and my colleagues in the Department of English, the Queen's University of Belfast, Basil Bigg and Roger Prior, for their help. I am also extremely grateful to Mrs Cilla Craig and Miss Vera Gordon for their patience and skill during the vicissitudes of preparing the typescript.

NOTE ON THE TEXT

In most cases I have used the earliest texts available. Where there are later editions of any work I have generally checked the earliest edition with them, using later readings if these seemed clearer for modern readers. The texts have been left largely unaltered, except that long 's' (ſ) wherever it occurred has been changed to short 's' and apostrophes supplied for possessives. In the few cases where there are established modern texts, as with the Scott–Saintsbury edition of Dryden or Osborn's edition of Spence's *Anecdotes*, I have used them. For quotation and reference to Rochester's own poetry I have used Pinto's edition of the poems (second edition, revised 1964) as the most readily obtainable for the reader. This is referred to as Pinto throughout.

Introduction

The history of Rochester criticism illustrates almost all the ways imaginable in which the critic can be deflected from a reasonably objective view of the poetry. Accordingly, this collection of critical comments on Rochester from his contemporaries through to the beginning of the twentieth century contains comparatively little that can help the modern reader to come to a fair estimate of the poems as poems, but is a mine of information both about the ways criticism can be deflected by non-critical considerations—ethical or religious bias, the inadequate or ill-judged application of historical or biographical information—and at the same time it is a record of changing attitudes, moral and aesthetic, over more than two centuries. In selecting the material I have been concerned firstly to give an adequate and representative coverage of critical opinion over these years. To have confined myself to the contemporary response to Rochester's poetry would have been to record critical judgment at its most partial, for during his lifetime Rochester was even more controversial as a man than as a poet. While he was alive, it was almost impossible to judge his literary achievement without entering into the controversies that surrounded him as a patron of literature, notorious rake, reputed atheist and finally Christian penitent; and even after his death criticism remained as much concerned with his character as with his poetry.

A surprising amount of comment on his own contemporaries is still extant, more perhaps than for any other literary figure of the Restoration, though by modern standards the record is meagre and confusingly mixed with biographical tittle-tattle and non-literary polemic. I have tried to include as much of this early material as possible, both because of its intrinsic interest and because some of it is hard to come by. Just as interesting, though often just as confused, is the response of subsequent generations, and there are valiant attempts over the years, by Thomas Rymer, by Dr Johnson to some extent, by Emile Forgues, for instance, to free literary judgments from the religious and moral dogma. Modern criticism can be dated roughly from the time when the critic could escape from the clutch of moral bigotry and read the poetry without either being excited by the promise of pornography or being blinkered by the assumption of moral superiority. By 1903—the date of the last two pieces in this collection—to defend Rochester's poetry was no longer regarded as perverse; nor was there a virtue in simply condemning it. But it is not finally, I think, until Whibley's excellent essay on 'The Court Poets' in volume 8 of the *Cambridge History of English Literature* (1912) that one gets the feeling, at least in extended critical discussion, that here at last is a critic willing to take the poetry on its own merits and quite independently of the myth that had grown up round Rochester's life. It is appropriate therefore to end on the threshold of modern critical attitudes with two pieces that show vividly both the continuing prejudices that surrounded the poet, illustrated from Thomas Longueville's book (No. 78), and a fair example of the attempts being made to see Rochester's work for its true worth. Courthorpe in this last extract (No. 79) is still referring to 'floods of indescribable filth' in the accepted nineteenth-century manner, but he is also attempting to come to genuinely literary judgments. With Whibley therefore I feel we arrive at a new phase of Rochester criticism, the modern phase, with its increasing understanding of Rochester as a literary artist.

EDITIONS OF THE POETRY

The availability of Rochester's poetry and the critical comments follow a related pattern: until the middle of the eighteenth century there were many editions; then came a gradual falling off, until the nineteenth century, when there were very few reprints; and it is not until the twentieth century that his poetry has become readily available again. Similarly, during his lifetime and in the first part of the eighteenth century he was a much discussed figure both as man and poet; between 1750 and 1850 interest waned, and what comment there was tended to become increasingly hostile. Thomas Park's judgment in 1806 that 'This Lord's licentious productions too forcibly warrant the sentence of outlawry that decorum and taste have passed upon them' (No. 52) seems to sum up the prevailing opinion. After 1850 interest begins to pick up and once again the record becomes fuller and more rewarding.

There is no complete bibliography of Rochester's writings, and the complex relationship of the various texts has never been thoroughly explored, although in *Attribution in Restoration Poetry* David Vieth has established three major lines of descent for the seventeenth- and earlier eighteenth-century editions. The overall picture is clear, however. The publications in the seventeenth century are more or less honest attempts to collect together what was known or assumed to be by Rochester. No collection of the poetry was published during his lifetime, though some of his lyrics found their way into miscellanies and several of his poems were printed in single sheet issues, 'broadsides', before 1680. Almost immediately after his death a collection of poems was issued described as *Poems on several Occasions by the Right Honourable the E. of R—*.[1] This purported to come from Antwerp, though it, and several subsequent editions, were in fact printed surreptitiously in London. The 1680 'editions', of which there were at least ten, provide the best editions before the twentieth century in spite of their surreptitious entry into the world, their obvious bid for the market in pornography, and though they are in fact anthologies and not solely Rochester's work. A new and in some ways more careful edition of the poetry, heavily bowdlerized, and therefore less comprehensive or authentic, was published by Jacob Tonson with an (unsigned) introduction by Thomas Rymer in 1691. These two texts, with reprints in 1695 and 1696, are the chief seventeenth-century printed sources. A large number of manuscript collections containing Rochester's poetry also survive from the period. Gentlemen writers were not expected to publish for profit and besides, censorship laws during Charles II's reign discouraged publication of the satire and pornography that featured largely in this court poetry. In addition to the poems, Rochester's play *Valentinian* was published separately in 1685 and a collection of letters in 1697 and 1699.

The beginning of the eighteenth century saw a flood of Rochester publications. These editions can be divided into those that are primarily concerned to make Rochester's poetry available as literature and those supplying the pornographic market. In the early eighteenth century, the literary texts derive from Tonson's edition, six reprints of which were published, with alterations, up to 1732. Next, in 1779, came Steevens's extensive selection with a preface by Dr Johnson (No. 47). A number of later selections are based on this edition. The pornographic texts were mostly published under the title *The Works of the Earls of Rochester and Roscommon*, of which there are at least twenty-eight separate editions following the first in 1707. Altogether between 1700 and 1750 there were at least twenty-seven editions of the poetry, excluding smaller selections; and between 1750 and 1800 there were about seventeen, if we include the extensive selection in Steevens's edition and the selections that derive from it. Between 1800 and 1850 there were only five editions —all selections—and between 1850 and 1900 only two extensive selections, though a few of his poems appeared in anthologies. Since 1900 the number of editions has risen again and there have been at least eleven editions either of the complete poems or of a substantial selection of them. There have also been editions of the complete works and of the Rochester-Savile correspondence.

BIOGRAPHICAL LITERATURE

Like the editions, the literature on Rochester himself can be divided into the clean and the unclean. On the one hand there is the series of religious homilies, which retell the story of Rochester's death-bed suffering and repentance, both to warn the reader of the dangers of the immoral life and to illustrate the Christian thesis that it is never too late to repent. On the other hand there are the accounts of Rochester's life that lay stress on his amatory or bacchic adventures (with incidents often invented by the writer) clearly designed for the same readers that bought the pornographic poetry. This titillating 'Rochesteriana', which continues throughout the eighteenth century and into the nineteenth, often threw up works of almost pure invention, such as William Dugdale's obscene *Singular Life, Amatory Adventures and Extraordinary Intrigues of John Wilmot* (1864). In the nineteenth century, too, there were a number of novels concerning Rochester's life. Perhaps the oddest of all these fictions is the series of stories said by a certain Mlle Kruizhanovskaya, a medium, to have been dictated to her, presumably in French, by the poet's spirit.[2] Apparently Rochester was a name to conjure with even in the reign of Queen Victoria.

Just as odd in their own way are the religious tracts that tell of Rochester's wicked life and spectacular conversion. These too went on into the nineteenth century with such publications as *The Repentance and Happy Death of the Celebrated Earl of Rochester* (1814), several times reprinted, and *The Conversion of the Earl of Rochester* (1840), a Religious Tract Society publication (No. 61). The earliest attempt to present Rochester's life as a religious parable was Gilbert Burnet's *Some Passages of the Life and Death . . . of Rochester* (No. 10), which Johnson extolled as a masterpiece in its own right. This is the most informative and valuable early document on Rochester, but we should remember that its prime purpose, like the later tracts, was to disseminate Christian propaganda. It was immensely popular and went on reprinting until the second half of the nineteenth century. Its popularity seems to have been at a height between 1800 and 1820, at the very time when interest in the poetry was at its nadir. Obviously it was thought that the poetry and the piety did not mix. Almost as popular as Burnet's work, and often reprinted with it, was Robert Parsons's funeral sermon (No. 9).

Because attitudes towards Rochester's poetry were closely bound up with attitudes towards him as a man, the editor faces the problem of where to draw the line between biographical and critical material. Generally I have tried to avoid the salacious or hagiological gossip, but occasionally I have included biographical excerpts either because they contain interesting observations on Rochester's writings or because they throw light on Rochester's literary personality. Aubrey's brief life (No. 29) and the excerpt from Wood's *Athenae Oxonienses* (No. 27) also provide the basic facts of Rochester's life and can be used as points of reference whenever biographical information is wanted. Burnet's *Life* is given entire as a key document for the understanding of Rochester's state of mind. It is not really a conventional *Life* but a series of interviews in which Rochester talks about his own attitudes and is given the orthodox, if sometimes cooked-up, replies point by point by Burnet.

EARLY PRAISE

The critical material falls into four main periods. The early period, running roughly from the early 1670s, when his poetry is first commented on, to the end of the seventeenth century, is distinguished by its partisanship. Writers are either strongly for or equally strongly against Rochester as both man and writer. We can never know whether men like Sir Francis Fane or John Crowne really believed their flattery of Rochester's genius; they were interested parties; and when Dryden tells Rochester he is 'above any incense I can give you' (No. 3b), we can only recall that within four or five years he is referring to Rochester's poetic gifts as 'a trifling kind of fancy' (No. 3c). There is, however, rather more consistency about Dryden's attitude to Rochester than might be supposed from this contrast. Even in the flattering Dedication of *Marriage à la Mode*, Dryden slily puts the emphasis not on Rochester's achievement, but on his potential and this, it is suggested, will remain as potential because Rochester is 'above the narrow praises which poesy could give you' (No. 3a). For Dryden, Rochester is the amateur, the dilettante, who can afford to dabble in poetry but whose dabblings no self-respecting professional would take too seriously. Dryden with his sense of the high seriousness of poetry was also expert at demolishing a rival's reputation (poor Shadwell, of enviable talents, has still not recovered from the drubbing he got in *Mac Flecknoe*) and Rochester, a much more formidable opponent in every way, has also suffered in his literary reputation through Dryden's well calculated slurs. The exact cause of Dryden's quarrel with Rochester is unknown, but on the evidence of his Preface to *All for Love*, Dryden took great offence at Rochester's lines in the *Allusion to Horace* (1675). This poem is a clever adaptation of the tenth satire of book one of Horace's *Satires*. It begins:

Well Sir, 'tis granted, I said D[*ryden's*] Rhimes,
Were stoln, unequal, nay, dull many times:
What foolish *Patron*, is there found of his,
So blindly partial, to deny me this?
But that his *Plays*, embroider'd up and down,
With *Wit* and *Learning*, justly pleas'd the *Town*,
In the same *Paper*, I as freely own,
Yet having this allow'd, the heavy *Mass*,
That stuffs up his loose volumes must not pass.[3]

Later in the poem Rochester returns to his attack to scoff at Dryden's attempts to emulate the humour of the Wits. The following lines (71–80), however, are complimentary by the standards of the age:

D[*ryden*], in vain try'd this nice way of wit,
For he to be a tearing *Blade* thought fit,
But when he would be sharp, he still was blunt:
To frisk his frollique fancy, he'd cry Cunt,
Wou'd give the *Ladies*, a dry *Bawdy* bob,
And thus he got the name of *Poet Squab*.
But to be just, 'twill to his praise be found,
His *Excellencies* more than faults abound;
Nor dare I from his sacred temples tear
That *Lawrel*, which he best deserves to wear.

In his Preface Dryden pretends that he thinks the author of the *Allusion* is one of Rochester's 'zanies' but he must have known its real author. In fact, Rochester's attack was not as severe as it has been made out to be by the satirical standards of the time, and Dryden is perhaps being a little over-touchy.

Sometimes the contemporary compliments to Rochester are sincere. In the opinion of Marvell (recorded in Aubrey's *Brief Life of Marvell*) 'the Earl of Rochester was the only man in England that had the true veine of satyre'. Marvell's compliment is that of the sophisticated practitioner of poetry, while Pepys's regretful 'As he is past writing any more so bad in one sense, so I despair of any man surviving him to write so good in another' (Letter to W. Hewer, 4 November 1680) probably reflects the feelings of countless ordinary readers until well on into the eighteenth century, to judge by the frequency of the editions. The other great Restoration diarist, John Evelyn, merely records that Rochester was 'a very profane wit'. Allusions to Rochester are frequent in the popular satire of the time as we can see in the recent Yale collection of *Poems on Affairs of State* as well as excerpts given in this collection (Nos. 6, 20). An anonymous commentator has scrawled on a copy of Mulgrave's *An Essay upon Satire* now in the British Museum library (Harleian MS 7317) a reference to Rochester as 'One of the finest men England ever bred, a great and admir'd Wit. . .'[4] Another less complimentary remark from a satire of the late 1680s, 'The Reformation of Manners', tells us 'One man reads Milton, forty Rochester' (*Poems on Affairs of State*, 1703, ii. 371). There is a record, even at this early date, of Rochester's poetry crossing the Atlantic. In a commonplace book of a New Englander, John Saffin (1632–1740), ten rather garbled lines of the poem *Upon Nothing* are written down without comment, suggesting perhaps oral transmission.[5]

During his lifetime any compliment to Rochester, like Lee's dedication of his tragedy *Nero* (No. 2a), is clearly suspect, but Lee's praise in the *Princess of Cleves* (No. 2b) referring to his death, is a touching public tribute. The spate of funeral elegies in 1680 are perhaps the most eloquent witness to his popularity as a poet. These are from a wide ranging section of the literary world. It was not only courtiers who lamented 'Strephon's' passing: Oldham and Aphra Behn were professional poets —Oldham, a staunchly independent moralist, Aphra Behn a playwright with some aspirations towards inclusion among the wits. Ann Wharton, a relative of Rochester, was an aristocratic amateur poet of melancholic rather than witty tendencies. Flatman was an Oxford academic far removed from the London Court, while his friend Samuel Woodford was an Anglican priest. Of the prose commemorators Burnet and Parsons also were priests. The only tribute from the circle of wit proper was Wolseley's Preface to *Valentinian*.

All this suggests that Rochester was accepted as a major poet by a wide cross-section of the reading public of his day and not just by a small fashionable clique, as has sometimes been assumed. Some of the elegies—those of Flatman (No. 17), Samuel Woodford (No. 18), Samuel Holland (No. 19)—stress the Christian significance of his life; as such, they give little information on Rochester as a writer, except to witness fo his great reputation as a literary figure. Much more interesting are the tour elegies that concentrate on his literary achievement and influence, and of these Oldham's *Bion* (No. 12) is the most interesting of all. Oldham, in the *Satire against Virtue*, 1676, had brilliantly attacked the poet's immorality by using Rochester's own technique of impersonation: the poem takes the form of a speech by Rochester himself attacking virtue. In the elegy Oldham has paid generous homage to the man who taught him how to write poetry:

If I am reckon'd not unblest in Song,
'Tis what I ow to thy all-teaching tongue,
Others thy Flocks, thy Lands, thy Riches have,
To me thou didst thy Pipe, and Skill vouchsafe.

Aphra Behn's elegy, in sprightly verse, concentrates on the loss of a great satirist:

Satyr has lost its art, its sting is gone,
The Fop and Cully now may be undone; [i.e. unportrayed]
That dear instructing Rage is now allay'd,
And no sharp Pen does tell 'em how they've stray'd . . .

It is surprising how often contemporaries of 'the mad Earl' (as Hearne liked to call him) stress his role as teacher and reformer. Anne Wharton's lines have this emphasis, celebrating his learning, his natural ability and his 'instructing' purpose, but like Aphra Behn she seems to think of him first as a satirist. Of all these elegies hers had the longest currency, still appearing in nineteenth-century editions of Rochester's poems (for example *The Cabinet of Love*, 1821) and the complimentary lines it inspired from Waller, Jack Howe and Robert Wolseley (Nos. 14b–d) seem to suggest that it was regarded with special favour by her contemporaries. Anne Wharton was a relative of Rochester and presumably knew him personally. The fourth elegy, the anonymous 'Alas what dark benighting Clouds or shade' (No. 15), while it also mentions that Rochester's purpose was 'to correct the proud' and celebrates his great poetic talent, hovers between a literary and eschatological interest in Rochester. Its account of Rochester's personal virtues strains our credulity, but here and there there are some informative hints about the contemporary response to the poetry, such as the suggestion that some found the verse obscure and needing the author's exposition (possibly a reference to the paradoxical *Satire against Mankind*).

Burnet's so-called *Life* and Parsons's funeral sermon on Rochester must also be considered as elegies (in his Preface Burnet refers to his work as 'celebrating the praises of the dead') and like some of the verse elegies their purpose is to stress the Christian significance of Rochester's life and death. Rochester had only been dead a couple of months when we find John Tillotson, later Archbishop of Canterbury, entering into his commonplace book for 1 October 1680: 'My Lord of Rochester . . . the greatest instance any age hath afforded: not for his own sake, as St. Paul was not, who yet was no enemy to God and religion, but by mistake. I cannot think, but that it was intended for some greater good to others' (Birch's *Life of Tillotson*, 1752, p. 74). And Rochester was scarcely dead when Tillotson was writing to a friend on 2 August, 'I am sorry, that an example, which might have been of so much use and advantage to the world, is so soon taken from us' (Birch, p. 73). Similarly Rochester's friend George Saville, Earl of Halifax, referring to Rochester's death in a letter to Burnet, is more concerned with the repentance than with the poetry (Marshall, *A Supplement to the History of Woodstock Manor*, 1874, p. 28). It was inevitable in an age as dominated by Christian thinking as the Restoration that this emphasis should be placed on the religious significance of Rochester's life. Burnet's most valuable contribution is the insight he gives us into the kind of mind that produced the poetry, a mind which combines an earnest, almost desperate desire to believe in something, with a tough scepticism that refuses to allow him to accept anything that his intellect does not fully understand. Burnet brings out Rochester's honesty both in his understanding of his own motives and in his frankness in talking about them: 'he would often break forth into such hard expressions concerning himself, as would be indecent for another to repeat' (p. 73). A remarkable example of this self-criticism is preserved in the gruesome 'Conference with a Post Boy' (Pinto, lxxx). Burnet takes Rochester's poetic genius for granted, remarking that 'few men ever had a bolder flight of fancy more steadily governed by judgment than he had.' The mention of judgment (intellectual control) is worth remarking and conforms with the picture Burnet gives of Rochester as a studious and not unlearned man, as well as a debauchee. Parsons's much shorter sermon (No. 9), though it is much less informative about the man, is as informative about the poet. Again the poetry is highly praised, Parsons singling out the importance of paradox. But his rather questionable belief that Rochester would have become a great religious poet is prompted by his desire to emphasize the sincerity of Rochester's conversion to Christianity. It is Parsons who records Rochester's death-bed wish that his 'profane and lewd writings' should be burnt (*Sermon*, 1680, pp. 28–9). Like Anne Wharton, Burnet and later Antony Wood (echoing Parsons), Parsons emphasizes not only Rochester's natural talents, but his learning and application 'rare, if not peculiar to him, amongst those of his quality'. Others who knew him differed about this. Dryden, we have already seen, had no great opinion of the seriousness of his attitudes and Rochester's tutor, Gifford, maintained that 'my Lord understood very little or no Greek, and that he had but little Latin, and therefore 'tis a great mistake in making him (as Burnet and Wood have done) so great a Master of Classick Learning' (*Hearne's Remarks and Collections*, ed. C. E. Doble, 1889, iii. 263). Hearne backs this up with an opinion of a 'Mr. Collins of Magdalen' that Rochester 'understood little or nothing of Greek' (*ibid.* iii. 273).

ATTACK AND DEFENCE

Just as Rochester inspired eulogy from his contemporaries, so he also found himself under constant attack. It would have been surprising if a man whose opinions and behaviour were so unorthodox had escaped censure, given the authoritarian temper of the age. The attacks are usually of two kinds: attacks on his personality (accusations of cowardice, malice, atheism, licentiousness) or attacks, like Dryden's and Mulgrave's, on his alleged incompetence as a poet. His controversial personality gave rise to a large number of poems in which he is satirized, sometimes gently and sympathetically by friends like Sedley and the Earl of Dorset, sometimes with great asperity, as in the attacks of Scroope and Mulgrave. Rochester's ability to inspire enmity among the professional writers is illustrated not only by Dryden's attack, but also in Otway's bitter condemnation of him as 'Lord Lampoon' in *The Poet's Complaint to his Muse*. Employing a device Rochester had himself developed, Oldham, in the *Satire on Virtue*, uses Rochester as a persona for condemning himself. The convention was continued after his death in poems like *Rochester's Ghost* (1682) and the poem of Thomas Durfey included in this collection (No. 25). In these poems Rochester's ghost returns to earth to condemn his own past life and the conduct of other debauchees. Sometimes the device is used simply to condemn others, as in 'Rochester's Farewell' (1680). Vieth gives a full account of this anti-Rochester literature in his *Attribution in Restoration Poetry* (ch. 6).

Robert Wolseley's 'Preface', attached to the publication of Rochester's play *Valentinian* in 1685, is the first extended criticism of Rochester's work. It is not an attempt at an impartial assessment but a defence of the poetry against Mulgrave's attacks in the *Essay upon Poetry* (1682) (No. 7b) and to a lesser extent in the *Essay upon Satire* (1679) (No. 7a). In the *Essay upon Poetry* Mulgrave concentrates his attention on the bawdiness of Rochester's songs and implies that Rochester lacked wit (meaning poetic invention). Wolseley, though he refers to Rochester's fame as a satirist, is primarily concerned to defend the lyric poetry on the grounds that excellence in poetry is independent of content and that the ability to make a good poem out of uncongenial material is the hallmark of the great poet. The ingenuity or wit of the poet to make something out of nothing is a common theme in Renaissance criticism. It is well expressed in Philip Massinger's lines in praise of a burlesque poem:

> It shewed more art in Virgil to relate,
> And make it worth the hearing, his Gnat's fate;
> Then to conceive what those great Mindes must be
> That sought and found out fruit full Italie.[6]

Paradoxical poetry, praising 'things without honour', was an established genre in the sixteenth and seventeenth centuries—Rochester's *Upon Nothing* and Donne's *Nocturnal upon St. Lucie's Day* are two widely differing examples of this kind.[7] Wolseley's defence is thus couched in aesthetic terms; he defends Rochester's poetic inventiveness. While he concedes that objection may be made against the content of Rochester's poetry on moral gounds (pp. 195–6), he argues that his poetic genius is too well known and too widely admitted to be brought into question. Throughout the essay he is not so much attempting to demonstrate Rochester's greatness as a poet as trying to demolish Mulgrave's objections.

Rymer's 'Preface' to the 1691 edition of the poems attempts a more dispassionately critical approach to the poetry. Unfortunately the exact circumstances of Rymer's commission are unknown. The 1691 volume of Rochester's poems, *Poems etc. on Several Occasions*, published by Jacob Tonson, has until recently been treated as the best early edition of the poetry. Prinz and Pinto suggest that it may have been 'produced with the approval of the Earl's family and friends' (Pinto ed., xli), but there is no real evidence for this. There is no doubt that it was a genuine attempt to produce a standard collection of Rochester's poetry that would be acceptable to the reading public at large, and Rymer's 'Preface', with its stress on the literary value of the poems, would help to establish the serious nature of the publication. Tonson, who was presumably the editor, was a reputable publisher and the bowdlerization that characterizes it would certainly be regarded as a virtue in the 1690s. Thomas Rymer seems to have known one of Rochester's intimates, Sir Fleetwood Shepherd; it is not known whether he knew Rochester himself. He is most likely to have been asked to contribute the Preface as the most distinguished English critic of literature next to Dryden—who could hardly have been expected to praise his old enemy. Whether Rymer was chosen because he was sympathetic, or was sympathetic because he was chosen there is no way of telling. The Preface is objective in its approach, hinting at Rochester's lack of discipline as a poet, a charge related to the earlier charge of 'amateurism', but also—and correctly—stressing the extraordinary energy, 'a strength, a spirit, and manly vigour' of Rochester's style. This is the central quality of Rochester's satire (as it must be of any great poet) and significantly, it is primarily the satire that Rymer discusses. In a more general way at the end of the Preface he mentions the paradoxical element in Rochester's poetry, the enigmatic interplay of serious and comic, so perceptively that we wish the Preface had been longer.

REPUTATION IN THE EARLY EIGHTEENTH CENTURY

In the last decade of the seventeenth century Rochester's reputation seemed to suffer a minor eclipse. This can be understood partly as the effect of the piety and seriousness of the court of William and Mary. The new poetic fashions persuaded even Swift, the greatest comic genius of the age, to try his hand at solemn Pindarics. For this short period the cultural climate was characterized by a prudery more Victorian than Restoration or Augustan. We should not be surprised that the young Addison (whom C. S. Lewis has characterized as a Victorian before his time) fails to mention John Wilmot in his galaxy of English Poets in *An Account of the Greatest English Poets* (1694), and that Samuel Cobb omits him from his *Poetae Britannici* of 1700. In spite of this temporary eclipse, there is evidence at the turn of the century that Rochester is still being widely read and some evidence about who is reading him. Joseph Addison later occasionally mentions Rochester and acknowledges (in a *Spectator* essay, 1712), that *Upon Nothing* is an 'admirable Poem' though 'upon that barren subject'. His friend Steele twice quotes the lines on Sedley from the *Allusion to Horace* in the same *Spectator* essays, for Steele Rochester's poetry seems to have had a particular fascination, and there are a number of references to Rochester in Steele's work.[8]

That another popular writer, Daniel Defoe, held Rochester in great esteem can be seen from the excerpts from the *Review* quoted (No. 35). Moll Flanders twice refers to Rochester, quoting two lines from *Artemesia* on love (Everyman ed., p. 62) and lines from the song 'Phyllis, be gentler, I advise' (Everyman ed., p. 55). That Moll could be expected to know Rochester's poetry so well, and that readers of Defoe's novels should be able to pick up the allusion suggests a very wide reading audience for Rochester in the 1720s. Even as late as 1749 Fielding expects his reader to pick up a casual reference in *Tom Jones* (Everyman. i. 104). This, however, like Rochester's influence on the libertine heroes in Richardson's *Pamela* and *Clarissa*, is more a tribute to Rochester's notoriety as a man than to his fame as a poet. References to Rochester over the period are more common in popular than in polite literature, but it is strange that Swift makes no references to him, because his work shows Rochester's influence.

Rochester's reputation as a poet reached a peak in the 1720s. Voltaire's estimate of him as a man of genius and great poet (No. 41), a view that was no doubt picked up during his stay in England between 1726 and 1729, probably reflects the prevailing opinion of polite society at that time in England. His assertion in the epistle on Rochester and Waller that Rochester's name is 'universally known' is exaggerated, but Rochester was familiar to French-speaking audiences not only through the writings of St Evremond which Voltaire mentions, but in Hamilton's *Memoirs of Grammont* (No. 36). St Evremond held Rochester in high esteem, writing in a letter to Ninon de Lanclos in 1698 that he 'had more wit than any man in England' (*Letters of Saint Evremond*, ed. Hayward, (1930), p. 323). Grammont, a French nobleman who spent some time in exile at Charles II's Court, expresses his admiration for Rochester more equivocally. Edmund Waller, in a letter to St Evremond, recalls a dinner conversation in which Grammont told Rochester that 'if he could by any means divest himself of one half of his wit, the other half would make him the most agreeable man in the world' ('Stephen Collet' [Thomas Byerley] *Relics of Literature*, (1823), p. 52). Rochester is also briefly mentioned in Bayle's encyclopaedic *Dictionary* (No. 33), and there were translations into French of Burnet's *Life* published in 1716 and 1743. There were also translations of the *Life* into German in 1698, 1732, 1735 and 1775 and into Dutch. None of Rochester's poetry was available in French until 1753 and the *Satire against Mankind* was published in a German prose translation in 1757.

In England Rochester continued to be championed as a poet and wit throughout the first half of the eighteenth century. The veteran critic John Dennis uses Rochester's name to illustrate the brilliance of the Restoration literary scene in contrast to what he regarded as the literary decadence of his own generation (No. 32). In *The Advancement and Reformation of Modern Poetry* (1701), (No. 32b) Dennis attacks Rochester's immorality, but this work is addressed to Rochester's arch-enemy Mulgrave and is not consistent with Dennis's usual attitudes. Comment on Rochester's poetry from 1700 to 1750 is almost always complimentary and even Giles Jacob (No. 38), while he deplores the immorality of the Restoration, is nonetheless full of admiration for Rochester's poetry. Most indicative of the general esteem of the 1720s and '30s is the learned Spence's shocked reaction to Pope's suggestion that the Earl of Dorset was the better poet: 'What, better than Rochester?' (1734), (No. 40). Spence's high regard for Rochester's poetry is evident in the *Historical Remarks on the English Poets* (1732–3), (No. 40) where he is singled out for praise as exceptional even in an age that was 'very rich in satire'.

There were, in this period, as we might expect, strong reservations about Rochester's character as a man and about the immorality of some of his poetry. These doubts are illustrated by a delightful remark of the Duchess of Montagu in a letter to her daughter-in-law Lady Mary in 1724: the Duchess describes a marriage of which she disapproves as 'the nastiest thing I ever heard in my life . . . There is nothing in my Lord Rochester's verses that makes one more ashamed.' But generally reservations about the immorality of the man and his poetry are not allowed to qualify the praise for the quality of the verse.

Pope's attitudes to Rochester are equivocal. The remarks recorded by Spence are mostly unflattering, or, at best, faint praise. Like Dryden, Pope seems to have considered Rochester a dilettante in literature, calling him a 'holiday writer' (No. 40d) and dismissing the whole tradition of the courtly wit of 'either Charles's days' (*Imitations of Horace II*, i. 108) as 'The Mob of Gentlemen who wrote with ease'. Elsewhere Pope comments on Rochester's 'bad versification' (No. 40e), though from Pope's point of view this meant not adopting as strict a view of the heroic couplet as his own. His early verses *On Silence* are deliberately modelled on *Upon Nothing* and his allusions to Rochester in the *Imitations of Horace*, written between 1733 and 1738, show that the poetry recurred to him late in life. At some stage in his career, too, he took the trouble to annotate his copy of the 1696 edition of Rochester's poems (now in the New York Public Library). Even more interestingly Pope took considerable pains in his own revised version of Mulgrave's *Essay upon*

Satire, which he published in his edition of Mulgrave's works (1723), to omit all censure of Rochester's poetry. For instance Mulgrave's line:

> Rochester I despise for his mere want of wit.

becomes in Pope's version:

> Last enters Rochester of sprightly wit.

A curious poem written about 1739 shows Pope's ambivalent attitude to Rochester. He calls the poem 'On lying in the Earl of Rochester's Bed at Atterbury' and tells us rather contradictorily:

> That here he lov'd, or here expir'd,
> Begets no numbers grave or gay.

Another of Pope's friends (later his enemy) Lady Mary Wortley Montagu shows a knowledge of Rochester's poetry: in a letter of 1759 alluding (it seems) to *Artemesia* and expecting the allusion to be understood, and in an earlier letter (1752), she gives it as her opinion that Richardson's *Pamela* will do more harm than the works of Rochester.

OPINIONS 1750–1800

By the 1750s, however, Lady Mary's views were definitely behind the times, for by now sympathy with Rochester's libertine attitudes and comic view of life was on the wane. Not only his immoral career, but the poetry itself, tended to be condemned outright on moral grounds. Even among his contemporaries there were people who attacked the poetry as immoral. Mulgrave we have already seen, attacked Rochester for the obscenity of his songs. But more typical of this early period is the equivocal attitude that Pepys expresses of a writer so good in one sense, so bad in another. Anthony Wood records the same mixed reaction:

> They [the poems of the 1680 volume] are full of obscenity and prophaneness, and are more fit (tho' excellent in their kind) to be read by Bedlamites, than pretenders to vertue and modesty.

The paradox of a man who would have been better if he had written worse came to be resolved by denying that he wrote well; to Walpole as we shall see he was a bad poet as well as a bad man. The shift towards this simple solution to the problem, which Wolseley had tried to tackle in the Preface to *Valentinian*, is already noticeable in the *Life of Sedley* of 1722 (No. 39):

They [the poems of Rochester and the other Court Wits] are not fit to be read by People whose Religion and Modesty have not quite forsaken them; and which, had those grosser Parts been left out, would justly have passed for the most polite Poetry that the World ever saw.

The confusion between aesthetic and moral standards may be accepted as inevitable, but writers were obviously determined to ignore the truth that Wolseley had pointed out that 'my Lord writ a great number [of poems] without the least obsceneness in 'em.' Besides, a selection of carefully gelded poems were readily available both in the Tonson editions and later in Steevens's selection.

The first out-and-out condemnation of both man and poems was Robert Shiels's account in '*Mr. Cibber's' Lives of the Poets* (1753) (No. 43). Shiels was not averse to profiting from Rochester's scandalous reputation, for he reproduced many of the anecdotes—some spurious—that had gathered round Rochester's life, but his dislike of the poems was unequivocal, though he acknowledged the exceptional natural talents of the man. He was concerned not to allow the vicious influence of the poetry to spread and refused to discuss it. By 1757 another Scot, the great David Hume, was informing his readers that 'the very name of Rochester is offensive to modern ears.' This did not, incidentally, prevent his contemporaries from buying copies of the poems in large numbers. Hume acknowledged Rochester's great talent as a poet, but refused to discuss the poetry except to condemn it—admittedly, here Hume was merely making a catalogue of Restoration poets as part of his general history of the period and therefore an extended discussion was anyway not his intention. He placed Rochester second, after Dryden, in his list of literary figures of the age. Walpole's attack on Rochester, 1758 (No. 45), took the process of denigration a stage further. Walpole was not willing to concede even natural talent and made his condemnation more severe by accepting the possibility that poetry could be both good *and* indecent: 'Indecency is far from conferring wit; but it does not destroy it neither.' Having said this he then goes on to argue that Rochester's poetry is without merit. The age which produced Rochester was barbarous, the favourable judgments of his contemporaries Wood and Marvell, absurd. Walpole, though he purports to judge the poetry as poetry, bases his criticism on a narrow moral judgment, a judgment that ignores Wolseley's caveat and the evidence of the bowdlerized editions. Walpole's determination to condemn is an excellent if sad example of the way in which a sensitive and intelligent man can adopt the unreasoned prejudices of an increasingly moralistic climate of opinion.

Not all comment in this period, however, is hostile. The *Biographia Britannica* (1766) article on Rochester, which records his waywardness as a man and quotes Walpole's opinions, also expresses admiration for the poetry: 'His style was clear and strong, and when he used figures they were very lively, yet far enough out of the common road.' This article, it should be noted, is reserved for a supplement of the *Biographia*, suggesting that Rochester is no longer regarded as an inevitable inclusion even in such an extensive compilation. In this growing climate of disapproval and neglect Johnson's *Life of Rochester* (No. 47) stands out as something of an exception. He is at any rate determined not to be misled by the cant of the period. Johnson's own highly moral view of life permits him no sympathy with the Restoration libertine's attitudes, but he is willing to try to separate his opinion of the poet's morals from his opinion of the morality of the poetry, though he is not entirely successful in this. As in the other *Lives of the Poets*, Johnson adopts a threefold division in this essay, first giving us the more important biographical facts and discussing Rochester's character (though these two parts are not kept separate) and then turning to a discussion of literary merits. The biographical material is largely taken from Burnet's *Life*, which Johnson mentions as a book 'the critick ought to read for its elegance, the philosopher for its arguments, and the saint for its piety'—I have followed Johnson in regarding it as 'an injury to the reader to offer him an abridgement'. The critical section is independent of earlier sources, though the judgments Johnson offers are open to question. It is possible that Johnson did not closely look at Rochester's work. At this time, although Rochester editions were still selling well, they were mostly of the popular, salacious kind which a critic like Johnson would disregard. At a more sophisticated level one would guess that Rochester was read as light entertainment and would therefore no longer warrant the treatment that Johnson gave to the poets like Milton, Dryden and Pope, though Steevens's selection shows that the polite reader expected Rochester to be represented in an extended collection of English poetry. Symptomatic of Johnson's lack of interest is his over-reliance on his memory. He misquotes Scroope's *Defence of Satire* and a line of the *Satire against Mankind* as 'a saying' of Rochester. Imperfect memory also probably explains Johnson's extraordinary judgment that Rochester's songs 'have no particular character', for had he re-examined them he could hardly have come to this conclusion. He mentions none of them specifically and possibly he was simply working on an impression he had formed of Restoration lyric in general. Most modern critics agree that Rochester's songs are, in Dr Leavis's words, 'peculiarly individual utterances' (*Revaluation*, p. 35), and this seems also to have been the view of Rochester's contemporaries. For example Parsons stresses Rochester's originality in the funeral sermon (No. 9):

> Whoever reads his composures, will find all things in them so peculiarly Great, New, and Excellent, that he will easily pronounce, that tho he has lent to many others, yet he has borrowed of none.

Johnson's comments on the satire are more specific. He shows his customary shrewdness in his caution about what can be accepted as Rochester's, mentioning only poems that are certainly authentic. He is complimentary about the *Allusion to Horace*, approving the ingenuity with which Rochester has manipulated Horace's verse to fit his own times. *Upon Nothing* he regards as 'the strongest effort of his [Rochester's] Muse'. Johnson was not the first to single out *Upon Nothing* for special praise. Giles Jacob thought it 'an excellent piece' (No. 38), but no one had hitherto suggested that it was the best of Rochester's poems. It is clever and has moments of power, yet it is essentially a play poem—as Forgues and Whibley later pointed out—and not to be seriously compared with the great satires. Unfortunately Johnson's judgment was followed by many later critics.

Of the other satires Johnson mentions some 'Verses to Lord Mulgrave' without comment. A lampoon in reply to Carr Scroope's *Defence of Satire* (presumably the lines beginning 'To rack and torture thy unmeaning Brain') is described as a vigorous piece. On the great *Satire against Mankind* Johnson remarks that 'Rochester can only claim what remains when all Boileau's part is taken away'—an argument he had disregarded in dealing with the more closely imitative *Allusion to Horace*.

At the root of Johnson's failure in this essay lies, one would guess, his great hurry to complete his commission. He had been given only a few weeks to prepare the first volume of *Lives*. The essay also suffers in spite of Johnson's relative detachment, from the prevalent weakness of Rochester criticism, of judging the poetry in terms of the man. For instance, Johnson takes it for granted that Rochester was too preoccupied with his debaucheries to take his writing seriously and goes on to argue from this that 'his pieces are commonly short'. Even if we did not have textual and biographical information to suggest that Rochester worked over his poetry it is apparent enough that his finest works—*Artemesia, Timon, Tunbridge Wells* and the *Satire against Mankind* are his longest. Also underlying Johnson's judgment is the Renaissance dogma that a good writer must be a good man. Though Johnson is too wise to adopt a sentimental or simple-minded view of what a good man is, not surprisingly he finds it difficult to include John Wilmot in that category. This prejudice colours the whole of Johnson's *Life* and is nowhere more evident than in the last lines:

> In all his works there is a spriteliness and vigour, and every where may be found tokens of a mind which study might have carried to excellence. What more can be expected from a life spent in ostentatious contempt of regularity, and ended before the abilities of many other men began to be displayed?

Johnson's opinions, expressed with their customary force and air of conviction, echo through the comments of writers throughout the nineteenth century. (See for example Nos. 49, 50 and the quotation from Stephen Collet, p. 20.)

THE EARLY NINETEENTH CENTURY

For all its faults Johnson's *Life of Rochester* is the last extended assessment of Rochester for many years to show any sympathy with his poetry. The new century witnessed both a steady decline not just in sympathetic comment but in any comment at all. Editions of the poetry became fewer. Silence is as significant as comment. Coleridge, for instance, for all his great interest in the seventeenth century, never mentions Rochester. This neglect is not easy to explain. Possibly Coleridge never entirely grew out of his youthful dislike of 'that school of French poetry, condensed and invigorated by English understanding': as he describes the Augustan poets in Chapter I of the *Biographia Literaria*. We might have expected Byron to be sympathetic, yet he only mentions Rochester once or twice in passing. What comment there is on the poetry is largely hostile, even when there is some interest in the man. There is still a glimmer of appreciation from Malone in his edition of Dryden's prose (1800). He gives a very unflattering picture of Rochester's literary relationships, but he does concede that he is a poet of distinction who 'wanted not [Dryden's] aid to be remembered'. Ree's *Cyclopedia* (1819) is more damning, it quotes Walpole's strictures with approval and adds, inaccurately, 'as for his poetical compositions they were for the most part lampoons or amatory effusions, the titles of which would stain the page of biography.' Thomas Byerley, under the pseudonym of Stephen Collet, sums up the attitude of his contemporaries in his *Relics of Literature* (1823). The opening phrase is taken from Johnson's *Life*: 'Although the blaze of this nobleman's reputation is not yet quite extinguished, it is principally as a great wit, a great libertine, and a great penitent, that he is at present known.' There are still however, interesting asides and signs that some intelligent readers are finding enjoyment in this Augustan poet. Isaac D'Israeli, for instance, calls Rochester 'a great satirist', a remark splendidly independent of the prejudices of his age. In his *Quarrels of Authors* (1814) (No. 53) he remarks that Rochester gives us an important insight into the nature of satire in suggesting to Burnet that it is prompted by revenge. In the same year a noble compliment to Rochester comes from Germany's greatest poet. It is not apparent whether Goethe knew the author of the passage he quotes from the *Satire against Mankind* in his *Autobiography* (1814) (No. 54). That he admired it profoundly and felt its full force is indicated by the context, where he uses the lines to illustrate the habitual melancholy of poets, remarking that 'whole volumes' could be written as a commentary on the text. A little later, in the lectures on the English poets of 1818, Hazlitt says just enough about Rochester to make us wish he had said much more. Hazlitt seems on the point of turning Rochester into a Romantic cult hero: 'his contempt for everything that others respect, almost amounts to sublimity.' Almost, but not quite, for there is in his poetry an Augustan decorum and restraint that was coming under bitter attack from some of Hazlitt's contemporaries—though Pope was the chief target. It is surprising, nevertheless, as Street remarks at the end of the nineteenth century (No. 74), that a romantic Rochester was not created, for his rebelliousness and outspokenness would have fitted him for the role. Possibly the neo-classicism in Restoration literature and art did not provide the right background for a Romantic hero, and Rochester, for all his rebelliousness, was very much a man and poet of his age. For whatever reason, then, Rochester was not accepted as a substitute for Lord Byron, with whom he was occasionally compared.

1850–1900

By the time Forgues came to write his two fascinating essays on Rochester for the French (and French-speaking European) public in 1857, there were signs that some of the old puritanical prejudices were dying. Exactly why this gradual shift towards more tolerant attitudes was taking place it is impossible to say. Why, for instance, did Henry Hallam (No. 60) read Rochester's satirical poetry (along with most of the other satire of the day) 'with nothing but disgust' in 1839, yet twenty-five years later not only admit Rochester's 'considerable and varied genius', but praise the lyrics, which he had not discussed in his earlier edition, as doing 'credit to the Caroline period'? It was not merely a personal change of opinion, and Hallam is still not *very* complimentary; it is a gradual changing of the general climate of opinion. This change is possibly reflected in an interesting comment by Gilchrist in his *Life of Blake* (1864) that society in Blake's day was much more puritanical than it was in his own. Additional evidence is provided by the change in the article on Rochester in the *Encyclopaedia Britannica* from the seventh edition (1842) to the ninth (1886). The article in the seventh edition is similar to those of earlier editions; it is largely biographical and confines itself, in commenting on the poetry, to quoting Walpole's strictures. The edition of 1860, the eighth, though still largely biographical, describes the poetry as possessing 'liveliness and vigour' and quotes Dr Johnson's qualified approval in place of Walpole. The ninth edition (No. 72) is still more complimentary. Condemnation of Rochester's poetry on narrow moral grounds is still quite common to the end of the nineteenth century, but more commentators are willing to be tolerant, to treat the verse on its merits and especially to admire the lyrics. These fifty years up to about 1900 are the only time in the history of Rochester criticism that we find the lyrics preferred to the satires.

The article by 'S.H.' in the *Gentleman's Magazine* of 1851 (No. 63) on Rochester and Nell Gwyn is a good example of the cautious tolerance that appears at mid-century. The usual comments are made about Rochester's indecency, but his poetry is also recognized as a valuable record of Restoration society and although this is a historical rather than a critical interest, it acknowledges the realism of the satires, an important quality that had been lost sight of. 'S.H.' is even willing, as few commentators have been, to take sides with Rochester against Dryden, by pointing out that the comments on Dryden in the *Allusion to Horace* are not unjust.

Forgues's articles in the *Revue des Deux Mondes* (August and September 1857) also stress the realism of Rochester's attitudes and the value of the verse as a record of Restoration society. Accordingly he is interested in the satire, and especially in two satires that had previously received little critical attention, *Timon* and *Tunbridge Wells*. His view of Rochester as a poet is uncomplimentary: though the best of the Restoration poets, he is of an inferior order, a Petronius, not a Juvenal or Persius. The value of the poems, he says, exists 'only for literary history and for studious explorers of former times'. The historical interest partly explains why he is willing to devote two long articles to this largely unknown English poet at a time when nothing comparable was to be found in English. Knowledge of Rochester on the Continent had never entirely died out, as we know from Goethe's quotation from the *Satire against Mankind* (No. 54). In France, Victor Hugo had included Rochester anachronistically as a character in his early drama *Cromwell* (1827), and he had appeared as a character in several slightly earlier plays (see Prinz *Rochester*, pp. 440–1), but the more serious French interest had evaporated. Forgues's concern with Rochester is something new. He is not without the kind of moral bias that had blinkered English judgments for so long, and he is just as ready as his English contemporaries to raise his hands in horror at the profligacy of Charles' reign, but he is also willing to look beyond this. From time to time he ventures critical judgments, and these are not entirely consistent with his overall view of Rochester's poetry as only of historical importance. In this literary criticism he shows independence of mind. The poem that Johnson extols, *Upon Nothing*, he considered 'of secondary importance', objecting to its epigrammatic method and that it is satirical where it ought to be philosophical. He dislikes the *Satire against Mankind* largely because of its pessimistic view of mankind. In this he shows his chief weakness as a critical commentator, his concern purely with what is being said and his lack of sensitivity about the poetic method. He shows an inability to respond to the force and energy of this poem, an energy that had so obviously impressed Goethe (No. 54) and, a little later, Tennyson (No. 68). It is not surprising then that he values more highly what he calls the 'humbler pieces', the comic satire, where he can enjoy the social comment without being called upon to respond to the ingenuity and power of the verse.

There is no evidence that Forgues was read by nineteenth-century English commentators, but in England too there is an increase in serious interest in Rochester's work at this date. Gilfillan (No. 66) and Taine (No. 67) might complain about Rochester's wickedness; Henry Morley might be contemptuous (No. 70); the well-read might ignore and misquote, but things were changing. On the one side there is some cruel evidence of just how little he was read: in Abbott and Campbell's *Life of Jowett*, the authors admit that they had to get learned help to identify three (garbled) lines of the *Satire against Mankind* (No. 68) and the letter from which the lines are recorded refers to them as 'some eighteenth-century verses'. An avid reader like Joseph Hunter can pass Rochester by without more than a glance. In his extensive manuscript collection of comments on the English poets Hunter reports of Rochester: 'I have cared so little about this person that I have not a single notice of him in the original book of notes for these articles.' On the other hand Jowett is seen enjoying the *Satire against Mankind* and Tennyson was fond of quoting from the poem (No. 68). Charles Cowden Clarke in the *Comic Writers of England* (1871) (No. 69) deals with Rochester at some length; interested as he is in the gossip surrounding Rochester, he does not ignore the poetry and is not uncomplimentary about it. It is interesting that he assumes, unjustifiably, that Marvell must have shared the nineteenth century's high estimate of Butler in preference to Rochester. By 1880 Edmund Gosse, though concerned with Rochester's nastiness, can present him as an exquisite lyrical poet and this view is echoed again by Oliver Elton in the last year of the century (No. 76). But nineteenth-century criticism of Rochester suffered from errors and misinformation. Elton, for example, accepts the story that Rochester had behaved spitefully towards Settle, Crowne and Otway, though it is not supported by the evidence. He is also handicapped by the uncertainty of the Rochester canon at this date. Like most of his predecessors he accepts poems that are probably not Rochester's (for instance *The Session of the Poets* and the lyric 'I cannot change as others do'). But then it is only since the publication of Vieth's edition of the poems in 1968, that the critic has been able to accept or reject poems with some degree of confidence.

MODERN CRITICISM

Rochester's reputation as a poet, never very high in the nineteenth century, has at last come into its own, though there is still no outstanding critical assessment. With the new edition of the poems by Vieth and the pioneering work of scholars like Prinz, Pinto, Thorpe and Wilson good texts are now available. The first modern edition was the *Collected Works* edited by John Hayward in 1926. This contains Rochester's play *Valentinian* as well as the poems and an extensive selection of letters, but suffers from the inclusion of much spurious material. Pinto's edition of the poetry in 1953, the first to establish the canon of Rochester's work, has now been superseded by Vieth's edition of the *Complete Poems*

(1968). There have also been several extensive selections of the poetry and a facsimile edition of *Poems on Several Occasions, 1680*, with an excellent introduction, by James Thorpe. A scholarly edition of the correspondence between Rochester and his friend Henry Savile edited by J. H. Wilson was published in 1941. The publication of these editions was greatly facilitated by the important bibliographical work of J. Prinz, *John Wilmot, Earl of Rochester: His Life and Writings* (1926). There has also been a distinct advance in sifting the authentic from the spurious in the details of Rochester's life. The most notable contributions to this are the book of Prinz already mentioned, Pinto's biography *Enthusiast in Wit*, a revised version of a biography first published in 1935 under the title *Rochester, Portrait of a Restoration Poet*, and J. H. Wilson's *The Court Wits of the Restoration* (1948).

Modern criticism, however, begins before these editions became available in Whibley's essay on the Court Poets in the *Cambridge History of English Literature* (vol. 8, 1912). The essay covers the work of the poets of Charles II's Court and gives us a resumé of Rochester's life. Whibley makes the inevitable mistakes of attribution and of accepting apocryphal biographical material, but when he writes about the poetry (pp. 213–15) he has a sure touch. He dismisses Johnson's praise of *Upon Nothing* by calling the poem, perhaps rather immoderately, 'a piece of ingenuity, unworthy his talent' and makes the point that Wolseley had made 227 years earlier and that hardly anyone had heeded, that a great many of Rochester's poems are unsalacious and can safely be judged 'upon their very high merits'. He sees that Rochester's claim to be a major poet must rest on the satire and argues that his skill as a satirist is a combination of 'nature' and 'art'. Nor is he to be put off by Pope's accusations of Rochester's 'incorrectness'—'He wrote the heroic couplet with a life and freedom that few have excelled'—though he acknowledges, as any honest critic must, that Rochester was no perfectionist. Rochester's use of the heroic couplet is much freer than either Pope's or Dryden's, and while this loses sometimes in precision it often gains in the wider range of rhythmic effects it allows. Whibley seems to have been the first modern critic to notice this. It is worth mentioning in passing that Rochester's flexible use of the couplet is to be explained in terms of the Renaissance theory of decorum which required a rough metre for satire. For Whibley the *Satire against Mankind* is Rochester's finest achievement, and he praises it for its energy and power. The lyrics he considers far less important, and his comments on them are fewer and less interesting. His praise of the 'imitation' of Quarles, for instance,

'Why do'st thou shade thy lovely face?' seems exaggerated. There is, in any case, considerable uncertainty that this poem is by Rochester; Vieth does not include it in his new edition, describing it as 'merely an adaptation of Quarles's *Emblemes*'. Whibley is the first critic of Rochester's poetry since the earlier eighteenth century to appreciate something of Rochester's true stature as a poet and to understand where his strength lies. He rejects as irrelevant to the poetry both the diabolical rake and the careless gentleman of the Rochester legends and sees him as a poet of both natural gifts and great technical skill. Much is inevitably left out in such a short space and Whibley's essay contains no more than a sketch of a thorough appreciation of the poetry.

With the appearance of the new editions there have been important contributions towards a re-assessment of the poetry. These have tended to be more concerned with sources and influences than with critical evaluation. There have been explorations of Rochester's thought, especially in the *Satire against Mankind*, of his use of conventional verse forms and of his place in literary history. Inevitably too, there has been continuing discussion of the problems concerned with the authenticity of the poems and the biography. Critical evaluation, until very recently, has tended to interpret the poetry from what we know of the man. Rochester's personality has obvious fascinations for a generation like ours that has grown up to regard his libertinism as morally acceptable. Critics, of which Pinto is perhaps the most distinguished, find Rochester highly sympathetic as a man and prefer those poems where he seems to be speaking in his own person. Thus Pinto gives high praise to the lyrics like 'Absent from thee I languish still' and 'All my past life is mine no more' where strong emotion is expressed. This is the 'romantic' Rochester, and certainly these occasional outbursts of emotion are one facet of his work. They are, however, one extreme of a range that extends in the other direction to the complete disengagement of poems like *The Maim'd Debauchee*, the *Song of a Young Lady to her Ancient Lover* and the mock song 'I cannot swive as others do'.

In more recent criticism some attempt has been made to redress the bias towards a personal interpretation of the poems by stressing Rochester's skill in disengaging himself from his work, the quality that Keats called 'negative capability'. In a recent British Academy lecture, for instance, Anne Righter demonstrates Rochester's use of irony. David Vieth is also largely concerned with this detachment in his *Attribution in Restoration Poetry* (1963). This is primarily a bibliographical work, but contains a number of important critical observations. He shows that in both *A very Heroicall Epistle in Answer to Ephelia* and in *An Epistolary Essay from M.G. to O.B.* the comic hero is a caricature of the Earl of Mulgrave and not, as was often assumed earlier, Rochester speaking in his own person. What were earlier taken to be autobiographical poems are shown to be mock heroic, in which the absurd boasting of the hero is the object of satire. The tendency of Vieth's critical comments, even clearer in the introduction to his edition of the poems, is to demonstrate the ironic detachment of Rochester's satirical techniques, and in showing this he has done more than any other critic to free the poetry from the shadow of the poet. Vieth, however, tends to ignore the more passionate, personal utterances that form an essential part of both lyric and satire and the critic is still awaited who can see the interplay of the two sides of Rochester's art, the emotion and the detachment, as part of the complex unity of his work.

NOTES

1 The earliest known version of this, the 'Huntington' edition, was published in photographic facsimile by James Thorpe, *Princeton Studies in English*, No. 30, 1950.

2 *Episode de la Vie de Tibère, œuvre medianimique dictée par l'esprit de J.-W. Rochester* (1886), *Le Pharaon Mernephtah* (1888), *Herculanum* (1889) etc.

3 Pinto, lv. ll. 1–9. The 'patron' of line 3 is Rochester's enemy the Earl of Mulgrave.

4 Recorded in John Hayward's edition of *Letters of Saint Evremond* (1930), p. 323.

5 N. S. Grabo, *Notes and Queries* 207 (1962), pp. 392–3.

6 *Wit Restor'd* (1658), p. 142.

7 For an excellent account of this tradition see Rosalie Colie's *Paradoxia Epidemica* (1966).

8 See *The Occasional Verse of Richard Steele*, ed. Blanchard (1952), p. xv.

CONTEMPORARY COMMENTS

1672–80

1. John Crowne on Rochester

1672

From the dedication of 'The History of Charles VIII of France', *Dramatic Works*, ed. J. Maidment and W. H. Logan (1873), i. 127–8.

'Starcht Jonny Crowne', 1640?–1703?, as Rochester called him, was one of the more successful of the professional writers of stage comedies in the reign of Charles II and was a favourite of the King. Rochester patronized him for a time.

I am fortunate enough in your Lordship's approbation, and can dispense with the rest of mankind. And this I am bold to affirm though I have not the Honour of much acquaintance with your Lordship; for it is sufficient that I have seen in some little sketches of your Pen, excellent Masteries and a Spirit inimitable; and that I have been entertained by others with the wit, which your Lordship with a gentile and careless freedom, sprinkles in your ordinary converse; and often supplies vulgar and necessitous wits wherewith to enrich themselves, and sometimes to treat their friends; and when your Lordship is pleased to ascend above us, you do it with a strange readiness and agility of mind, and by swift and easy motions attain to heights, which others by much climbing, dull industry, and constraint cannot reach. Nor is this vast wit crowded together in a little soul, where it wants freedom, and is uneasy, but fills up the spaces of a large and generous mind, infinitely delighting to oblige all, but especially to encourage any blossoming merits; and ready to forgive large and voluminous faults for the sake of any one thing tolerably said or done.

2. Nathanael Lee, two references to Rochester

1674; 1681

Nathanael Lee, 1653–92, was a professional writer of heroic tragedy. His career illustrates well the humiliations the professional writers had to suffer during this period. The first excerpt given here is another example of the sycophancy expected of a professional towards the nobility, but the second extract where Rochester figures as 'Rosidore', first pointed out as a reference to Rochester by Thorn-Drury, seems to be unsolicited and sincere. In addition to 'Rosidore' the character of 'Nemours' is also based on Rochester. Pinto finds echoes of Rochester's translation of lines from Seneca's *Troas* and *Upon Nothing* in the passage (*Enthusiast in Wit*, p. 233).

(a) From the dedication of *Nero* (1674):

From the Criticks, whose Fury I dread, those Kill-men, and more than *Jews*, I appeal to your Lordship, as the Saint did to *Caesar*: To you, whose Judgment vie's remark with your Grandure, who are as absolutely Lord of Wit, as those Prevaricators are its Slaves: To you, who by excellent Reading and Conversation with the pleasantly Wise, have justly limited the mighty Sallies of an overflowing Fancy; whose Sayings astonish the Censorious, and whose Writings are so exactly ingenious, Princes treasure them in their Memory as things divine. This is so far from Flattery and Untruth, that it appears rather an impertinent kind of asserting what every Man knows; as if I should gravely tell the World 'tis Day at Noon. . . . ('Nero', *Dramatick Works of Nathanael Lee* (1734) iii. 76)

(b) From Act I scene 2, *The Princess of Cleves*, produced September 1681:

VIDAME . . . he that was the Life, the Soul of Pleasure,
Count *Rosidore* is dead.

NEMOURS Then we may say
Wit was, and Satire is a Carcase now.
I thought his last Debauch wou'd be his Death—
But is it certain?

VIDAME Yes, I saw him Dust,
I saw the mighty Thing a nothing made,
Huddled with Worms, and swept to that cold Den,
Where Kings lie crumbl'd just like other Men.

NEMOURS Nay then let's rave and elegize together,
Where *Rosidore* is now but common Clay,
Whom every wiser Emmet bears away,
And lays him up against a Winter's Day.

He was the Spirit of Wit—and had such an Art in guilding his Failures, that it was hard not to love his Faults: He never spoke a witty thing twice, tho' to different Persons; his Imperfections were catching, and his Genius was so luxuriant, that he was forc'd to tame it with a Hesitation in his Speech to keep it in view—But, Oh! how awkward, how insipid, how poor and wretchedly dull is the Imitation of those that have all the Affectation of his Verse, and none of his Wit!

('The Princess of Cleves', *Dramatick Works of Nathanael Lee* (1733) i. 17–18)

3. John Dryden on Rochester

1673; 1678

The first and second of these passages were written when Dryden was enjoying Rochester's patronage. The exact cause of the estrangement between the two poets, which led to Dryden's sharp attack on Rochester in the Preface to *All for Love*, is not known. There may have been resentment that Dryden sought the patronage of Rochester's enemy, the Earl of Mulgrave, and Dryden's references to Rochester's *Allusion to Horace* in the Preface suggest that the poet laureate resented the criticisms of himself contained there (see Introduction pp. 5–6). For whatever reason relations continued to deteriorate, Dryden aiding Mulgrave in his attack on Rochester in the *Essay upon Satire* (see note on Mulgave, No. 7). In December 1679 Dryden was attacked by a gang in Rose Alley, London, probably at Rochester's instigation. Rochester is not mentioned by name in the 'Preface'—it would have been too risky to oppose a nobleman of such eminence openly—but there has never been any doubt for whom the attack was intended. Rochester's best work, the formal satires, were written after the two pieces of flattery and before the attack in the Preface.

(a) Extract from Dedication of *Marriage à la Mode* (March 1673)

But, my Lord, I ought to have considered, that you are as great a judge, as you are a patron; and that in praising you ill, I should incur a higher note of ingratitude, than that I thought to have avoided. I stand in need of all your accustomed goodness for the dedication of this play; which, though perhaps it be the best of my comedies, is yet so faulty, that I should have feared you for my critic, if I had not, with some policy, given you the trouble of being my protector. Wit seems to have lodged itself more nobly in this age, than in any of the former; and people of my mean condition are only writers, because some of the nobility, and your Lordship in the first place, are above the narrow praises which poesy could give you. But, let those who love to see themselves exceeded, encourage your Lordship in so dangerous a quality; for my own part, I must confess, that I have so much of self-interest, as to be content with reading some papers of your verses, without desiring you should proceed to a scene, or play; with the common prudence of those who are worsted in a duel, and declare they are satisfied, when they are first wounded. Your Lordship has but another step to make, and from the patron of wit, you may become its tyrant; and oppress our little reputations with more ease than you now protect them. But these, my Lord, are designs, which I am sure you harbour not, any more than the French king is contriving the conquest of the Swissers. (*Dramatic Works of John Dryden*, ed. Scott-Saintsbury, 18 vols., Edinburgh 1882, iv. 256–7.)

(b) Extract from letter from Dryden to Rochester, April/May 1673:

And now the Shame of seeing my self overpayd so much for an ill Dedication,[1] has made me almost repent of my Addresse. I find it is not for me to contend any way with your Lordship, who can write better on the meanest Subject than I can on the best. I have onely ingag'd my selfe in a new debt, when I had hop'd to cancell a part of the old one: And shou'd either have chosen some other Patron, whom it was in my power to have oblig'd by speaking better of him than he deserv'd, or have made your Lordship onely a hearty Dedication of the respect and Honour I had for you, without giveing you the occasion to conquer me, as you have done, at my own Weapon. My onely relief is, that what I have written is publique, and I am so much my own friend, as to conceale your Lordship's letter for that which would have given Vanity to any other poet, has onely given me confusion. You see, my Lord, how far you have pushed me; I dare not own the honour you have done me, for fear of showing it to my own disadvantage. You are that Rerum Natura of your own Lucretius, *Ipsa suis pollens opibus, nihil indiga nostri*:[2] You are above any Incense I can give you; and have all the happiness of an idle life, join'd with the good Nature of an Active. Your friends in town are ready to envy the leisure you have given your self in the Country: though they know you are onely their Steward, and that you treasure up but so much health, as you intend to spend on them in

[1] The dedication of *Marriage à la Mode*, which Rochester had evidently liked. The letter from Rochester which this letter answers has not survived.

[2] 'Strong in its own qualities, needing nothing from us' (*De Rerum Natura*, ii. 650). A reference to Rochester's translation of a few lines from Lucretius' *De Rerum Natura*, II, 646–51 (Pinto, xi, p. 50).

Winter. In the meane time you have withdrawn your selfe from attendance, the curse of Courts. You may thinke of what you please, and that as little as you please; (for in my opinion), thinking it selfe, is a kind of paine to a witty man; he finds so much more in it to disquiet, than to please him. (*The Letters of John Dryden*, ed. C. E. Ward (Durham N.C., 1942), pp. 8–9.)

(c) 'Preface' to *All for Love* (extract) (1678):

But, if I come closer to those who are allowed for witty men, either by the advantage of their quality, or by common fame, and affirm that neither are they qualified to decide sovereignly concerning poetry, I shall yet have a strong party of my opinion; for most of them severally will exclude the rest, either from the number of witty men, or at least of able judges. But here again they are all indulgent to themselves; and every one who believes himself a wit, that is, every man, will pretend at the same time to a right of judging. But to press it yet further, there are many witty men, but few poets; neither have all poets a taste of tragedy. And this is the rock on which they are daily splitting. Poetry, which is a picture of nature, must generally please; but it is not to be understood that all parts of it must please every man; therefore is not tragedy to be judged by a witty man, whose taste is only confined to comedy. Nor is every man, who loves tragedy, a sufficient judge of it; he must understand the excellences of it too, or he will only prove a blind admirer, not a critic. From hence it comes that so many satires on poets, and censures of their writings, fly abroad. Men of pleasant conversation (at least esteemed so), and endued with a trifling kind of fancy, perhaps helped out with some smattering of Latin, are ambitious to distinguish themselves from the herd of gentlemen, by their poetry—

Rarus enim ferme sensus communis in illa Fortuna.[1]

And is not this a wretched affectation, not to be contented with what fortune has done for them, and sit down quietly with their estates, but they must call their wits in question, and needlessly expose their nakedness to public view? Not considering that they are not to expect the same approbation from sober men, which they have found from their flatterers after the third bottle. If a little glittering in discourse has passed them on us for witty men, where was the necessity of undeceiving the world? Would a man who has an ill title to an estate, but yet is in

[1] 'For in those high places a feeling for others is rarely to be found' (Juvenal *Satires*, VIII. 73–4).

possession of it; would he bring it of his own accord, to be tried at Westminster? We who write, if we want the talent, yet have the excuse that we do it for a poor subsistence; but what can be urged in their defence, who, not having the vocation of poverty to scribble, out of mere wantonness take pains to make themselves ridiculous? Horace was certainly in the right, where he said, 'that no man is satisfied with his own condition.' A poet is not pleased, because he is not rich; and the rich are discontented, because the poets will not admit them of their number. Thus the case is hard with writers: If they succeed not, they must starve; and if they do, some malicious satire is prepared to level them, for daring to please without their leave. But while they are so eager to destroy the fame of others, their ambition is manifest in their concernment; some poem of their own is to be produced, and the slaves are to be laid flat with their faces on the ground, that the monarch may appear in the greater majesty.

Dionysius and Nero had the same longings, but with all their power they could never bring their business well about. 'Tis true, they proclaimed themselves poets by sound of trumpet; and poets they were, upon pain of death to any man who durst call them otherwise. The audience had a fine time on't, you may imagine; they sat in a bodily fear, and looked as demurely as they could: for it was a hanging matter to laugh unseasonably; and the tyrants were suspicious, as they had reason, that their subjects had them in the wind; so, every man, in his own defence, set as good a face upon the business as he could. It was known beforehand that the monarchs were to be crowned laureates; but when the show was over, and an honest man was suffered to depart quietly, he took out his laughter which he had stifled, with a firm resolution never more to see an emperor's play, though he had been ten years a-making it. In the meantime the true poets were they who made the best markets, for they had wit enough to yield the prize with a good grace, and not contend with him who had thirty legions. They were sure to be rewarded, if they confessed themselves bad writers, and that was somewhat better than to be martyrs for their reputation. Lucan's example was enough to teach them manners; and after he was put to death, for overcoming Nero, the emperor carried it without dispute for the best poet in his dominions. No man was ambitious of that grinning honour; for if he heard the malicious trumpeter proclaiming his name before his betters, he knew there was but one way with him. Mæcenas took another course, and we know he was more than a great man, for he was witty too: But finding himself far gone in poetry, which Seneca assures us was not his talent,[1] he thought it his best way to be well with Virgil and with Horace; that at least he might be a poet at the second hand; and we see how happily it has succeeded with him; for his own bad poetry is forgotten, and their panegyrics of him still remain. But they who should be our patrons are for no such expensive ways to fame; they have much of the poetry of Mæcenas, but little of his liberality. They are for persecuting Horace and Virgil, in the persons of their successors; for such is every man who has any part of their soul and fire, though in a less degree. Some of their little zanies yet go further; for they are persecutors even of Horace himself, as far as they are able, by their ignorant and vile imitations of him; by making an unjust use of his authority, and turning his artillery against his friends. But how would he disdain to be copied by such hands! I dare answer for him, he would be more uneasy in their company, than he was with Crispinus, their forefather, in the Holy Way; and would no more have allowed them a place amongst the critics, than he would Demetrius the mimic, and Tigellius the buffoon

> *—Demetri, teque, Tigelli,*[2]
> *Discipulorum inter jubeo plorare cathedras.*

With what scorn would he look down on such miserable translators, who make doggerel of his Latin, mistake his meaning, misapply his censures, and often contradict their own? He is fixed as a landmark to set out the bounds of poetry

> *—Saxum antiquum, ingens,—*[3]
> *Limes agro positus, litem ut discerneret arvis.*

But other arms than theirs, and other sinews are required, to raise the weight of such an author; and when they would toss him against enemies—

> *Genua labant, gelidus concrevit frigore sanguis.*[4]
> *Tum lapis ipse, viri vacuum per inane volatus,*
> *Nec spatium evasit totum, nec pertulit ictum.*

[1] Seneca, *Epistulae Morales*, 114.

[2] 'I order you, Demetrius and you, Tigellius, to wail among the desks of your pupils.' (Horace, *Satires*, I. x, 90–1.)

[3]
> An Antique Stone he saw, the Common Bound
> Of Neighb'ring Fields; and Barrier of the Ground.

(Virgil, *Aeneid*, xii. 897–8, in Dryden's own translation, 1300–1.)

[4]
> His knocking Knees are bent beneath the Load:
> And shiv'ring Cold congeals his vital Blood,
> The Stone drops from his arms: and falling short,
> For want of Vigour, mocks his vain Effort.

(Virgil, *Aeneid*, xii. 905–7, in Dryden's translation, 1308–1311.)

For my part, I would wish no other revenge, either for myself, or the rest of the poets, from this rhyming judge of the twelvepenny gallery, this legitimate son of Sternhold,[1] than that he would subscribe his name to his censure, or (not to tax him beyond his learning) set his mark. For, should he own himself publicly, and come from behind the lion's skin, they whom he condemns would be thankful to him, they whom he praises would choose to be condemned; and the magistrates, whom he has elected, would modestly withdraw from their employment, to avoid the scandal of his nomination. The sharpness of his satire, next to himself, falls most heavily on his friends, and they ought never to forgive him for commending them perpetually the wrong way, and sometimes by contraries. If he have a friend, whose hastiness in writing is his greatest fault, Horace would have taught him to have minced the matter, and to have called it readiness of thought, and a flowing fancy; for friendship will allow a man to christen an imperfection by the name of some neighbour virtue—

Vellem in amicitia sic erraremus; et isti[2]
Errori nomen virtus posuisset honestum.

But he would never have allowed him to have called a slow man hasty, or a hasty writer a slow drudge,[3] as Juvenal explains it

—Canibus pigris, scabieque vetusta[4]
—Lævibus, et siccæ lambentibus ora lucernæ,
Nomen erit, Pardus, Tigris, Leo; si quid adhuc est
Quod fremit in terris violentius.

(*The Dramatic Works of John Dryden*, ed. Scott-Saintsbury, v, 331–7)

[1] A sixteenth-century versifier of the Psalms whose name became a stock word of abuse to describe the bad poet.

[2] 'I would wish we could make such mistakes in friendship and that right feeling would have given an honourable name to a mistake like that.' (Horace, *Satires*, I. iii. 41–2.)

[3] This clearly refers to lines in the *Allusion to Horace* (11, 41–3):

Of all our *Modern Wits* none seems to me,
Once to have toucht upon true *Comedy*,
But hasty *Shadwel*, and slow *Wicherley*.

Dryden misinterprets the passage, however. Rochester is referring to Shadwell's brisk and Wycherley's meagre output. Dryden refers to Shadwell's slowness in *Mac Flecknoe*, 11. 149–50.

[4] 'lazy hounds that are bald with chronic mange, and who lick the edges of a dry lamp, will be called "Leopard", "Tiger", "Lion", or any other animal in the world that roars more fiercely.' (Juvenal, *Satires*, vii. 34–7.)

4. Francis Fane on Rochester

1675; 1680

A grandson of Francis Fane, first Earl of Westmorland, Fane, after trying his hand at writing plays, retired to his country estate. He wrote in 1686 that he had 'long since devoted himself to a country life, . . . wanting patience to attend the leasure of the stage'. He seems to have known Rochester personally. He died in or about 1689.

(a) From the Dedication to Rochester of *Love in the Dark*:

All Poems in their Dedications, ought to return to your Lordship, as all Rivers to the Sea, from whose depth and saltness they are season'd and supply'd: none of them ever coming to your Lordship's hands, without receiving some of the rich Tinctures of your unerring Judgement, and running with much more clearness, having past so fine a strainer. If this receives any approbation in the World, I must ascribe it principally to your Lordship's partial recommendations, and impartial corrections. Your Lordship is the first person in the World, by whom I have been Highly and Heroically oblig'd: and if the first Impressions of Gratitude, may be as strong and captivating, as those of the first Love; they must needs be much more lasting and immutable, in my Passion for your Lordship; since the World affords no object so high and admirable, ever to work a change; your Lordship being the most accomplish'd of all Mankind, that I ever knew, read, or heard of, by Humane testimony. Eminent Beings are as hard to be believ'd, as they are to be understood and no Man can speak Truth of your Lordship's Superlative Endowments, without suspicion of Flattery; nor conceal them without conviction of Ignorance. That famous Temper of weight, so rarely found in Bodies, appears most Illustriously in your Lordship's Mind. Judgement, and Fancy, seldom concurring in other Men, in any small proportion, are possest by your Lordship in the highest degree that ever was allow'd the Soul of Man; yet with so happy and harmonious a mixture, that neither of them predominate nor usurp; but, like two peaceful Colleagues in Empire, agree within themselves, and govern the rest of the World, acting in your Lordship's noble, and elevated Mind, like Fire and Air in the upper Region, whose Purity makes them easily convertible, and mutually assistant, whilst they are always quarrelling and preying upon each other in gross inferior Bodies. What was favourably said of my Lord Bacon in his time, may much more justly be affirmed of your Lordship, in yours; that if ever there were a beam of Knowledge, immediately deriv'd from God, upon any Man, since the Creation, there is one upon your self. Others, by wearisome steps, and regular gradations, climb up to Knowledge; your Lordship is flown up to the top of the Hill: you are an Enthusiast in Wit; a Poet and Philosopher by Revelation; and have already in your tender Age, set out such new and glorious Lights in Poetry, yet these so orthodox and Unquestionable, that all the Heroes of Antiquity, must submit, or Homer and Virgil be judg'd Nonconformists. For my part, I account it one of the great felicities of my life, to have liv'd in your age; but much greater, to have had access to your Person, and to have been cherish'd and enlighten'd by the influences, and irradiations of so great a Luminary. For I must confess, I never return from your Lordship's most Charming and Instructive Conversation, but I am inspir'd with a new Genius, and improv'd in all those Sciences I ever coveted the knowledge of: I find my self not only a better Poet, a better Philosopher; but much more than these, a better Christian: your Lordship's miraculous Wit, and intellectual pow'rs being the greatest Argument that ever I could meet with, for the immateriality of the Soul, they being the highest exaltation of humane Nature; and, under Divine Authority, much more convincing to suspicious Reason, than all the Pedantick proofs of the most Learnedly peevish Disputants; so that, I hope, I shall be oblig'd to your Lordship, not only for my Reputation in this World, but my future Happiness in the next. (*Love in the Dark* (1675) Sigg. A 2ʳ–A 3ʳ.)

(b) To the late Earl of Rochester, upon the report of His Sickness in Town, being newly Recovered by His Lordship's advice in the Country. In Allusion to the Ode of Horace.

What means this tumult in my Veins,
These eccho'd Groans and Sympathetick pains?
Ah cruel Lord! Why do'st thou wound
Him whom so late thy pity found?
Or did'st thou spare my Life, that I
A nobler Death for thee should dy?

It is not possible, nor just,
The little Off-springs of the dust,
The Sun extinct should him survive,
By whose kind beams they're kept alive;
Oh! rather let me dy before,
Perish Ten Thousand more,
To spy the Bounds of th' indiscover'd shore,
Though with less hopes than they that sought the *Indian* Oar.
How dar'st thou bold disease surprize
The joy, and Glory of our eyes;
Mankind's delight, wits utmost Goal,
Heav'ns Masterpiece, spirit of Soul:
We need thee not to make his Fame more bright
    Officious Death, to lesser Stars requir'd,
Who never shine out clear, but in thy Night.
    He is all Flame, all Light,
And lives unenvy'd, though by all admir'd:
Free as the Angels in their blest Estate,
What none can reach, there's none will emulate.
Quench *Feaver*, quench thy too presumtuous heat,
    Tremble to Ice at so August a name,
Or if thou need'st wilt be by mischiefs great,
    Fire on, and set the World on Flame.
Had credulous *England*, fond of Foreign News,
    And from remotest parts the World above,
Receiv'd the *Indian Faith*, which none else does refuse,
Did Men believe, that after their remove
From Earth, they should enjoy the Friends they Love;
With all their Wit, their Rhetorick, and sense,
Which with immortal ease they could dispence:
What Crowds would leap into his *Funeral* Pile,
London would desert, Kingless be the Isle;
The *Strand* instead of Men, would Acrons yield
Whitehall a Meadow be, th' *Exchange* a Field.

(*Poems by Several Hands*, collected by Nahum Tate (1685), pp. 11–13)

5. Sir Carr Scroope, 'Answer by way of Epigram'

1677

From *Poems on Affairs of State*, ed. G. de F. Lord (1963), i. 373.

Sir Carr Scroope, 1649–80, was one of the lesser wits of Charles II's Court. This epigram is a reply to an attack by Rochester on Scroope, 'On the Supposed Author of a Late Poem in Defense of Satire' (Pinto, lxxiii), part of a series of attacks and counter-attacks by the two poets. The series is printed by Lord. The title of the Epigram is taken from the Gyldenstolpe MS version.

Rail on, poor feeble scribbler, speak of me
In as ill terms as the world speaks of thee.
Sit swelling in thy hole like a vex'd toad,
And all thy pox and malice spit abroad.
Thou canst blast no man's name by thy ill word:
Thy pen is full as harmless as thy sword.

6. Lines from an Anonymous Advice to Apollo

1678

From *Poems on Affairs of State* (1703), i, 200–1.

The type of poem represented here, in which the contemporary poets are reviewed in order, was popular during the Restoration. A similar poem, called 'A Session of the Poets' has been attributed to Rochester himself (Pinto, lvii) and though Vieth rejects it as spurious, Rochester may have had a hand in its composition.

Rochester's easie Muse does still improve
Each hour thy[1] little wealthy *World* of Love,
(That *World* in which each Muse is thought a Queen)
That he must be forgiv'n in Charity then;
Tho his sharp Satyrs have offended thee;
In charity to Love, who will decay,
When its delightful Muse (its only stay)
Is by thy Pow'r severely ta'ne away.
Forbear (then) Civil Wars, and strike not down
Love, who alone supports thy tott'ring Crown.

[1] i.e. Apollo's.

7. John Sheffield, Earl of Mulgrave, later Marquess of Normandy and Duke of Buckinghamshire, on Rochester

1679; 1682

John Sheffield, third Earl of Mulgrave, 1648–1721, was perhaps the chief of Rochester's enemies following a quarrel in 1669, and there are several poems by Rochester which satirize him (see Pinto, xxxvi. li. lxi). The antipathy between the two men was intensified by Mulgrave's patronage of Dryden. Dryden seems to have assisted Mulgrave in the composition of the *Essay upon Satire* and Rochester was under the erroneous impression that it was largely Dryden's work (see Rochester's letter to Savile 21 November 1679).

(a) Lines 230–69 of *An Essay upon Satire* (1679)

Rochester I despise for his mere want of wit
(Though thought to have a tail and cloven feet)
For while he mischief means to all mankind,
Himself alone the ill effect does find,
And so like witches justly suffers shame,
Whose harmless malice is so much the same.
False are his words, affected as his wit,
So often he does aim, so seldem hit;
To ev'ry face he cringes whilst he speaks,
But when the back is turn'd the head he breaks.
Mean in each motion, lewd in ev'ry limb,
Manners themselves are mischievous in him;
A proof that chance alone makes ev'ry creature,
A very Killigrew without good nature.[1]

[1] Henry Killigrew, one of the wilder rakes of Charles II's Court.

For what a Bessus hath he always liv'd,[1]
And his own kicking notably contriv'd?
For there's the folly that's still mix'd with fear:
Cowards more blows than any hero bear.
Of fighting sparks some may their pleasure say,
But 'tis a bolder thing to run away.
The world may well forgive him all his ill,
For ev'ry fault does prove his penance still;
Falsely he falls into some dang'rous noose,
And then as meanly labors to get loose;
A life so infamous it's better quitting,
Spent in base injuring and low submitting.
I'd like to have left out his poetry,
Forgot almost by all as well as me:
Sometimes he hath some humor, never wit,[2]
And if it ever (very rarely) hit,
'Tis under so much nasty rubbish laid,
To find it out's the cinder-woman's trade,
Who for the wretched remnants of a fire,
Must toil all day in ashes and in mire.
So lewdly dull his idle works appear,
The wretched text deserves no comment here,
There one poor thought's sometimes left all alone
For a whole page of dulness to atone.
'Mongst forty bad's one tolerable line,
Without expression, fancy, or design.

(from *Poems on Affairs of State*, ed. G. de F. Lord (1963), i. 412–13)

(b) Lines 63–4, 80–9 of *An Essay upon Poetry* (1682)

First then of *Songs*, that now so much abound:
Without his Song no Fop is to be found . . .
. . . Here as in all things else, is most unfit
Bawdry barefac'd, that poor pretence to Wit,—

[1] Bessus, a cowardly, bragging character in Beaumont and Fletcher's *King and no King*.

[2] The essence of the distinction here seems to be that humour is destructive, consisting mainly of ridicule, while wit involves imaginative invention. A little later the emotional connotation came to be reversed and humour came to be regarded as superior to wit, see for example Congreve's letter 'Concerning Humour in Comedy' (1695) Spingarn, iii. 242.

Such nauseous Songs as the late Convert made,[1]
Which justly call this censure on his Shade;
Not that warm thoughts of the transporting joy
Can shock the Chastest or the Nicest cloy,
But obscene words, too gross to move desire,
Like heaps of Fuel do but choak the Fire.
That Author's Name has undeserved praise,
Who pall'd the appetite he meant to raise.

(from J. E. Spingarn, *Critical Essays of the Seventeenth Century* (Oxford, 1908), ii. 288)

8. Charles Blount on Rochester's translation from Seneca

7 February 1680

'Letter to Strephon' [i.e. Rochester], *The Miscellaneous Works of Charles Blount* (1695), pp. 117–18.

Charles Blount, 1654–93, was an admirer of Hobbes and published a number of free thinking and deistic works.

My lord, I had the Honour Yesterday to receive from the Hands of an Humble Servant of your Lordship's, your most incomparable Version of that Passage of *Seneca's*, where he begins with,—*Post mortem nihil est, ipsaque mors nihil*,[2] etc.—and must confess, with your Lordship's Pardon, that I cannot but esteem the Translation to be, in some measure, a confutation of the Original; since what less than a divine and immortal

[1] Rochester was converted to Christianity on his deathbed in 1680.
[2] 'After Death nothing is, and nothing Death' (Rochester's translation), see Pinto, xxxix.

Mind could have produced what you have there written? Indeed, the Hand that wrote it may become *Lumber*, but sure, the Spirit that dictated it, can never be so: No, my Lord, your mighty Genius is a most sufficient Argument of its own Immortality; and more prevalent with me, than all the Harangues of the Parsons, or Sophistry of the Schoolmen.[1]

[1] The rest of the letter is a learned discussion of the immortality of the soul.

COMMENT AT ROCHESTER'S DEATH

1680 – 1700

9. Robert Parsons on Rochester

1680

Extract from *A Sermon preached at the Earl of Rochester's Funeral* (1680), pp. 7–9.

This famous sermon by Rochester's family chaplain was the first of a long line of cautionary publications in which Rochester features as the exemplary late penitent. First published in 1680, it had achieved its fourteenth edition by around 1730 and went on being published throughout the eighteenth and into the nineteenth century; the last edition (with Burnet's *Life*) is dated 1820.

His Quality[1] I shall take no notice of, there being so much of what was excellent and extraordinary in this great Person, that I have no room for any thing that is common to him with others.

A Wit he had so rare and fruitful in its Invention, and withall so choice and delicate in its Judgment, that there is nothing wanting in his Composures to give a full answer to that question, what and where Wit is? except the purity and choice of subject. For had such excellent seeds but fallen upon good ground, and instead of pitching upon a Beast or a Lust, been raised up on high, to celebrate the mysteries of the Divine Love, in Psalms, and Hymns, and Spiritual songs; I perswade my self we might by this time have receiv'd from his Pen as excellent an Idea of Divine Poetry, under the Gospel, useful to the teaching of Virtue, especially in this generation, as his profane Verses have been to destroy it. And I am confident, had God spared him a longer life, this would have been the whole business of it, as I know it was the vow and purpose of his Sickness.

[1] i.e. social rank.

His natural talent was excellent, but he had hugely improved it by Learning and Industry, being throughly acquainted with all Classick Authors, both Greek and Latin; a thing very rare, if not peculiar to him, amongst those of his quality. Which yet he used not, as other Poets have done, to translate or steal from them, but rather to better, and improve them by his own natural fancy. And whoever reads his Composures, will find all things in them so peculiarly Great, New, and Excellent, that he will easily pronounce, That tho he has lent to many others, yet he has borrowed of none; and that he has been as far from a sordid imitation of those before him, as he will be from being reach'd by those that follow him.

His other personal accomplishments in all the perfections of a Gentleman for the Court or the Country, whereof he was known by all men to be a very great Master, is no part of my business to describe or understand: and whatever they were in themselves, I am sure they were but miserable Comforters to him, since they only minister'd to his sins, and made his example the more fatal and dangerous; for so we may own, (nay I am obliged by him not to hide, but to shew the rocks, which others may avoid) that he was once one of the *greatest of Sinners*.

And truly none but one so great in parts could be so; as the chiefest of the Angels for knowledge and power became most dangerous. His Sins were like his Parts, (for from them corrupted they sprang), all of them high and extraordinary. He seem'd to affect something singular and paradoxical in his Impieties, as well as in his Writings, above the reach and thought of other men; taking as much pains to draw others in, and to pervert the right ways of virtue, as the Apostles and Primitive Saints, *to save their own souls, and them that heard them.* For this was the heightning and amazing circumstance of his sins, that he was so diligent and industrious to recommend and propagate them; not like those of old that *hated the light*, but those the Prophet mentions, *Isiah 3.9. who declare their sin as Sodom, and hide it not*, that *take it upon their shoulders, and bind it to them as a Crown*; framing Arguments for Sin, making Proselytes to it, and writing Panegyricks upon Vice; singing Praises to the great enemy of God, and casting down Coronets and Crowns before his Throne.

Nay so confirm'd was he in Sin, that he lived, and oftentimes almost died, a Martyr for it.

10. Gilbert Burnet, *Some Passages of the Life and Death of Rochester*

1680

Gilbert Burnet was born in Edinburgh in 1643. After a distinguished ecclesiastical career in Scotland he became chaplain to Charles II and, soon after William III's accession to the throne in 1688, which he had furthered, was made Bishop of Salisbury. He died in 1715. The *Life of Rochester*, here printed in full, had a phenomenal success, published first in 1680 and thereafter in repeated editions and reprints (including translation into French, Dutch and German) until as late as 1876. It is discussed in the Introduction pp. 9–10. The text reproduced is that of the first edition. For a list of editions, though incomplete, see Clarke and Foxcroft's *Life of Gilbert Burnet* (Cambridge, 1907), pp. 526–7 and Prinz, *op. cit.*, pp. 414–18.

From the Preface:

I have endeavoured to give his character as fully as I could take it: for, I who saw him only in one light, in a sedate and quiet temper, when he was under a great decay of strength and loss of spirits, cannot give his picture with that life and advantage that others may who knew him when his parts were more bright and lively; yet the composure he was then in may perhaps be supposed to balance any abatement of his usual vigour, which the declination of his health brought him under. I have written this discourse with as much care, and have considered it as narrowly, as I could. I am sure I have said nothing but truth: I have done it slowly, and often used my second thoughts in it, not being so much concerned in the censures which might fall on myself, as cautious that nothing should pass that might obstruct my only design of writing, which is the doing what I can towards the reforming a loose and lewd age. And if such a signal instance, concurring with all the evidence that we have for our most holy faith, has no effect on those who are running the same course, it is much to be feared they are given up to a reprobate sense.

SOME PASSAGES OF THE LIFE AND DEATH OF JOHN EARL OF ROCHESTER

JOHN WILMOT, Earl of Rochester, was born in April, Anno Dom. 1648. His father was *Henry* Earl of *Rochester*, but best known by the title of the Lord *Wilmot*, who bore so great a part in all the late wars, that mention is often made of him in the History: And had the chief share in the Honour of the preservation of his Majesty that now Reigns, after *Worcester* fight, and the conveying him from Place to Place, till he happily escaped into *France*: But dying before the King's Return, he left his Son little other Inheritance, but the Honour and Title derived to him, with the pretensions such eminent services gave him to the King's favour: these were carefully managed by the great prudence and discretion of his Mother, a Daughter of that Noble and ancient family of the *St. Johns* of *Wiltshire*, so that his education was carried on in all things suitably to his Quality.

When he was at School he was an extraordinary Proficient at his book: and those shining parts, which since have appeared with so much lustre; began then to shew themselves: He acquired the *Latin* to such perfection, that to his dying-day he retained a great relish of the fineness and Beauty of that Tongue: and was exactly versed in the incomparable Authors that writ about *Augustus's* time, whom he read often with that peculiar delight which the greatest Wits have ever found in those Studies.[1]

When he went to the *University* the general joy which over-ran the whole Nation upon his Majesty's *Restauration*, but was not regulated with that Sobriety and Temperance, that became a serious gratitude to God for so great a blessing, produced some of its ill effects on him: He began to love these disorders too much; His Tutor was that Eminent and Pious Divine Dr. *Blandford*, afterwards promoted to the Sees of *Oxford* and *Worcester*: And under his Inspection, he was committed to the more immediate care of Mr. *Phineas Berry*, a Fellow of Wadham

[1] See however my note to No. 27 for a different opinion.

College, a very learned and good-natured man; whom he afterwards ever used with much respect, and rewarded him as became a great man. But the humour of that time wrought so much on him, that he broke off the Course of his Studies; to which no means could ever effectually recall him; till when he was in *Italy* his Governor, Dr. *Balfour*, a learned and worthy man, now a Celebrated Physician in *Scotland*, his Native Country; drew him to read such Books, as were most likely to bring him back to love Learning and Study: and he often acknowledged to me, in particular three days before his Death, how much he was obliged to Love and Honour this his Governor, to whom he thought he owed more than to all the World, next after his Parents, for his Fidelity and Care of him, while he was under his trust. But no part of it affected him more sensibly, than that he engaged him by many tricks (so he expressed it) to delight in Books and reading; So that ever after he took occasion, in the Intervals of those woful Extravagancies that consumed most of his time to read much: and though the time was generally but indifferently employed, for the choice of the Subjects of his Studies was not always good, yet the habitual Love of Knowledge together with these fits of Study, had much awakened his Understanding, and prepared him for better things, when his mind should be so far changed as to relish them.

He came from his Travels in the 18th Year of his Age, and appeared at Court with as great Advantages as most ever had. He was a Graceful and well-shaped Person, tall, and well made, if not a little too slender: He was exactly well bred, and what by a modest behaviour natural to him, what by a Civility become almost as natural, his Conversation was easie and obliging. He had a strange Vivacity of thought, and vigour of expression: his Wit had a subtility and sublimity both, that were scarce imitable. His Style was clear and strong: When he used Figures they were very lively, and yet far enough out of the Common Road: he had made himself Master of Ancient and Modern Wit, and of the Modern *French* and *Italian* as well as the *English*. He loved to talk and write of Speculative Matters, and did it with so fine a thread, that even those who hated the Subjects that his Fancy ran upon, yet could not but be charmed with his way of treating them. *Boileau* among the *French*, and *Cowley* among the *English* Wits, were those he admired most. Sometimes other men's thoughts mixed with his Composures, but that flowed rather from the Impressions they made on him when he read them, by which they came to return upon him as his own thoughts; than that he servilely copied from any. Few men ever had a bolder flight of fancy, more steadily governed by Judgment than he had. No wonder a young man so made, and so improved was very acceptable in a Court.

Soon after his coming thither he laid hold on the first Occasion that offered to shew his readiness to hazard his life in the Defence and Service of his Country. In *winter* 1665 he went with the Earl of *Sandwich* to Sea, when he was sent to lie for the *Dutch East-India* Fleet; and was in the *Revenge*, Commanded by Sir *Thomas Tiddiman*, when the Attack was made on the Port of *Bergen* in *Norway*, the *Dutch* ships having got into that *Port*. It was as desperate an Attempt as ever was made: during the whole Action, the Earl of *Rochester* shewed as brave and as resolute a Courage as was possible: A Person of Honour told me he heard the Lord *Clifford*, who was in the same Ship, often magnifie his Courage at that time very highly. Nor did the Rigours of the Season, the hardness of the Voyage, and the extream danger he had been in, deter him from running the like on the very next Occasion; for the *Summer* following he went to Sea again, without communicating his design to his nearest Relations. He went aboard the Ship Commanded by Sir *Edward Spragge* the day before the great Sea-fight of that Year: Almost all the Volunteers that were in the same Ship were killed. Mr. *Middleton* (brother to Sir *Hugh Middleton*) was shot in the Arms. During the Action, Sir *Edward Spragge* not being satisfied with the behaviour of one of the Captains, could not easily find a person that would chearfully venture through so much danger to carry his Commands to that Captain. This Lord offered himself to the Service; and went in a little Boat, through all the shot, and delivered his Message, and returned back to Sir *Edward*: which was much commended by all that saw it. He thought it necessary to begin his life with these Demonstrations of his Courage in an Element and way of fighting, which is acknowledged to be the greatest trial of clear and undaunted Valour.[1]

He had so entirely laid down the Intemperance that was growing on him before his Travels, that at his Return he hated nothing more. But falling into Company that loved these Excesses, he was, though not without difficulty, and by many steps, brought back to it again. And the natural heat of his fancy, being inflamed by Wine, made him so extravagantly pleasant, that many, to be more diverted by that humor, studied to engage him deeper and deeper in Intemperance: which at length did so entirely subdue him; that, as he told me, for five years together he was continually Drunk: not all the while under the visible

[1] Rochester's courage however was often called in question, see for example Scroope's *Epigram* (No. 5).

effect of it, but his blood was so inflamed, that he was not in all that time cool enough to be perfectly Master of himself. This led him to say and do many wild and unaccountable things: By this, he said, he had broke the firm constitution of his Health, that seemed so strong, that nothing was too hard for it; and he had suffered so much in his Reputation, that he almost dispaired to recover it. There were two Principles in his natural temper, that being heighten'd by that heat carried him to great excesses: a violent love of Pleasure, and a disposition to extravagant Mirth. The one involved him in great sensuality: the other led him to many odd Adventures and *Frollicks*, in which he was oft in hazard of his life. The one being the same irregular appetite in his Mind, that the other was in his Body, which made him think nothing diverting that was not extravagant. And though in cold blood he was a generous and good-natured man, yet he would go far in his heats, after any thing that might turn to a Jest or matter of Diversion: He said to me, He never improved his Interest at Court, to do a premeditate Mischief to other persons. Yet he laid out his Wit very freely in *Libels* and *Satyrs*, in which he had a peculiar Talent of mixing his Wit with his Malice, and fitting both with such apt words, that Men were tempted to be pleased with them: from thence his Composures came to be easily known, for few had such a way of tempering these together as he had; so that, when any thing extraordinary that way came out, as a Child is fathered sometimes by its Resemblance, so it was laid at his Door as its Parent and Author.

These Exercises in the course of his life were not always equally pleasant to him; he had often sad Intervals and severe Reflections on them: and though then he had not these awakened in him by any deep Principle of Religion, yet the horror that Nature raised in him, especially in some Sicknesses, made him too easie to receive some ill Principles, which others endeavoured to possess him with; so that he was too soon brought to set himself too secure, and fortifie his Mind against that, by dispossessing it all he could of the belief or apprehensions of Religion. The Licentiousness of his temper, with the briskness of his Wit, disposed him to love the Conversation of those who divided their time between lewd Actions and irregular Mirth. And so he came to bend his Wit, and direct his Studies and Endeavours to support and strengthen these ill Principles both in himself and others.

An accident fell out after this, which confirmed him more in these courses: when he went to Sea in the year 1665, there happened to be in the same Ship with him Mr. *Mountague* and another Gentleman of

Quality, these two, the former especially, seemed persuaded that they should never return into *England*. Mr. *Mountague* said, He was sure of it: the other was not so positive. The Earl of *Rochester*, and the last of these, entred into a formal Engagement, not without Ceremonies of Religion, that if either of them died, he should appear, and give the other notice of the future State, if there was any. But Mr. *Mountague* would not enter into the Bond. When the day came that they thought to have taken the *Dutch*-Fleet in the Port of *Bergen*, Mr. *Mountague* though he had such a strong Presage in his Mind of his approaching death, yet he generously staid all the while in the place of greatest danger: The other Gentleman signalized his Courage in a most undaunted manner, till near the end of the Action; when he fell on a sudden into such a trembling that he could scarce stand; and Mr. *Mountague* going to him to hold him up, as they were in each other's Arms, a Cannon Ball killed him outright, and carried away Mr. *Mountague*'s Belly, so that he died within an hour after. The Earl of *Rochester* told me that these presages they had in their minds made some impression on him, that there were separated beings: and that the Soul, either by a natural sagacity, or some secret Notice communicated to it, had a sort of Divination: But that Gentleman's never appearing was a great snare to him, during the rest of his life. Though when he told me this, he could not but acknowledge, it was an unreasonable thing for him, to think that Beings in another State were not under such Laws and Limits, that they could not command their own motions, but as the Supream Power should order them; and that one who had so corrupted the Natural Principles of Truth, as he had, had no reason to expect that such an extraordinary thing should be done for his Conviction.

He told me of another odd Presage that one had of his approaching Death in the Lady *Warre's*, his mother-in-law's house: The Chaplain had dreamt that such a day he should die, but being by all the Family put out of the belief of it, he had almost forgot it; till the Evening before at Supper, there being Thirteen at Table; according to a fond conceit that one of these must soon die, One of the young Ladies pointed to him, that he was to die. He remembering his Dream fell into some disorder and the Lady *Warre* reproving him for his Superstition, he said, He was confident he was to die before Morning, but he being in perfect health, it was not much minded. It was *Saturday*-night, and he was to Preach next day. He went to his Chamber and sat up late, as appeared by the burning of his Candle, and he had been preparing his Notes for his Sermon, but was found dead in his Bed the next Morning: These things he said made him inclined to believe, the Soul was a substance distinct from matter: and this often returned into his thoughts. But that which perfected his perswasion about it, was, that in the Sickness which brought him so near death before I first knew him, when his Spirits were so low and spent, that he could not move nor stir, and he did not think to live an hour; He said, his Reason and Judgment were so clear and strong, that from thence he was fully persuaded that Death was not the spending or dissolution of the Soul; but only the separation of it from matter. He had in that Sickness great Remorses for his past Life, but he afterwards told me, They were rather general and dark Horrours, than any Convictions of sinning against God. He was sorry he had lived so as to wast his strength so soon, or that he had brought such an ill name upon himself, and had an Agony in his Mind about it, which he knew not well how to express: But at such times, though he complied with his Friends in suffering Divines to be sent for, he said, He had no great mind to it: and that it was but a piece of his breeding, to desire them to pray by him, in which he joyned little himself.

As to the Supreme Being, he had always some Impression of one: and professed often to me, That he had never known an entire *Atheist*, who fully believed there was no God.[1] Yet when he explained his Notion of this Being, it amounted to no more than a vast power, that had none of the Attributes of Goodness or Justice we ascribe to the Deity: These were his thoughts about Religion, as himself told me. For Morality, he freely own'd to me, that though he talked of it, as a fine thing, yet this was only because he thought it a decent way of speaking, and that as they went always in Cloaths, though in their Frollicks they would have chosen sometimes to have gone naked, if they had not feared the people: So though some of them found it necessary for human life to talk of Morality, yet he confessed they cared not for it, further than the reputation of it was necessary for their credit, and affairs: of which he gave me many Instances, as their professing and swearing Friendship, where they hated mortally; their Oaths and Imprecations in their Addresses to Women, which they intended never to make good; the pleasure they took in defaming innocent Persons, and spreading false reports of some, perhaps in Revenge, because they could not engage them to comply with their ill Designs: The delight they had in making people quarrel; their unjust usage of their Creditors, and putting them

[1] cf. The recollection of Rochester's tutor Giffard 'Mr. Giffard, says my Lord, I have been guilty of Extravagances, but I will assure you I am no Atheist.' Thomas Hearne, *Remarks and Collections*, ed. Doble, 1889, iii. 263.

off by any deceitful Promise they could invent, that might deliver them from present Importunity. So that in detestation of these Courses he would often break forth into such hard Expressions concerning himself, as would be indecent for another to repeat.[1]

Such had been his Principles and Practices in a Course of many years which had almost quite extinguish'd the natural Propensities in him to Justice and Vertue: He would often go into the Country, and be for some months wholly imployed in Study, or the Sallies of his Wit: which he came to direct chiefly to *Satyre*. And this he often defended to me; by saying there were some people that could not be kept in Order, or admonished but in this way. I replied, That it might be granted that a grave way of *Satyre* was sometimes no improfitable way of Reproof. Yet they who used it only out of spite, and mixed Lies with Truth, sparing nothing that might adorn their *Poems* or gratifie their Revenge, could not excuse that way of Reproach, by which the Innocent often suffer: since the most malicious things, if wittily expressed, might stick to and blemish the best men in the World, and the malice of a Libel could hardly consist with the Charity of an Admonition. To this he answered, A man could not write with life, unless he were heated by Revenge; For to make a *Satyre* without Resentments, upon the cold Notions of *Phylosophy*, was as if a man would in cold blood, cut men's throats who had never offended him: And he said, the lies in these Libels came often in as Ornaments that could not be spared without spoiling the beauty of the *Poem*.

For his other Studies, they were divided between the Comical and witty Writings of the Antients and Moderns, the *Roman* Authors, and Books of Physick: which the ill state of health he was fallen into, made more necessary to himself: and which qualifi'd him for an odd adventure, which I shall but just mention. Being under an unlucky Accident, which obliged him to keep out of the way; He disguised himself, so that his nearest Friends could not have known him, and set up in *Tower-Street* for an *Italian Mountebank*, where he had a Stage, and practised Physick for some Weeks not without success. In his latter years, he read Books of History more. He took pleasure to disguise himself as a *Porter*, or as a *Beggar*; sometimes to follow some mean Amours, which, for the variety of them, he affected. At other times, merely for diversion, he would go about in odd shapes, in which he acted his part so naturally, that even those who were in the secret, and saw him in these shapes, could perceive nothing by which he might be discovered.

[1] One of these attacks on himself survives in the *Lines to a Postboy* (Pinto, lxxx).

I have now made the Description of his former Life, and Principles, as fully as I thought necessary, to answer my End in Writing: And yet with those reserves, that I hope I have given no just cause of offence to any. I have said nothing but what I had from his own mouth, and have avoided the mentioning of the more particular Passages of his life, of which he told me not a few: But since others were concerned in them, whose good only I design, I will say nothing that may either provoke or blemish them. It is their Reformation, and not their Disgrace, I desire: This tender consideration of others has made me suppress many remarkable and useful things, he told me: But finding that, though I should name none, yet I must at least Relate such Circumstances, as would give too great Occasion for the *Reader* to conjecture concerning the Persons intended, right or wrong, either of which were inconvenient enough, I have chosen to pass them quite over. But I hope those that know how much they were engaged with him in his ill Courses, will be somewhat touched with this tenderness I express towards them: and be thereby the rather induced to reflect on their Ways, and to consider without prejudice or passion what a sense this Noble Lord had of their case, when he came at last seriously to reflect upon his own.

I now turn to those parts of this *Narrative*, wherein I myself bore some share, and which I am to deliver upon the Observations I made, after a long and free Conversation with him for some months. I was not long in his Company, when he told me, He should treat me with more freedom than he had ever used to men of my Profession. He would conceal none of his Principles from me, but lay his thoughts open without any Disguise; nor would he do it to maintain Debate, or shew his Wit, but plainly tell me what stuck with him; and protested to me, That he was not so engaged to his old Maxims as to resolve not to change, but that if he could be convinc'd, he would choose rather to be of another mind; He said, He would impartially Weigh what I should lay before him, and tell me freely when it did convince him and when it did not. He expressed this disposition of mind to me in a manner so frank, that I could not but believe him, and be much taken with his way of Discourse: So we entered into almost all the parts of Natural and Revealed Religion, and of Morality. He seemed pleased, and in a great measure satisfied, with what I said upon many of these Heads: And though our freest Conversation was when we were alone, yet upon several Occasions other persons were Witnesses to it. I understood from many hands that my Company was not distasteful to him, and that the Subjects about which we talked most were not unacceptable: and he expressed himself often, not ill pleased with many things I said to him, and particularly when I visited him in his last Sickness, so that I hope it may not be altogether unprofitable to publish the substance of those matters about which We argued so freely, with our reasoning upon them: And perhaps what had some effects on him, may be not altogether ineffectual upon others. I followed him with such Arguments as I saw were most likely to prevail with him: and my not urging other Reasons, proceeded not from any distrust I had of their force, but from the necessity of using those that were most proper for him. He was then in a low state of health, and seemed to be slowly recovering of a great Disease: He was in the Milk-Diet, and apt to fall into Hectical-Fits; any accident weakened him; so that he thought he could not live long; And when he went from *London*, he said, He believed he should never come to Town more. Yet during his being in Town he was so well, that he went often abroad, and had great Vivacity of Spirit. So that he was under no such decay, as either darkened or weakened his Understanding; Nor was he any way troubled with the Spleen, or Vapours, or under the power of Melancholy. What he was then, compared to what he had been formerly, I could not so well judge, who had seen him but twice before. Others have told me they perceived no difference in his parts. This I mention more particularly, that it may not be thought that Melancholy, or the want of Spirits, made him more inclined to receive any Impressions: for indeed I never discovered any such thing in him.

Having thus opened the way to the Heads of our Discourse, I shall next mention them. The *three* chief things We talked about, were *Morality*, *Natural Religion*, and *Revealed Religion*, *Christianity* in particular. For *Morality*, He confessed, he saw the necessity of it, both for the Government of the World, and for the preservation of Health, Life, and Friendship: and was very much ashamed of his former Practices, rather because he had made himself a Beast, and had brought pain and sickness on his Body, and had suffered much in his Reputation, than from any deep sense of a Supream being or another State: But so far this went with him, that he resolved firmly to change the Course of his Life; which he thought he should effect by the study of *Philosophy*, and had not a few no less solid than pleasant Notions concerning the folly and madness of Vice: but he confessed he had no remorse for his past Actions, as Offences against God, but only as Injuries to himself and to Mankind.

Upon this Subject I shewed him the Defects of *Philosophy*, for reforming the World: That it was a matter of Speculation, which but few either had the leisure, or the capacity to enquire into. But the Principle that must reform Mankind, must be obvious to every Man's Understanding. That *Philosophy* in matters of Morality, beyond the great lines of our Duty, had no very certain fixed Rule, but in the lesser Offices and Instances of our Duty went much by the Fancies of Men and Customs of Nations; and consequently could not have Authority enough to bear down the Propensities of Nature, Appetite, or Passion: For which I instanced in these two Points; The *One* was, About that *Maxim* of the *Stoicks*, to extirpate all sort of Passion and concern for any thing. That, take it by one hand, seemed desirable, because, if it could be accomplish'd, it would make all the accidents of life easie; but I think it cannot, because Nature after all our striving against it, will still return to itself: Yet on the other hand it dissolved the Bonds of Nature and Friendship, and slackened Industry which will move but dully, without an inward heat: And if it delivered a man from any Troubles, it deprived him of the chief pleasures of Life, which arise from Friendship. The *other* was concerning the restraint of pleasure, how far that was to go. Upon this he told me the two *Maxims* of his *Morality* then were, that he should do nothing to the hurt of any other, or that might prejudice his own health: And he thought that all pleasure, when it did not interfere with these, was to be indulged as the gratification of our natural Appetites. It seemed unreasonable to imagine these were put into a man only to be restrained, or curbed to such a narrowness: This he applied to the free use of Wine and Women.

To this I answered, That if Appetites being Natural, was an Argument for the indulging them, then the revengeful might as well alledge it for Murder, and the Covetous for stealing; whose Appetites are no less keen on those Objects; and yet it is acknowledg'd that these Appetites ought to be curb'd. If the difference is urged from the Injury that another Person receives, the Injury is as great, if a Man's Wife is defiled, or his Daughter corrupted: and it is impossible for a man to let his Appetites loose to Vagrant Lusts, and not to transgress in these particulars: So there was no curing the Disorders, that must arise from thence, but by regulating these Appetites: And why should we not as well think that God intended our brutish and sensual Appetites should be governed by our Reason, as that the fierceness of beasts should be managed and tamed by the Wisdom, and for the use of Man? So that it is no real absurdity to grant that Appetites were put into Men on purpose to exercise their Reason in the Restraint and Government of them: which to be able to do, Ministers a higher and more lasting pleasure to a Man, than to give them their full scope and range. And if other Rules of *Philosophy* be observed, such as the avoiding those Objects that stir Passion; Nothing raises higher Passions than ungovern'd Lust; nothing darkens the Understanding, and depresses a man's mind more, nor is any thing managed with more frequent Returns of other Immoralities, such as Oaths and Imprecations which are only intended to compass what is desired: The expence that is necessary to maintain these Irregularities makes a man false in his other dealings. All this he freely confessed was true, Upon which I urged, that, if it was reasonable for a man to regulate his Appetite in things which he knew were hurtful to him; Was it not as reasonable for God to prescribe a Regulation of those Appetites, whose unrestrained Course did produce such mischievous effects. That it could not be denied, but doing to others what we would have others do unto us, was a just Rule: Those men then that knew how extremely sensible they themselves would be of the dishonour of their Families in the case of their Wives or Daughters, must needs condemn themselves, for doing that which they could not bear from another: And if the peace of Mankind, and the entire satisfaction of our whole life, ought to be one of the chief measures of our Actions, then let all the World judge, Whether a Man that confines his Appetite, and lives contented at home, is not much happier, than those that let their Desires run after forbidden Objects. The thing being granted to be better in it self, then the question falls between the restraint of Appetite in some Instances, and the freedom of a man's thoughts, the soundness of his health, his application to Affairs, with the easiness of his whole life. Whether the one is not to be done before the other? As to the difficulty of such a restraint, though it is not easie to be done, when a man allows himself many liberties, in which it is not possible to stop; Yet those who avoid the Occasions that may kindle these impure Flames, and keep themselves well employed, find the Victory and Dominion over them no such impossible, or hard matter, as may seem at first view. So that though the *Philosophy* and *Morality* of this Point were plain; Yet there is not strength enough in that Principle to subdue Nature, and Appetite. Upon this I urged, that *Morality* could not be a strong thing, unless a man were determined by a Law within himself: for if he only measured himself by Decency, or the Laws of the Land, this would teach him only to use such caution in his ill Practices, that they should not break out too visibly: but would never carry him to an inward and universal probity: That Vertue was of so complicated a Nature, that, unless a man came entirely within its discipline, he could not adhere stedfastly to any one

Precept; for Vices are often made necessary supports to one another. That this cannot be done, either steddily, or with any satisfaction, unless the Mind does inwardly comply with, and delight in the Dictates of Virtue. And that could not be effected, except a man's nature were internally regenerated, and changed by a higher Principle: Till that came about, corrupt Nature would be strong, and *Philosophy* but feeble: especially when it strugled with such Appetites or Passions as were much kindled, or deeply rooted in the Constitution of one's Body. This, he said, sounded to him like *Enthusiasme*, or *Canting*: He had no notion of it, and so could not understand it: He comprehended the Dictates of *Reason* and *Philosophy*, in which as the Mind became much conversant, there would soon follow as he believed, a greater easiness in obeying its precepts: I told him on the other hand, that all his Speculations of *Philosophy* would not serve him in any stead, to the reforming of his Nature and Life, till he applied himself to God for inward assistances. It was certain, that the Impressions made in his Reason governed him, as they were lively presented to him: but these are so apt to slip out of our Memory, and we so apt to turn our thoughts from them, and at some times the contrary Impressions are so strong, that let a man set up a reasoning in his Mind against them, he finds that Celebrated saying of the Poet,

Video meliora, proboque; deteriora sequor

'I see what is better, and approve it; but follow what is worse', to be all that *Philosophy* will amount to. Whereas those who upon such Occasions apply themselves to God, by earnest Prayer, feel a disengagement from such Impressions, and themselves endued with a power to resist them. So that those bonds which formerly held them, fall off.

This he said must be the effect of a heat in Nature: it was only the strong diversion of the thoughts, that gave the seeming Victory, and he did not doubt but if one could turn to a *Problem* in *Euclid*, or to Write a Copy of Verses, it would have the same effect. To this I answered, That if such Methods did only divert the thoughts, there might be some force in what he said: but if they not only drove out such Inclinations, but begat Impressions contrary to them, and brought men into a new disposition and habit of mind; then he must confess there was somewhat more than a diversion, in these changes, which were brought on our minds by true Devotion. I added, that Reason and Experience were the things that determined our perswasions: that Experience without Reason may be thought the delusion of our Fancy, so Reason without Experience had not so convincing an Operation: But these two meeting together, must needs give a man all the satisfaction he can desire. He could not say, It was unreasonable to believe that the Supream Being might make some thoughts stir in our Minds with more or less force, as it pleased: Especially the force of these motions being, for the most part, according to the Impression that was made on our Brains: which that power that directed the whole frame of Nature, could make grow deeper as it pleased. It was also reasonable to suppose God a Being of such goodness that he would give his assistance to such as desired it: For though he might upon some greater Occasions in an extraordinary manner turn some people's minds; Yet since he had endued Man with a faculty of Reason, it is fit that men should employ that, as far as they could; and beg his assistance: which certainly they can do. All this seemed reasonable, and at least probable: Now good men, who felt, upon their frequent Applications to God in prayer, a freedom from those ill Impressions, that formerly subdued them, an inward love to Vertue and true Goodness, and easiness and delight in all the parts of Holiness, which was fed and cherished in them by a seriousness in Prayer, and did languish as that went off, had as real a perception of an inward strength in their Minds, that did rise and fall with true Devotion, as they perceived the strength of their Bodies increased or abated, according as they had or wanted good nourishment.

After many Discourses upon this Subject, he still continued to think all was the effect of Fancy: He said, That he understood nothing of it, but acknowledged that he thought they were very happy whose Fancies were under the power of such Impressions; since they had somewhat on which their thoughts rested and centred: But when I saw him in his last Sickness, he then told me, He had another sense of what we had talked concerning prayer and inward assistances. This Subject led us to discourse of God, and of the Notion of Religion in general. He believed there was a Supream Being: He could not think the World was made by chance, and the regular Course of Nature seemed to demonstrate the Eternal Power of its Author. This, he said, he could never shake off; but when he came to explain his Notion of the Deity, he said, he looked on it as a vast Power that wrought every thing by the necessity of its Nature: and thought that God had none of those Affections of Love or Hatred, which breed perturbation in us, and by consequence he could not see that there was to be either reward or punishment. He thought our Conceptions of God were so low, that we had better not think much of him: And to love God seemed to him a presumptuous thing, and the heat of fanciful men. Therefore he believed there should be no other Religious Worship, but a general Celebration of that Being, in some short Hymn: All the other parts of Worship he esteemed the Inventions of Priests, to make the World believe they had a Secret of Incensing and Appeasing God as they pleased. In a word, he was neither perswaded that there was a a special Providence about humane Affairs; nor that Prayers were of much use, since that was to look on God as a weak Being, that would be overcome with Importunities. And for the state after death, though he thought the Soul did not dissolve at death; Yet he doubted much of Rewards or Punishments: the one he thought too high for us to attain, by our slight Services; and the other was too extream to be inflicted for Sin. This was the substance of his Speculations about God and Religion.

I told him his Notion of God was so low, that the Supreme Being seemed to be nothing but Nature. For if that Being had no freedom, nor choice of its own Actions, nor operated by Wisdom or Goodness, all those Reasons which led him to acknowledge a God, were contrary to this Conceit; for if the Order of the Universe perswaded him to think there was a God, He must at the same time conceive him to be both Wise and Good, as well as powerful, since these all appear'd equally in the Creation: though his Wisdom and Goodness had ways of exerting themselves, that were far beyond our Notions or Measures. If God was Wise and Good, he would naturally love, and be pleased with those that resembled him in these Perfections, and dislike those that were opposite to him. Every Rational Being naturally loves itself, and is delighted in others like itself, and is averse from what is not so. Truth is a Rational Nature's acting in conformity to itself in all things, and goodness is an Inclination to promote the happiness of other Beings: so Truth and Goodness were the essential perfections of every reasonable Being, and certainly most eminently in the Deity: *nor* does his Mercy or Love raise Passion or Perturbation in Him; for we feel that to be a weakness in ourselves, which indeed only flows from a want of power, or skill to do what we wish or desire: It is also reasonable to believe God would assist the Endeavours of the Good, with some helps suitable to their Nature. And that it could not be imagined, that those who imitated him, should not be especially favoured by him: and therefore since this did not appear in this State, it was most reasonable to think it should be in another, where the rewards shall be an admission to a more perfect State of Conformity to God, with the felicity that follows it, and the Punishments should be a total exclusion from him, with all the horrour and darkness that must follow that. These seemed to be the natural

Results of such several Courses of life, as well as the Effects of Divine Justice, Rewarding or punishing. For since he believed the Soul had a distinct subsistance, separated from the Body; Upon its dissolution, there was no reason to think it passed into a State of utter Oblivion, of what it had been in formerly: but that as the reflections on the good or evil it had done, must raise joy or horrour in it; So those good or ill Dispositions accompanying the departed Souls, they must either rise up to a higher Perfection, or sink to a more depraved and miserable State. In this life variety of Affairs and objects do much cool and divert our Minds; and are on the one hand often great temptations to the good, and give the bad some ease in their trouble; but in a State wherein the Soul shall be separated from sensible things, and employed in a more quick and sublime way of Operation, this must very much exalt the Joys and Improvements of the good, and as much heighten the horrour and rage of the Wicked. So that it seemed a vain thing to pretend to believe a Supream Being, that is Wise and Good as well as great, and not to think a discrimination will be made between the Good and Bad, which, it is manifest, is not fully done in this life.

As for the Government of the World, if We believe the Supream Power made it, there is no reason to think he does not govern it: For all that we can fancy against it, is the distraction which that Infinite Variety of Second Causes, and the care of their Concernments, must give to the first, if it inspects them all. But as among men, those of weaker Capacities are wholly taken up with some one thing, whereas those of more enlarged powers can, without distraction, have many things within their care, as the Eye can at one view receive a great Variety of Objects, in that narrow Compass, without confusion; So if we conceive the Divine Understanding to be as far above ours, as his Power of creating and framing the whole Universe, is above our limited activity; We will no more think the Government of the World a distraction to him: and if we have once overcome this prejudice, We shall be ready to acknowledge a Providence directing all Affairs; a care well becoming the Great Creator.

As for Worshipping Him, if we imagine Our Worship is a thing that adds to his happiness, or gives him such a fond Pleasure as weak people have to hear themselves commended, or that our repeated Addresses do overcome Him through our mere Importunity, We have certainly very unworthy thoughts of him. The true ends of Worship come within another consideration: which is this, A man is never entirely Reformed, till a new Principle governs his thoughts: nothing makes that Principle so strong, as deep and frequent Meditations of God; whose Nature, though it be far above our Comprehension, yet his Goodness and Wisdom are such Perfections as fall within our Imagination: And he that thinks often of God, and considers him as governing the World, and as ever observing all his Actions, will feel a very sensible effect of such Meditations, as they grow more lively and frequent with him; so the end of Religious Worship either publick or private, is to make the Apprehensions of God, have a deeper root and a stronger influence on us. The frequent returns of these are necessary: Lest if we allow of too long intervals between them, these Impressions may grow feebler, and other Suggestions may come in their room; And the Returns of Prayer are not to be considered as Favours extorted by mere Importunity, but as Rewards conferred on men so well disposed, and prepared for them: according to the Promises that God has made, for answering our Prayers: thereby to engage and nourish a devout temper in us, which is the chief root of all true Holiness and Vertue.

It is true we cannot have suitable Notions of the Divine Essence; as indeed we have no just *Idea* of any Essence whatsoever: Since we commonly consider all things, either by their outward *Figure*, or by their Effects: and from thence make Inferences what their Nature must be. So though we cannot frame any perfect Image in our Minds of the Divinity, Yet we may from the Discoveries God has made of Himself, form such Conceptions of Him, as may possess our Minds with great Reverence for Him, and beget in us such a Love of those Perfections as to engage us to imitate them. For when we say we love God; the meaning is, We love that Being that is Holy, Just, Good, Wise; and infinitely perfect: And loving these Attributes in that Object will certainly carry us to desire them in ourselves. For whatever We love in another, We naturally, according to the degree of our love, endeavour to resemble it. In sum, the Loving and Worshipping God, though they are just and reasonable returns and expressions of the sense we have of his Goodness to us; Yet they are exacted of us not only as a Tribute to God, but as a mean to beget in us a Conformity to his Nature, which is the chief end of pure and undefiled Religion.

If some Men, have at several times, found out Inventions to corrupt this, and cheat the World; it is nothing but what occurs in every sort of Employment, to which men betake themselves. *Mountebanks* Corrupt *Physick*; *Petty-Foggers* have entangled the matters of Property, and all Professions have been vitiated by the Knaveries of a number of their Calling.

With all these Discourses he was not equally satisfied: He seemed convinced that the Impressions of God being much in Men's minds, would be a powerful means to reform the World: and did not seem determined against Providence; But for the next State, he thought it more likely that the Soul began anew, and that her sense of what she had done in this Body, lying in the figures that are made in the Brain, as soon as she dislodged, all these perished, and that the Soul went into some other State to begin a new Course. But I said on this Head, That this was at best a conjecture, raised in him by his fancy: for he could give no reason to prove it true; Nor was all the remembrance our Souls had of past things seated in some material figures lodged in the Brain; Though it could not be denied but a great deal of it lay in the Brain. That we have many abstracted Notions and *Ideas* of immaterial things which depend not on bodily Figures: Some Sins, such as Falsehood and ill-Nature were seated in the Mind, as Lust and Appetite were in the Body: And as the whole Body was the Receptacle of the Soul, and the Eyes and Ears were the Organs of Seeing and Hearing, so was the Brain the Seat of Memory: Yet the power and faculty of Memory, as well as of Seeing and Hearing, lay in the Mind: and so it was no unconceivable thing that either the Soul by its own strength, or by the means of some subtiler Organs, which might be fitted for it in another state, should still remember as well as think. But indeed We know so little of the Nature of our Souls, that it is a vain thing for us to raise an *Hypothesis* out of the conjectures We have about it, or to reject one, because of some difficulties that occur to us; since it is as hard to understand how we remember things now, as how We shall do it in another State; only we are sure we do it now, and so we shall be then, when we do it.

When I pressed him with the secret Joys that a good Man felt, particularly as he drew near Death, and the Horrours of ill men especially at that time; He was willing to ascribe it to the Impressions they had from their Education: But he often confessed, that whether the business of Religion was true or not, he thought those who had the perswasions of it, and lived so that they had quiet in their Consciences, and believed God governed the World, and acquiesced in his Providence, and had the hope of an endless blessedness in another State, the happiest men in the World: And said, He would give all that he was Master of, to be under those Perswasions, and to have the Supports and Joys that must needs flow from them. I told him the main Root of all Corruptions in Men's Principles was their ill life; Which as it darkened their Minds, and disabled them from discerning better things, so it made it necessary for them to seek out such Opinions as might give them ease from those Clamours, that would otherwise have been raised within them: He did not deny but that, after the doing of some things, he felt great and severe Challenges within himself; But he said, He felt not these after some others which I would perhaps call far greater Sins, than those that affected him more sensibly: This I said, might flow from the Disorders he had cast himself into, which had corrupted his judgment, and vitiated his tast of things; and by his long continuance in, and frequent repeating of some Immoralities, he had made them so familiar to him, that they were become as it were natural: And then it was no wonder if he had not so exact a sense of what was Good or Evil; as a Feaverish man cannot judge of Tasts.

He did acknowledge the whole Systeme of Religion, if believed, was a greater foundation of quiet than any other thing whatsoever: for all the quiet he had in his mind, was, that he could not think so good a Being as the Deity would make him miserable. I asked if when by the ill course of his life he had brought so many Diseases on his Body, he could blame God for it; or expect that he should deliver him from them by a Miracle. He confessed there was no reason for that: I then urged, that if sin should cast the mind by a natural Effect, into endless Horrours and Agonies, which being seated in a Being not subject to Death, must last for ever, unless some Miraculous Power interposed, could he accuse God for that which was the effect of his own choice and ill life.

He said, They were happy that believed: for it was not in every man's power.

And upon this we discoursed long about *Revealed Religion*. He said, He did not understand the business of Inspiration; He believed the Penmen of the Scriptures had heats and honesty, and so writ: but could not comprehend how God should reveal his Secrets to Mankind. Why was not Man made a Creature more disposed for Religion, and better Illuminated? He could not apprehend how there should be any corruption in the Nature of Man, or a Lapse derived from *Adam*. God's communicating his Mind to one Man, was the putting it in his power to cheat the World: For Prophecies and Miracles, the World had been always full of strange Stories; for the boldness and cunning of Contrivers meeting with the Simplicity and Credulity of the People, things were easily received; and, being once received, passed down without contradiction. The Incoherences of Stile in the Scriptures, the odd Transitions, the seeming Contradictions, chiefly about the Order of time, the Cruelties enjoined the *Israelities* in destroying the *Canaanites*,

Circumcision, and many other Rites of the *Jewish* Worship; seemed to him unsuitable to the Divine Nature; And the first three Chapters of *Genesis* he thought could not be true, unless they were Parables. This was the substance of what he Excepted to *Revealed Religion* in general, and to the *Old Testament* in particular.

I answerd to all this, that believing a thing upon the testimony of another, in other matters where there was no reason to suspect the testimony, chiefly where it was confirmed by other Circumstances, was not only a reasonable thing, but it was the hinge on which all the Government and Justice in the World depended: Since all the Courts of Justice proceed upon the Evidence given by Witnesses; for the use of Writings is but a thing more lately brought into the World. So then if the credibility of the thing, the innocence and disinterestedness of the Witnesses, the number of them, and the publickest Confirmations that could possibly be given, do concur to perswade us of any matter of Fact, it is a vain thing to say, because it is possible for so many men to agree in a Lye, that therefore these have done it. In all other things a man gives his assent when the credibility is strong on the one side, and there appears nothing on the other side to ballance it. So such numbers agreeing in their Testimony to these Miracles; for instance of our Saviour's calling *Lazarus* out of the Grave the fourth day after he was buried, and his own rising again after he was certainly dead; If there had been never so many Impostures in the World, no man can with any reasonable colour pretend this was one. We find both by the *Jewish* and *Roman* Writers that lived in that time, that our Saviour was Crucified: and that all his Disciples and Followers believed certainly that he rose again. They believed this upon the Testimony of the Apostles, and of many hundreds who saw it, and died confirming it: They went about to perswade the World of it, with great Zeal, though they knew they were to get nothing by it, but Reproach and Sufferings: and by many wonders which they wrought they confirmed their Testimony. Now to avoid all this, by saying it is possible this might be a Contrivance, and to give no presumption to make it so much as probable, that it was so, is in plain *English* to say, *We are resolved let the Evidence be what it will, We will not believe it.*

He said, If a man says he cannot believe, what help is there? for he was not master of his own Belief, and believing was at highest but a probable Opinion. To this I answered, That if a man will let a wanton conceit possess his fancy against these things and never consider the Evidence for Religion on the other hand, but reject it upon a slight view of it, he ought not to say he cannot, but he will not believe: and while a man lives an ill course of life, he is not fitly qualified to examine the matter aright. Let him grow calm and virtuous, and upon due application examine things fairly, and then let him pronounce according to his Conscience, if to take it at its lowest, the Reasons on the one hand are not much stronger than they are on the other. For I found he was so possessed with the general conceit that a mixture of Knaves and Fools had made all extraordinary things be easily believed, that it carried him away to determine the matter, without so much as looking on the Historical Evidence for the truth of *Christianity*, which he had not enquired into, but had bent all his Wit and Study to the support of the other side. As for that, that believing is at best but an Opinion; if the Evidence be but probable, it is so: but if it be such that it cannot be questioned, it grows as certain as knowledge: For we are no less certain that there is a great Town called *Constantinople*, the Seat of the *Ottoman* Empire, than that there is another called *London*. We as little doubt that Queen *Elizabeth* once reigned, as that King *Charles* now Reigns in *England*. So that believing may be as certain, and as little subject to doubting as seeing or knowing.

There are two sorts of believing Divine matters; the one is wrought in us by our comparing all the evidences of matter of Fact, for the confirmation of *Revealed Religion*; with the Prophecies in the Scripture; where things were punctually predicted, some Ages before their completion; not in dark and doubtful words, uttered like Oracles, which might bend to any Event, but in plain terms, as the foretelling that *Cyrus* by name should send the *Jews* back from the Captivity, after the fixed period of seventy years: The History of the *Syrian* and *Egyptian* Kings, so punctually foretold by *Daniel*, and the Prediction of the destruction of *Jerusalem*, with many Circumstances relating to it, made by our *Saviour*; joyning these to the excellent Rule and Design of the Scripture in matters of *Morality*, it is at least as reasonable to believe this as any thing else in the World. Yet such a believing as this is only a general perswasion in the Mind, which has not that effect, till a man, applying himself to the Directions set down in the Scriptures (which upon such Evidence cannot be denied, to be as reasonable, as for a man to follow the Prescriptions of a learned Physitian, and when the Rules are both good and easie, to submit to them for the recovering of his health) and by following these, finds a power entring within him, that frees him from the slavery of his Appetites and Passions, that exalts his Mind above the accidents of life, and spreads an inward purity in his

Heart, from which a serene and calm Joy arises within him: And good men by the efficacy these Methods have upon them, and from the returns of their prayers, and other endeavours, grow assured that these things are true, and answerable to the Promises they find registred in Scripture. All this, he said, might be fancy: But to this I answered, That as it were unreasonable to tell a man that is abroad, and knows he is awake, that perhaps he is in a dream, and in his Bed, and only thinks he is abroad, or that as some go about in their sleep, so he may be asleep still; So good and religious men know, though others might be abused, by their fancies, that they are under no such deception: and find they are neither hot nor *Enthusiastical*, but under the power of calm and clear Principles. All this he said he did not understand, and that it was to assert or beg the thing in question, which he could not comprehend.

As for the possibility of Revelation, it was a vain thing to deny it: For as God gives us the sense of seeing material Objects by our Eyes, and opened in some a capacity of apprehending high and sublime things, of which other men seemed utterly incapable: So it was a weak assertion that God cannot awaken a power in some men's Minds, to apprehend and know some things, in such a manner that others are not capable of it. This is not half so incredible to us as sight is to a blind man, who yet may be convinced there is a strange power of seeing that governs men, of which he finds himself deprived. As for the capacity put into such men's hands to deceive the World, We are at the same time to consider, that besides the probity of their tempers, it cannot be thought but God can so forcibly bind up a man in some things, that it should not be in his power to deliver them otherwise then as he gives him in Commission: besides, the Confirmation of Miracles are [*sic*] a divine Credential to warrant such persons in what they deliver to the World: which cannot be imagined can be joyned to a Lye, since this were to put the Omnipotence of God, to attest that which no honest man will do. For the business of the Fall of Man, and other things of which we cannot perhaps give ourselves a perfect account: We who cannot fathom the Secrets of the Councel of God, do very unreasonably to take on us to reject an excellent Systeme of good and holy Rules, because we cannot satisfie our selves about some difficulties in them. Common Experience tells us, There is a great disorder in our Natures, which is not easily rectified: all *Philosophers* were sensible of it, and every man that designs to govern himself by Reason, feels the struggle between it and nature: So that it is plain, there is a Lapse of the high powers of the Soul.

But why, said he, could not this be rectified by some plain Rules given; but men must come and shew a trick, to perswade the World they speak to them in the Name of God? I Answered, That Religion being a design to recover and save Mankind, was to be so opened as to awaken and work upon all sorts of people: and generally men of a simplicity of Mind, were those that were the fittest Objects for God to shew his favour to; Therefore it was necessary that Messengers sent from Heaven should appear with such alarming Evidences as might awaken the World, and prepare them, by some astonishing Signs, to listen to the Doctrine they were to deliver. *Philosophy*, that was only a matter of fine Speculation, had few Votaries: And as there was no Authority in it to bind the World to believe its Dictates, so they were only received by some of nobler and refined Natures, who could apply themselves to, and delight in such Notions. But true Religion was to be built on a Foundation, that should carry more weight on it, and to have such Convictions, as might not only reach those who were already disposed to receive them, but rouse up such as without great and sensible excitation would have otherwise slept on in their ill Courses.

Upon this and some such Occasions, I told him, I saw the ill use he made of his Wit, by which he slurred the gravest things with a slight dash of his Fancy: and the pleasure he found in such wanton Expressions, as calling the doing of Miracles, *the shewing of a trick*, did really keep him from examining them, with that care which such things required.

For the *Old Testament*, We are so remote from that time, We have so little knowledge of the Language in which it was writ, have so imperfect an account of the History of those Ages, know nothing of their Customs, Forms of Speech, and the several Periods they might have, by which they reckoned their time, that it is rather a wonder We should understand so much of it, than that many passages in it should be so dark to us. The chief use it has to us *Christians*, is, that, from Writings which the *Jews* acknowledged to be divinely inspired, it is manifest the *Messias* was promised before the destruction of their Temple: which being done long ago; and these Prophecies agreeing to our Saviour, and to no other, Here is a great Confirmation given to the Gospel. But though many things in these Books could not be understood by us, who live above 3000 years after the chief of them were written, it is no such extraordinary matter.

For that of the Destruction of the *Canaanites* by the *Israelites*, It is to be considered, that if God had sent a Plague among them all, that could not have been found fault with. If then God had a Right to take away their Lives, without Injustice or Cruelty, he had a Right to appoint others to do it, as well as to execute it by a more immediate way: And the taking away people by the Sword, is a much gentler way of dying, than to be smitten with a Plague or a Famine. And for the Children that were Innocent of their Fathers' faults, God could in another State make that up to them. So all the difficulty is, Why were the *Israelites* commanded to execute a thing of such Barbarity? But this will not seem so hard, if we consider that this was to be no Precedent, for future times; since they did not do it but upon special Warrant and Commission from Heaven, evidenc'd to all the World by such mighty Miracles as did plainly shew, That they were particularly design'd by God to be the Executioners of his Justice: And God by employing them in so severe a Service, intended to possess them with great horrour of Idolatry, which was punished in so extream a manner.

For the Rites of their Religion, We can ill judge of them, Except We perfectly understood the Idolatries round about them: To which we find they were much inclined: So they were to be bent by other Rites to an extreme aversion from them: And yet, by the pomp of many of their Ceremonies and Sacrifices, great Indulgences were given to a people naturally fond of a visible splendour in Religious Worship. In all which, if we cannot descend to such satisfactory Answers, in every particular, as a curious man would desire, it is no wonder. The long interval of time, and other accidents, have worn out those things which were necessary to give us a clearer light into the meaning of them. And for the story of the Creation, how far some things in it may be Parabolical, and how far Historical, has been much disputed: there is nothing in it that may not be historically true. For if it be acknowledged that Spirits can form Voices in the Air, for which we have as good Authority as for any thing in History; then it is no wonder that *Eve* being so lately created, might be deceived, and think a *Serpent* spake to her, when the Evil Spirit framed the Voice.

But in all these things I told him he was in the wrong way, when he examined the business of Religion, by some dark parts of Scripture: Therefore I desired him to consider the whole Contexture of the *Christian Religion*, the Rules it gives, and the Methods it prescribes. Nothing can conduce more to the peace, order and happiness of the World, than to be governed by its Rules. Nothing is more for the Interests of every man in particular: The Rules of Sobriety, Temperance and Moderation, were the best Preservers of life, and which was perhaps more, of Health. Humility, Contempt of the Vanities of the World, and the being well employed, raised a man's Mind to a freedom from the Follies and Temptations that haunted the greatest part. Nothing was so generous and great as to supply the Necessities of the Poor and to forgive Injuries: Nothing raised and maintained a man's Reputation so much, as to be exactly just, and merciful; Kind, Charitable and Compassionate; Nothing opened the powers of a man's Soul so much as a calm Temper, a serene Mind, free of Passion and Disorder; Nothing made Societies, Families, and Neighbourhoods so happy, as when these Rules, which the Gospel prescribes, took place, *Of doing as we would have others do to us, and loving our Neighbours as our selves.*

The *Christian Worship* was also plain and simple; suitable to so pure a Doctrine. The Ceremonies of it were few and significant, as the admission to it by a washing with Water, and the Memorial of our Saviour's Death in *Bread* and *Wine*; The motives in it to perswade to this Purity, were strong: That God sees us, and will Judge us for all our Actions: That we shall be for ever happy or miserable, as we pass our Lives here: The Example of our Saviour's Life, and the great expressions of his Love in Dying for us, are mighty Engagements to Obey and Imitate him. The plain way of Expression used by our Saviour and his Apostles, shews there was no Artifice, where there was so much Simplicity used: There were no Secrets kept only among the Priests, but every thing was open to all *Christians*: The Rewards of Holiness are not entirely put over to another State, but good men are specially blest with peace in their Consciences, great Joy in the Confidence they have of the Love of God, and of seeing Him for ever: And often a signal Course of Blessings follows them in their whole Lives; But if at other times Calamities fell on them, these were so much mitigated by the Patience they were taught, and the inward Assistances, with which they were furnished, that even those Crosses were converted to Blessings.

I desired he would lay all these things together, and see what he could except to them, to make him think this was a Contrivance. Interest appears in all Humane contrivances; Our Saviour plainly had none; He avoided Applause, withdrew Himself from the Offers of a Crown: He submitted to Poverty and Reproach, and much Contradiction in his Life, and to a most ignominious and painful Death. His Apostles had none neither, They did not pretend either to Power or Wealth; But delivered a Doctrine that must needs condemn them, if they ever made such use of it: They declared their Commission fully without reserves till other times; They Recorded their own Weakness; Some of them wrought with their own hands; and when they received the Charities of their Converts, it was not so much to supply their own Necessities, as to distribute to others: They knew they were to suffer much for giving their Testimonies, to what they had seen and heard: In which so many in a thing so visible, as Christ's Resurrection and Ascension, and the Effusion of the Holy Ghost which He had promised, could not be deceived: And they gave such publick Confirmations of it by the Wonders they themselves wrought, that great multitudes were converted to a Doctrine, which, besides the opposition it gave to Lust and Passion, was born down and Persecuted for three hundred years: and yet its force was such, that it not only weathered out all those Storms, but even grew and spread vastly under them. *Pliny* about threescore years after, found their Numbers great and their Lives Innocent: and even *Lucian* amidst all his Raillery, gives a high Testimony to their Charity and Contempt of Life, and the other Vertues of the *Christians*; which is likewise more than once done by Malice itself, *Julian* the Apostate.

If a man will lay all this in one Ballance, and compare with it the few Exceptions brought to it, he will soon find how strong the one, and how slight the other are. Therefore it was an improper way, to begin at some Cavils about some Passages in the *New Testament*, or the *Old*, and from thence to prepossess one's Mind against the whole. The right method had been first to consider the whole matter, and from so general a view to descend to more particular Enquiries: whereas they suffered their Minds to be forestalled with Prejudices; so that they never examined the matter impartially.

To the greatest part of this he seemed to assent, only he excepted to the belief of Mysteries in the *Christian Religion*; which he thought no man could do, since it is not in a man's power to believe that which he cannot comprehend, and of which he can have no Notion. The believing Mysteries, he said, made way for all the Jugglings of Priests; for they getting the people under them in that Point, set out to them what they pleased; and giving it a hard Name, and calling it a *Mystery*, The people were tamed, and easily believed it. The restraining a man from the use of Women, Except one in the way of Marriage, and denying the remedy of Divorce, he thought unreasonable impositions on the Freedom of Mankind: And the business of the Clergy, and their Maintenance, with the belief of some Authority and Power conveyed in their Orders, lookt, as he thought, like a piece of Contrivance: and why, said he, must a man tell me, I cannot be saved, unless I believe things against my Reason, and then that I must pay him for telling me of them? These were all the Exceptions which at any time I heard from him to *Christianity*. To which I made these Answers.

For Mysteries it is plain there is in every thing somewhat that is unaccountable. How Animals or Men are formed in their Mothers' bellies, how Seeds grow in the Earth, how the Soul dwells in the Body, and acts and moves it; How we retain the Figures of so many words or things in our Memories, and how we draw them out so easily and orderly in our Thoughts or Discourses? How Sight and Hearing were so quick and distinct, how we move, and how Bodies were compounded and united? These things if we follow them into all the Difficulties, that we may raise about them, will appear every whit as unaccountable as any Mystery of Religion: And a blind or deaf man would judge Sight or Hearing as incredible, as any Mystery may be judged by us: For our Reason is not equal to them. In the same rank, different degrees of Age or Capacity raise some far above others: So that Children cannot fathom the Learning, nor weak persons the Councels, of more illuminated Minds: Therefore it was no wonder if we could not understand the Divine Essence: We cannot imagine how two such different Natures as a Soul and a Body should so unite together, and be mutually affected with one another's Concerns, and how the Soul has one Principle of Reason, by which it acts Intellectually, and another of life by which it joyns to the Body, and acts Vitally; two Principles so widely differing both in their Nature and Operation, and yet united in one and the same Person. There might be as many hard Arguments brought against the possibility of these things, which yet every one knows to be true, from Speculative Notions, as against the Mysteries mentioned in the Scriptures. As that of the *Trinity*, That in one essence there are three different Principles of Operation, which, for want of terms fit to express them by, We call *Persons*, and are called in Scripture *The Father, Son, and Holy Ghost*, and that the Second of these did unite Himself in a most intimate manner with the Humane Nature of Jesus Christ: And that the Sufferings he underwent, were accepted of God as a Sacrifice for our Sins; Who thereupon conferred on Him a Power of granting Eternal Life to all that submit to the Terms on which He offers it; And that the matter of which our Bodies once consisted, which may as justly be called the Bodies we laid down at our Deaths, as these can be said to be the Bodies which we formerly lived in, being refined and made more spiritual, shall be reunited to our Souls, and become a fit Instrument for them in a more perfect Estate; and that God inwardly bends and moves our Wills by such Impressions, as he can make on our Bodies and Minds.

These, which are the chief Mysteries of our Religion, are neither so unreasonable, that any other Objection lies against them, but this, that they agree not with our Common Notions, nor so unaccountable that somewhat like them, cannot be assigned in other things, which are believed really to be, though the manner of them cannot be apprehended: So this ought not to be any just Objection to the submission of our Reason to what we cannot so well conceive, provided our belief of it be well grounded. There have been too many Niceties brought in indeed, rather to darken than explain these: They have been defended by weak Arguments, and illustrated by Similies not always so very apt and pertinent. And new subtilties have been added, which have rather perplexed than cleared them. All this cannot be denied; the Opposition of *Hereticks* anciently, occasioned too much Curiosity among the *Fathers*: Which the *Schoolmen* have wonderfully advanced of late times. But if Mysteries were received, rather in the simplicity in which they are delivered in the Scriptures, than according to the descantings of fanciful men upon them, they would not appear much more incredible, than some of the common Objects of sense and perception. And it is a needless fear that if some Mysteries are acknowledged, which are plainly mentioned in the *New Testament*, it will then be in the power of the Priests to add more at their pleasure. For it is an absurd Inference from our being bound to assent to some Truths about the Divine Essence, of which the manner is not understood, to argue that therefore in an Object presented duly to our Senses, such as *Bread* and *Wine*, We should be bound to believe against their Testimony, that it is not what our Senses perceived it to be, but the whole *Flesh* and *Blood* of *Christ*; an entire Body being in every Crumb and drop of it. It is not indeed in a man's power to believe thus against his Sense and Reason, where the Object is proportioned to them, and fitly applied, and the Organs are under no indisposition or disorder. It is certain that no Mystery is to be admitted, but upon very clear and express Authorities from Scripture, which could not reasonably be understood in any other sense. And though a man cannot form an explicit Notion of a Mystery, for then it would be no longer a Mystery, Yet in general, he may believe a thing to be, though he cannot give himself a particular account of the way of it: or rather though he cannot Answer some Objections which lie against it. We know We believe many such in Humane matters, which are more within our reach: and it is very unreasonable to say, We may not do it in Divine things, which are much more above our Apprehensions.

For the severe Restraint of the use of Women, it is hard to deny that Priviledge to Jesus Christ, as a Law-Giver, to lay such Restraints, as all inferiour Legislators do; who when they find the Liberties their Subjects take, prove hurtful to them, set such Limits, and make such Regulations, as they judge necessary and expedient. It cannot be said but the Restraint of Appetite is necessary in some Instances: and if it is necessary in these, perhaps other Restraints are no less necessary, to fortifie and secure these. For if it be acknowledged that Men have a property in their Wives and Daughters, so that to defile the one, or corrupt the other, is an unjust and injurious thing; It is certain, that except a man carefully governs his Appetites, he will break through these Restraints: and therefore our Saviour knowing that nothing could so effectually deliver the World from the mischief of unrestrained Appetite, as such a Confinement, might very reasonably enjoyn it. And in all such Cases We are to ballance the Inconveniences on both hands, and where we find they are heaviest, We are to acknowledge the Equity of the Law. On the one hand there is no prejudice, but the restraint of Appetite; On the other are the mischiefs of being given up to pleasure, of running inordinately into it, of breaking the quiet of our own Family at home, and of others abroad: the ingaging into much Passion, the doing many false and impious things to compass what is desired, the Wast of men's Estates, time, and health. Now let any man judge, Whether the prejudices on this side, are not greater, than that single one of the other side, of being denied some pleasure? For *Polygamy*, it is but reasonable since Women are equally concern'd in the Laws of Marriage, that they should be considered as well as Men: but, in a State of *Polygamy* they are under great misery and jealousie, and are indeed barbarously used. Man being also of a sociable Nature, Friendship and Converse were among the primitive Intendments of Marriage, in which as far as the man may excel the Wife in greatness of Mind and height of Knowledge, the Wife some way makes that up with her Affection and tender Care: So that from both happily mixed, there arises a Harmony, which is to vertuous Minds one of the greatest joys of life: But all this is gone in a state of *Polygamy*, which occasions perpetual Jarrings and Jealousies. And the Variety does but engage men to a freer Range of pleasure, which is not to be put in the Ballance with the far greater Mischiefs that must follow the other course. So that it is plain, Our Saviour considered the Nature of Man, what it could bear, and what was fit for it, when he so restrained us in these our Liberties. And for Divorce, a power to break that Bond would too much encourage married persons in the little quarrellings that may rise between them; If it were in their power to depart one from another. For when they know that cannot be, and that they must live and die together, it does naturally incline them to lay down their Resentments, and to endeavour to live as well together as they can. So the Law of the Gospel being a Law of Love, designed to engage *Christians* to mutual love; It was fit that all such Provisions should be made, as might advance and maintain it; and all such Liberties be taken away, as are apt to enkindle and foment strife. This might fall in some instances to be uneasie and hard enough, but Laws consider what falls out most commonly, and cannot provide for all particular Cases. The best Laws are in some Instances very great grievances. But the Advantages being ballanced with the Inconveniences, Measures are to be taken accordingly. Upon this whole matter I said, That pleasure stood in opposition to other Considerations of great Weight, and so the decision was easie—And since our Saviour offers us so great Rewards, It is but reasonable He have a Priviledge of loading these Promises with such Conditions, as are not in themselves grateful to our natural Inclinations: For all that propose high Rewards, have thereby a right to exact difficult performances.

To this he said, We are sure the terms are difficult, but are not so sure of the Rewards. Upon this I told him, That we have the same assurance of the Rewards that we have of the other parts of *Christian Religion*. We have the Promises of God made to us by Christ, confirmed by many Miracles: We have the Earnests of these, in the quiet and peace which follow a good Conscience; and in the Resurrection of Him from the dead, who hath promised to raise us up. So that the Reward is sufficiently assured to us: And there is no reason it should be given to us, before the Conditions are performed, on which the Promises are made. It is but reasonable we should trust God, and do our Duty, *In hopes of that eternal Life, which God, who cannot lie, hath promised.* The Difficulties are not so great, as those which sometimes the commonest concerns of Life bring upon us: The learning some Trades or Sciences, the governing our Health and Affairs, bring us often under as great straits. So that it ought to be no just prejudice, that there are some things in Religion that are uneasie, since this is rather the effect of our corrupt Natures, which are farther deprav'd by vicious habits, and can hardly turn to any new course of life, without some pain, than of the Dictates of *Christian-*

ity, which are in themselves just and reasonable, and will be easie to us when renew'd, and in a good measure restor'd to our Primitive Integrity.

As for the Exceptions he had to the Maintenance of the Clergy, and the Authority to which they pretended; if they stretched their Designs too far, the Gospel did plainly reprove them for it: So that it was very suitable to that Church, which was so grosly faulty this way, to take the Scriptures out of the hands of the people, since they do so manifestly disclaim all such practices. The Priests of the true *Christian Religion* have no secrets among them, which the World must not know, but are only an Order of Men dedicated to God, to attend on Sacred things, who ought to be holy in a more peculiar manner, since they are to handle the things of God. It was necessary that such persons should have a due Esteem paid them, and a fit Maintenance appointed for them: That so they might be preserved from the Contempt that follows Poverty, and the Distractions which the providing against it might otherwise involve them in: And as in the Order of the World, it was necessary for the support of Magistracy and Government, and for preserving its esteem, that some state be used (though it is a happiness when Great Men have Philosophical Minds, to despite the Pageantry of it.) So the plentiful supply of the Clergy, if well used and applied by them, will certainly turn to the Advantage of Religion. And if some men either through Ambition or Covetousness used indirect means, or servile Compliances, to aspire to such Dignities, and being possessed of them, applied their Wealth either to Luxury or Vain Pomp, or made great Fortunes out of it for their Families; these were personal failings in which the Doctrine of Christ was not concerned.

He upon that told me plainly, There was nothing that gave him, and many others, a more secret encouragement in their ill ways, than that those who pretended to believe, lived so that they could not be thought to be in earnest, when they said it: For he was sure *Religion* was either a mere Contrivance, or the most important thing that could be: So that if he once believed, he would set himself in great earnest to live suitably to it. The aspirings that he had observed at Court, of some of the Clergy, with the servile ways they took to attain to Preferment, and the Animosities among those of several Parties, about trifles, made him often think they suspected the things were not true, which in their Sermons and Discourses they so earnestly recommended. Of this he had gathered many Instances; I knew some of them were Mistakes and Calumnies; Yet I could not deny but something of them might be too true: And I publish this the more freely, to put all that pretend to Religion, chiefly those that are dedicated to holy Functions, in mind of the great Obligation that lies on them to live suitably to their Profession: Since otherwise a great deal of the Irreligion and Atheism that is among us, may too justly be charged on them: for wicked men are delighted out of measure when they discover ill things in them, and conclude from thence not only that they are Hypocrites, but that Religion itself is a cheat.

But I said to him upon this Head, that though no good man could continue in the practice of any known sin, yet such might, by the violence or surprise of a Temptation, to which they are liable as much as others, be of a sudden overcome to do an ill thing, to their great grief all their life after. And then it was a very unjust Inference, Upon some few failings, to conclude that such men do not believe themselves. But how bad soever many are, it cannot be denied but there are also many both of the Clergy and Laity, who give great and real Demonstrations of the power Religion has over them; in their Contempt of the World, the strictness of their Lives, their readiness to forgive Injuries, to relieve the Poor, and to do good on all Occasions: and yet even these may have their failings, either in such things wherein their Constitutions are weak, or their Temptations strong and suddain: And in all such cases We are to judge of men, rather by the course of their Lives than by the Errors, that they through infirmity or surprise may have slipt into.

These were the chief Heads we have discoursed on; and as far as I can remember, I have faithfully repeated the substance of our Arguments: I have not concealed the strongest things he said to me; but though I have not enlarged on all the Excursions of his Wit in setting them off, Yet I have given them their full strength, as he expressed them, and as far as I could recollect, have used his own words: So that I am afraid some may censure me for setting down these things so largely, which Impious Men may make an ill use of, and gather together to encourage and defend themselves in their Vices: But if they will compare them with the Answers made to them, and the sense that so great and refined a Wit had of them afterwards, I hope they may through the blessing of God be not altogether ineffectual.

The issue of all our Discourses was this, He told me, He saw Vice and Impiety were as contrary to Humane Society, as wild Beasts let loose would be; and therefore he firmly resolved to change the whole method of his Life: to become strictly just and true, to be Chast and Temperate, to forbear Swearing and Irreligious Discourse, to Worship and Pray to his Maker: And that though he was not arrived at a full perswasion of *Christianity*, he would never employ his Wit more to run it down, or to corrupt others.

Of which I have since a farther assurance, from a Person of Quality, who conversed much with him, the last year of his life; to whom he would often say, That he was happy, if he did believe, and that he would never endeavour to draw him from it.

To all this I Answered, That a Vertuous Life would be very uneasie to him, unless Vicious Inclinations were removed: It would otherwise be a perpetual constraint. Nor could it be effected without an inward Principle to change him: and that was only to be had by applying himself to God for it in frequent and earnest Prayers. And I was sure if his Mind were once cleared of these Disorders, and cured of those Distempers, which Vice brought on it, so great an Understanding would soon see through all those flights of Wit that do feed Atheism and Irreligion: which have a false glittering in them, that dazles some weak-sighted Minds, who have not capacity enough to penetrate further than the Surfaces of things: and so they stick in these Toyls, which the strength of his Mind would soon break through, if it were once freed from those things that depressed and darkened it.

At this pass he was when he went from *London*, about the beginning of *April*: He had not been long in the Country when he thought he was so well, that being to go to his Estate in *Somersetshire* he rode thither Post. This heat and violent motion did so inflame an Ulcer, that was in his Bladder, that it raised a very great pain in those parts: Yet he with much difficulty came back by Coach to the Lodge at *Woodstock-Park*. He was then wounded both in Body and Mind: He understood Physick and his own Constitution and Distemper so well, that he concluded he could hardly recover: For the Ulcer broke and vast quantities of purulent matter passed with his Urine. But now the hand of God touched him, and as he told me, It was not only a general dark Melancholy over his Mind, such as he had formerly felt; but a most penetrating cutting Sorrow. So that though in his Body he suffered extream pain for some weeks, Yet the Agonies of his Mind sometimes swallowed up the sense of what he felt in his Body. He told me, and gave it me in charge, to tell it to one for whom he was much concern'd, that though there were nothing to come after this life, Yet all the Pleasures he had ever known in Sin, were not worth that torture he had felt in his Mind: He considered he had not only neglected and dishonoured, but had openly defied his Maker, and had drawn many others into the like Impieties:

So that he looked on himself as one that was in great danger of being damn'd. He then set himself wholly to turn to God unfeignedly, and to do all that was possible, in that little remainder of his life which was before him, to redeem those great portions of it, that he had formerly so ill employed. The Minister that attended constantly on him, was that good and worthy man Mr. *Parsons*, his Mother's Chaplain, who hath since his death Preached, according to the Directions he received from him, his Funeral Sermon: in which there are so many remarkable Passages, that I shall refer my *Reader* to them, and will repeat none of them here, that I may not thereby lessen his desire to edifie himself by that excellent Discourse, which has given so great and so general a satisfaction to all good and judicious *Readers*. I shall speak cursorily of every thing, but that which I had immediately from himself: He was visited every Week of his sickness by his *Diocesan*, that truly Primitive Prelate, the Lord Bishop of *Oxford*; who though he lived six miles from him, yet looked on this as so important a piece of his Pastoral Care, that he went often to him; and treated him with that decent plainness and freedom which is so natural to him; and took care also that he might not on terms more easy than safe, be at peace with himself. Dr. *Marshal*, the Learned and Worthy Rector of *Lincoln*-Colledge in *Oxford*, being the Minister of the Parish, was also frequently with him: and by these helps he was so directed and supported, that he might not on the one hand satisfie himself with too superficial a Repentance, nor on the other hand be out of measure oppressed with a Sorrow without hope. As soon as I heard he was ill, but yet in such a condition that I might write to him, I wrote a Letter to the best purpose I could. He ordered one that was then with him, to assure me it was very welcome to him: but not satisfied with that, he sent me an Answer, which, as the Countess of *Rochester*, his Mother told me, he dictated every word, and then signed it. I was once unwilling to have publish'd it, because of a Complement in it to myself, far above my merit, and not very well suiting with his Condition.

But the sense he expresses in it of the Change then wrought on him, hath upon second thoughts prevail'd with me to publish it, leaving out what concerns myself.

Woodstock Park, *Oxfordshire.*
June 25, 1680

My most Honour'd Dr. Burnett,

My Spirits and Body decay so equally together, that I shall write You a Letter as weak as I am in person. I begin to value Churchmen above all men in the World, &c. If God be yet pleased to spare me longer in this World, I hope in your Conversation to be exalted to that degree of Piety, that the World may see how much I abhor what I so long loved, and how much I glory in Repentance and in God's Service. Bestow your Prayers upon me, that God would spare me (if it be his good Will) to shew a true Repentance and Amendment of life for the time to come: or else, if the Lord pleaseth to put an end to my worldly being now, that He would mercifully accept of my Death-Bed Repentance, and perform that Promise that He hath been pleased to make, That at what time soever a Sinner doth Repent, He would receive him. Put up these Prayers, most dear Doctor, to Almighty God, for

Your most Obedient and
Languishing servant,
ROCHESTER

He told me, when I saw him, That he hoped I would come to him upon that general Insinuation of the desire he had of my Company; and he was loath to write more plainly: not knowing whether I could easily spare so much time. I told him, That on the other hand, I looked on it as a presumption to come so far, when he was in such excellent hands; and though perhaps the freedom formerly between us, might have excused it with those to whom it was known; yet it might have the appearance of so much Vanity to such as were strangers to it; So that till I received his Letter, I did not think it convenient to come to him: And then not hearing that there was any danger of a sudden change, I delayed going to him till the Twentieth of *July*. At my coming to his House an accident fell out not worth mentioning, but that some have made a story of it. His Servant, being a *Frenchman*, carried up my Name wrong, so that he mistook it for another, who had sent to him, that he would undertake his Cure, and he being resolved not to meddle with him, did not care to see him: This mistake lasted some hours, with which I was the better contented, because he was not then in such a condition, that my being about him could have been of any use to him: for that Night was like to have been his last. He had a *Convulsion-Fit*, and raved; but, *Opiates* being given him, after some hours rest, his raving left him so entirely, that it never again returned to him.

I cannot easily express the Transport he was in, when he awoke and saw me by him: He broke out in the tenderest Expressions concerning my kindness in coming so far to see *such* a *One*, using terms of great abhorrence concerning himself, which I forbear to relate. He told me, as his strength served him at several snatches, for he was then so low, that he could not hold up discourse long at once, what sense he had of his past life; what sad apprehension for having so offended his Maker, and dishonoured his Redeemer: What Horrours he had gone through, and how much his Mind was turned to call on God and on his Crucified Saviour; So that he hoped he should obtain Mercy, for he believed he had sincerely repented; and had now a calm in his Mind after that storm that he had been in for some Weeks. He had strong Apprehensions and Perswasions of his admittance to Heaven: of which he spake once not without some extraordinary Emotion. It was indeed the only time that he spake with any great warmth to me: For his Spirits were then low, and so far spent, that, though those about him told me, He had expressed formerly great fervor in his Devotions; Yet Nature was so much sunk, that these were in a great measure fallen off. But he made me pray often with him; and spoke of his Conversion to God as a thing now grown up in him to a settled and calm serenity. He was very anxious to know my Opinion of a Death-Bed Repentance. I told him, That before I gave any Resolution in that, it would be convenient that I should be acquainted more particularly with the Circumstances and Progress of his Repentance.

Upon this he satisfied me in many particulars. He said, He was now perswaded both of the truth of *Christianity*, and of the power of inward Grace, of which he gave me this strange account. He said, Mr. *Parsons*, in order to his Conviction, read to him the fifty-third *Chapter* of the Prophecie of *Isaiah*, and compared *that* with the History of our Saviour's Passion, that he might there see a Prophecie concerning it, written many Ages before it was done; which the *Jews*, that blasphemed Jesus Christ, still kept in their hands, as a Book divinely inspired. He said to me, *That as he heard it read, he felt an inward force upon him, which did so enlighten his Mind and convince him, that he could resist it no longer: For the words had an authority which did shoot like Raies or Beams in his Mind; so that he was not only convinced by the Reasonings he had about it, which satisfied his Understanding, but by a power which did so effectually constrain him, that he did ever after as firmly believe in his Saviour, as if he had seen him in the Clouds.* He had made it to be read so often to him, that he had got it by heart: and went through a great part of it in Discourse with me, with a sort of heavenly Pleasure, giving me his Reflections on it. Some few I remember, *Who hath believed our Report?* (Verse 1.) *Here*, he said, *was foretold the Opposition the Gospel was to meet with from such Wretches as he was. He hath no Form nor Comeliness, and when we shall see Him, there is no beauty that we should desire him.* (Verse 2.) On this he said, *The meanness of his appearance and Person has made vain and foolish people disparage Him, because he came not in such a Fool's-Coat as they delight in.* What he said on the other parts I do not well remember: and indeed I was so affected with what he said then to me, that the general transport I was under during the whole Discourse, made me less capable to remember these Particulars, as I wish I had done.

He told me, That he had thereupon received the Sacrament with great satisfaction and that was encreased by the pleasure he had in his Lady's receiving it with him: who had been for some years misled into the Communion of the Church of *Rome*, and he himself had been not a little Instrumental in procuring it, as he freely acknowledged. So that it was one of the joyfullest things that befel him in his Sickness, that he had seen that Mischief removed, in which he had so great a Hand: and during his whole Sickness, he expressed so much tenderness and true kindness to his Lady, that as it easily defaced the remembrance of every thing wherein he had been in fault formerly, so it drew from her the most passionate care and concern for him that was possible: which indeed deserves a higher Character than is decent to give of a Person yet alive. But I shall confine my Discourse to the Dead.

He told me, He had overcome all his Resentments to all the World; so that he bore ill-will to no Person, nor hated any upon personal accounts. He had given a true state of his Debts, and had ordered to pay them all, as far as his Estate that was not setled, could go: and was confident that if all that was owing to him were paid to his Executors, his Creditors would be all satisfied. He said, He found his Mind now possessed with another sense of things, than ever he had formerly: He did not repine under all his pain; and, in one of the sharpest Fits he was under while I was with him; He said, *He did willingly submit*; and looking up to Heaven, said, *God's holy Will be done, I bless Him for all He does to me.* He professed he was contented either to die or live, as should please God; And though it was a foolish thing for a man to pretend to choose, Whether he would die or live, yet he wished rather to die. He knew he could never be so well, that life should be comfortable to him. He was confident he should be happy if he died but he feared if he lived, he might Relapse: And then said he to me, *In what a condition shall I be if I Relapse after all this? But,* he said, *he trusted in the Grace and Goodness of God, and was resolved to avoid all those Temptations, that Course of Life, and Company, that were likely to insnare him: and he desired to live on no other account, but that he might, by the change of his Manners some way take off the high Scandal his former Behaviour had given.* All these things at several times, I had from him, besides some Messages, which very well became a dying Penitent to some of his former Friends, and a Charge to publish any thing concerning him, that might be a mean to reclaim others. *Praying God, that as his life had done much hurt, so his death might do some good.*

Having understood all these things from him, and being pressed to give him my Opinion plainly about his Eternal State; I told him, That, though the Promises of the Gospel did all depend upon a real change of Heart and Life, as the indispensible condition upon which they were made; and that it was scarce possible to know certainly whether our Hearts are changed, unless it appeared in our lives; and the Repentance of most dying men being like the howlings of condemned Prisoners for Pardon, which flowed from no sense of their Crimes, but from the horrour of approaching Death; there was little reason to encourage any to hope much from such Sorrowings: Yet certainly, if the Mind of a Sinner, even on a Death-Bed, be truly renewed and turned to God, so great is His Mercy, that He will receive him, even in that extremity. He said, *He was sure his Mind was entirely turned and though Horrour had given him his first awaking, yet that was now grown up into a settled Faith and Conversion.*

There is but one prejudice lies against all this, to defeat the good Ends of Divine Providence by it upon others, as well as on himself: and that is that it was a part of his Disease, and that the lowness of his Spirits made such an alteration in him, that he was not what he had formerly been; and this some have carried so far as to say, That he died mad: These Reports are raised by those who are unwilling that the last Thoughts or Words of a Person, every way so extraordinary, should have any effect either on themselves or others: And it is to be fear'd, that some may have so far seared their Consciences, and exceeded the common Measures of Sin and Infidelity, that neither this Testimony, nor one coming from the Dead, would signifie much towards their Conviction. That this Lord was either mad or stupid, is a thing so notoriously untrue, that it is the greatest Impudence for any that were about him to Report it; and a very unreasonable Credulity in others to believe it. All the while I was with him, after he had slept out the disorders of the Fit he was in the first Night, he was not only without Ravings; but had a clearness in his Thoughts, in his Memory, in his reflections on Things and Persons, far beyond what I ever saw in a Person so low in his strength. He was not able to hold out long in Discourse, for his Spirits failed: but once for half an hour, and often for a quarter of an hour, after he awakened, he had a Vivacity in his Discourse that was extraordinary, and in all things like himself. He called often for his Children, his Son the now Earl of Rochester, and his three Daughters, and spake to them with a sense and feeling that cannot be expressed in Writing. He called me once to look on them all, and said, *See how Good God has been to me, in giving me so many Blessings, and I have carried myself to Him like an ungracious and unthankful Dog.* He once talked a great deal to me of Public Affairs, and of many Persons and things, with the same clearness of thought and expression, that he had ever done before. So that by no sign, but his Weakness of Body, and giving over Discourse so soon, could I perceive a difference between what his Parts formerly were, and what they were then.

And that wherein the presence of his Mind appeared most, was in the total change of an ill habit grown so much upon him, that he could hardly govern himself, when he was any ways heated, three Minutes without falling into it; I mean *Swearing*. He had acknowledged to me the former Winter, that he abhorred it as a base and indecent thing, and had set himself much to break it off: but he confessed that he was so overpower'd by that ill Custom, that he could not speak with any warmth, without repeated Oaths, which, upon any sort of provocation, came almost naturally from him: But in his last Remorses this did so sensibly affect him, that by a resolute and constant watchfulness, the habit of it was perfectly master'd; So that, upon the returns of pain, which were very severe and frequent upon him, the last day I was with him, or upon such displeasures as people sick or in pain are apt to take of a sudden at those about them; On all these Occasions he never swore an Oath all the while I was there.

Once he was offended with the delay of one that he thought made not haste enough, with somewhat he called for, and said in a little heat, *That damned Fellow*: soon after I told him, I was glad to find his Style so reformed, and that he had so entirely overcome that ill habit of Swearing; Only that word of calling any *damned*, which had returned upon him, was not decent. His Answer was: *Oh that Language of Fiends, which was so familiar to me, hangs yet about me: Sure none has deserved more to be damned than I have done.* And after he had humbly asked God Pardon for it, he desired me to call the Person to him, that he might ask him forgiveness: but I told him that was needless for he had said it of one that did not hear it, and so could not be offended by it.

In this disposition of Mind did he continue all the while I was with him, four days together; He was then brought so low that all hope of

Recovery was gone. Much purulent matter came from him with his Urine, which he passed always with some pain; But one day with unexpressible torment: Yet he bore it decently, without breaking out into Repinings or impatient Complaints. He imagined he had a Stone in his Passage; but it being searched, none was found. The whole substance of his Body was drained by the Ulcer, and nothing was left but Skin and Bone: and by lying much on his Back, the parts there began to mortifie; But he had been formerly so low, that he seemed as much past all hopes of life as now: which made him one Morning after a full and sweet Night's rest procured by *Laudanum*, given him without his knowledge, to fancy it was an effort of Nature, and to begin to entertain some hopes of Recovery: For he said, He felt himself perfectly well, and that he had nothing ailing him, but an extreme weakness, which might go off in time: and then he entertained me with the Scheme he had laid down for the rest of his life, how retired, how strict, and how studious he intended to be: But this was soon over, for he quickly felt that it was only the effect of a good sleep, and that he was still in a very desperate state.

I thought to have left him on *Friday*, but, not without some Passion, he desired me to stay that day: there appeared no symptome of present death; and a Worthy Physitian then with him, told me, That though he was so low that an accident might carry him away on a suddain; Yet without that, he thought he might live yet some Weeks. So on *Saturday*, at Four of the Clock in the Morning I left him, being the *24th* of *July*. But I durst not take leave of him; for he had expressed so great an unwillingness to part with me the day before, that, if I had not presently yielded to one day's stay, it was like to have given him some trouble, therefore I thought it better to leave him without any Formality. Some hours after he asked for me, and when it was told him I was gone, he seem'd to be troubled, and said, *Has my Friend left me, then I shall die shortly*. After that he spake but once or twice till he died: He lay much silent: Once they heard him praying very devoutly. And on *Monday* about Two of the Clock in the Morning, he died, without any *Convulsion*, or so much as a groan.

THE CONCLUSION

Thus he lived, and thus he died in the Three-and-Thirtieth Year of his Age. Nature had fitted him for great things, and his Knowledge and Observation qualify'd him to have been one of the most extraordinary

Men, not only of his Nation, but of the Age he lived in; And I do verily believe, that if God had thought fit to have continued him longer in the World, he had been the Wonder and Delight of all that knew him. But the infinitly wise God knew better what was fit for him, and what the Age deserved. For men who have so cast off all sense of God and Religion, deserve not so signal a Blessing as the Example and Conviction which the rest of his life might have given them. And I am apt to think that the Divine Goodness took pity on him, and seeing the sincerity of his Repentance, would try and venture him no more in Circumstances of Temptation, perhaps too hard for Humane Frailty. Now he is at rest, and I am very confident enjoys the Fruits of his late, but sincere Repentance. But such as live, and still go on in their Sins and Impieties, and will not be awakened neither by this, nor the other Allarms that are about their Ears, are, it seems given up by God to a judicial Hardness and Impenitency.

Here is a publick Instance of One who lived of their Side, but could not die of it: And though none of all our Libertines understood better than he, the secret Mysteries of Sin, had more studied every thing that could support a man in it, and had more resisted all external means of Conviction than he had done; Yet when the hand of God inwardly touched him, he could no longer *kick against those Pricks*, but *humbled himself under that Mighty Hand*, and as he used often to say in his Prayers, *He who had so often denied Him, found then no other Shelter, but his Mercies and Compassions.*

I have written this Account with all the tenderness and caution I could use, and in whatsoever I may have failed, I have been strict in the truth of what I have related, remembering that of *Job, Will ye lie for God?* Religion has Strength and Evidence enough in it self, and needs no Support from Lyes, and made Stories. I do not pretend to have given the formal words that he said, though I have done that where I could remember them. But I have written this with the same Sincerity, that I would have done, had I known I had been to die immediately after I had finished it. I did not take Notes of our Discourses last Winter after we parted; so I may perhaps in the setting out of my Answers to him, have enlarged on several things both more fully and more regularly, than I could say them in such free Discourses as we had. I am not so sure of all I set down as said by me, as I am of all said by him to me. But yet the substance of the greatest part, even of that, is the same.

It remains that I humbly and earnestly beseech all that shall take this Book in their hands, that they will consider it entirely: and not wrest some parts to an ill intention. God, the Searcher of Hearts, knows with what Fidelity I have writ it: But if any will drink up only the Poison that may be in it, without taking also the Antidote here given to those ill Principles; or considering the sense that this great Person had of them, when he reflected seriously on them; and will rather confirm themselves in their ill ways, by the Scruples and Objections which I set down, than be edified by the other parts of it; As I will look on it as a great Infelicity, that I should have said any thing that may strengthen them in their Impieties; So the sincerity of my Intentions will, I doubt not, excuse me at his hands, to whom I offer up this small Service.

I have now performed, in the best manner I could, what was left on me by this Noble Lord, and have done with the part of an Historian. I shall in the next place say somewhat as a Divine. So extraordinary a Text does almost force a Sermon, though it is plain enough it self, and speaks with so loud a Voice, that those who are not awakened by it, will perhaps consider nothing that I can say. If our Libertines will become so far sober as to examine their former Course of Life, with that disengagement and impartiality, which they must acknowledge a wise man ought to use in things of greatest Consequence, and ballance the Account of what they have got by their Debaucheries, with the Mischiefs they have brought on themselves and others by them, they will soon see what a mad Bargain they have made. Some Diversion, Mirth, and Pleasure is all they can promise themselves; but to obtain this, how many Evils are they to suffer? how have many wasted their strength, brought many Diseases on their Bodies, and precipitated their Age in the pursuit of those things? and as they bring old Age early on themselves, so it becomes a miserable state of life to the greatest part of them; *Gouts*, *Stranguries*, and other Infirmities, being severe Reckonings for their past Follies; not to mention the more loathsome Diseases, with their no less loathsome and troublesome Cures, which they must often go through, who deliver themselves up to forbidden Pleasure. Many are disfigur'd beside, with the marks of their Intemperance and Lewdness, and which is yet sadder, an Infection is derived often-times on their Innocent, but unhappy Issue, who being descended from so vitiated an Original, suffer for their Excesses. Their Fortunes are profusely wasted, both by their neglect of their Affairs, they being so buried in Vice, that they cannot employ either their Time or Spirits, so much exhausted by Intemperance, to consider them; and by that Prodigal Expence which their Lusts put them upon. They suffer no less in their Credit, the chief mean to recover an intangled Estate; for that irregular

Expence forceth them to so many mean shifts, makes them so often false to all their Promises and Resolutions, that they must needs feel how much they have lost, that which a Gentleman, and Men of ingenuous tempers, do sometimes prefer even to life it self, their Honour and Reputation. Nor do they suffer less in the Nobler powers of their Minds, which, by a long course of such dissolute Practices, come to sink and degenerate so far, that not a few, whose first Blossoms gave the most promising Hopes, have so wither'd, as to becomes incapable of great and generous Undertakings, and to be disabled to every thing, but to wallow like Swine in the filth of Sensuality, their Spirits being dissipated, and their Minds so nummed, as to be wholly unfit for business, and even indisposed to think.

That this dear price should be paid for a little wild Mirth, or gross and corporal Pleasure, is a thing of such imparalleled Folly, that if there were not too many such Instances before us, it might seem incredible. To all this we must add the Horrours that their ill Actions raise in them, and the hard shifts they are put to to stave off these, either by being perpetually drunk or mad, or by an habitual disuse of thinking and reflecting on their Actions, and (if these Arts will not perfectly quiet them) by taking Sanctuary in such Atheistical Principles as may at least mitigate the sourness of their thoughts, though they cannot absolutely settle their Minds.

If the state of Mankind and Humane Societies are considered, what Mischiefs can be equal to those which follow these Courses? Such Persons are a plague wherever they come; they can neither be trusted nor beloved, having cast off both Truth and Goodness, which procure confidence and attract Love: they corrupt some by their ill Practices, and do irreparable Injuries to the rest; they run great Hazards, and put themselves to much trouble, and all this to do what is in their power to make Damnation as sure to themselves as possibly they can. What Influence this has on the whole Nation is but too visible; how the Bonds of Nature, Wedlock, and all other Relations, are quite broken. Vertue is thought an Antick Piece of Formality, and Religion the effect of Cowardice or Knavery: These are the Men that would Reform the World, by bringing it under a new System of Intellectual and Moral Principles; but bate them a few bold and lewd Jests, what have they ever done, or designed to do, to make them to be remembered, except it be with detestation? They are the Scorn of the present Age, and their Names must rot in the next. Here they have before them an Instance of one who was deeply corrupted with the Contagion which he first derived from Others, but unhappily heightened it much himself. He was a Master indeed, and not a bare trifler with Wit, as some of these are who repeat, and that but scurvily, what they may have heard from him or some others, and with Impudence and Laughter will face the World down, as if they were to teach it Wisdom; who, God knows, cannot follow one Thought a step further than as they have conned it; and take from them their borrow'd Wit and their mimical Humour, and they will presently appear what they indeed are, the least and lowest of Men.

If they will, or if they can think a little, I wish they would consider that by their own Principles, they cannot be sure that Religion is only a Contrivance, all they pretend to is only to weaken some Arguments that are brought for it: but they have not Brow enough to say, They can prove that their own Principles are true. So that at most they bring their Cause no higher, than that it is possible *Religion* may not be true. But still it is possible it may be true, and they have no shame left that will deny that it is also probable it may be true; and if so, then what mad Men are they who run so great a hazard for nothing? But their own Confession, it may be there is a God, a Judgment, and a Life to come; and if so, then He that believes these things, and lives according to them, as he enjoys a long course of Health and quiet of Mind, an innocent rellish of many true Pleasures, and the Serenities, which Vertue raises in him, with the good Will and Friendship which it procures him from others; So when he dies, if these things prove Mistakes, he does not outlive his Error, nor shall it afterwards raise trouble or disquiet in him if he ceases to be: But if these things be true, he shall be infinitely happy in that State, where his present small Services shall be so excessively rewarded. The *Libertines*, on the other side, as they know they must die, so the thoughts of Death must be always Melancholy to them, they can have no pleasant view of that which yet they know cannot be very far from them: The least painful *Idea* they can have of it is, that it is an extinction and ceasing to be; but they are not sure even of that. Some secret Whispers within make them, whether they will or not, tremble at the Apprehensions of another State; neither their Tinsel-Wit, nor superficial Learning, nor their impotent Assaults upon the weak side as they think of Religion, nor the boldest Notions of Impiety, will hold them up then. Of all which I now present so lively an *Instance*, as perhaps History can scarce parallel.

Here were parts so exalted by Nature, and improved by Study, and yet so corrupted and debased by Irreligion and Vice, that he who was made to be one of the Glories of his Age, was become a Proverb, and, if his Repentance had not interposed, would have been one of the greatest Reproaches of it. He knew well the small strength of that weak Cause, and at first despised, but afterwards abhorred it. He felt the Mischiefs, and saw the madness of it; and therefore though he lived to the scandal of many, he died as much to the Edification of all those who saw him; and, because they were but a small number, he desired that he might even when dead yet speak. He was willing nothing should be concealed that might cast Reproach on himself, and on Sin, and offer up Glory to God and Religion. So that though he lived a hainous Sinner, yet he died a most exemplary Penitent.

It would be a vain and Ridiculous Inference, for any from hence to draw Arguments about the abstruse Secrets of Predestination; and to conclude that if they are of the number of the Elect, they may live as they will, and that Divine Grace will at some time or other violently constrain them, and irresistibly work upon them: But as St. *Paul* was called to that Eminent Service, for which he was appointed, in so stupendous a manner, as is no warrant for others to expect such a Vocation; So if upon some signal Occasions such Conversions fall out, which, how far they are short of Miracles, I shall not determine, it is not only a vain but a pernicious Imagination, for any to go on in their ill ways, upon a fond Conceit and Expectation that the like will befal them: For whatsoever God's extraordinary dealings with some may be, We are sure His common way of Working is by offering these things to our rational Faculties, which, by the assistances of His Grace, if we improve them all we can, shall be certainly effectual for our Reformation; and if we neglect or abuse these, We put ourselves beyond the common Methods of God's Mercy, and have no reason to expect that Wonders should be wrought for our Conviction; which though they sometimes happen, that they may give an effectual Allarm for the awaking of others, yet it would destroy the whole design of Religion, if men should depend upon or look for such an extraordinary and forcible Operation of God's Grace.

And I hope that those who have had some sharp Reflections on their past Life, so as to be resolved to forsake their ill Courses, will not take the least encouragement to themselves in that desperate and unreasonable Resolution of putting off their Repentance till they can sin no longer, from the hopes I have express'd of this Lord's obtaining Mercy at the last; and from thence presume that they also shall be received, when they turn to God on their Death-beds: For what Mercy soever

God may shew to such as really were never inwardly touched before that time: Yet there is no reason to think that those who have dealt so disingenuously with God and their own Souls, as designedly to put off their turning to Him upon such Considerations, should then be accepted with Him. They may die suddenly, or by a Disease that may so disorder their Understandings, that they shall not be in any capacity of Reflecting on their past Lives. The inward Conversion of our Minds is not so in our power, that it can be effected without Divine Grace assisting. And there is no reason for those who have neglected these Assistances all their Lives, to expect them in so extraordinary a manner at their Death. Nor can one, especially in a Sickness, that is quick and critical, be able to do those things that are often indispensibly necessary to make his Repentance compleat: And even in a longer Disease, in which there are larger Opportunities for these things; Yet there is great Reason to doubt of a Repentance begun and kept up merely by Terrour, and not from any ingenuous Principle. In which, though I will not take on me to limit the Mercies of God, which are boundless, Yet this must be confessed, that to delay Repentance, with such a design, is to put the greatest Concernment we have upon the most dangerous and desperate Issue that is possible.

But they that will still go on in their Sins, and be so partial to them, as to use all endeavours to strengthen themselves in their evil Course, even by these very things which the Providence of God sets before them, for the casting down of these strong holds of Sin: What is to be said to such? it is to be feared, that if they obstinately persist, they will by degrees come within that Curse, *He that is Unjust, let him be Unjust still: and he that is Filthy, let him be Filthy still. But if our Gospel is hid, it is hid to them that are lost, in whom the god of this World hath blinded the Minds of them which believe not, lest the Light of the Glorious Gospel of Christ, who is the Image of God, should shine unto them.*

11. Gilbert Burnet, from the *History of the Reign of King Charles II*

Bishop Burnet's History of His own Time
(1753) i 370–2

The three most eminent wits of that time, on whom all the lively libels were fastened, were the Earls of Dorset, and Rochester, and Sir Charles Sidley . . . Wilmot Earl of Rochester, was naturally modest, till the Court corrupted him. His wit had in it a peculiar brightness, to which none could ever arrive. He gave himself up to all sorts of extravagance, and to the wildest frolicks that a wanton wit could devise. He would have gone about the streets as a beggar, and made love as a porter. He set up a stage as an Italian mountebank. He was for some years always drunk, and was ever doing some mischief. The King loved his company for the diversion it afforded, better than his person: And there was no love lost between them. He took his revenges in many libels. He found out a footman that knew all the Court, and he furnished him with a red coat and a musket as a centinel, and kept him all the winter long every night, at the doors of such ladies, as he believed might be in intrigues. In the Court a centinel is little minded, and is believed to be posted by a captain of the Guards to hinder a combat: So this man saw who walked about, and visited at forbidden hours. By this means Lord Rochester made many discoveries. And when he was well furnished with materials, he used to retire into the country for a month or two to write libels: Once being drunk he intended to give the King a libel that he had writ on some ladies: But by a mistake he gave him one written on himself. He fell into an ill habit of body: And in several fits of sickness he had deep remorses; for he was guilty both of much impiety, and of great immoralities. But as he recovered he threw these off, and turned again to his former ill courses. In the last year of his life I was much with him, and have writ a book of what pass'd between him and me: I do verily believe, he was then so entirely changed, that, if he had recovered, he would have made good all his resolutions. Sidley had a more sudden and copious wit, which furnished a perpetual run of discourse: But he was not so correct as Lord Dorset, nor so sparkling as Lord Rochester.

ELEGIES ON ROCHESTER'S DEATH

1680

12. John Oldham, *Bion, A Pastoral, in Imitation of the Greek of Moschus, bewailing the Death of the Earl of Rochester*

Works of John Oldham (1684) pp. 73–87.

John Oldham (1653–83), the most talented of Rochester's literary disciples, admired him as much as a poet as he disliked his immoral conduct as a man. Although first brought to general notice by Rochester and his friends, Oldham was too independent a man to accept open patronage. The following poem acknowledges the debt Oldham owed Rochester poetically. Bion was the name of the Greek poet mourned in an elegy attributed to Moschus.

Bion.

A Pastoral, in Imitation of the Greek of Moschus, bewailing the Death of the Earl of Rochester.

Mourn all ye Groves, in darker shades be seen,
Let Groans be heard, where gentle Winds have been:
Ye *Albion* Rivers, weep your Fountains dry,
And all ye Plants your moisture spend, and die;
Ye melancholy Flowers, which once were Men,
Lament, until you be transform'd agen:
Let every Rose pale as the Lilly be,
And Winter Frost seize the Anemone:
But thou, O *Hyacinth*, more vigorous grow
In mournful Letters thy sad glory show,
Enlarge thy grief, and flourish in thy wo:

For *Bion*, the beloved *Bion's* dead,
His voice is gone, his tuneful breath is fled.
Come all ye Muses, *come, adorn the Shepherd's Herse*
With never-fading Garlands, never-dying Verse.
Mourn ye sweet Nightingales in the thick Woods,
Tell the sad news to all the *British* Floods:
See it to *Isis*, and to *Cham* convey'd,
To *Thames*, to *Humber*, and to utmost *Tweed:*
And bid them waft the bitter tidings on,
How *Bion's* dead, how the lov'd Swain is gone,
And with him all the Art of graceful Song.
Come all ye Muses, *come, adorn the Shepherd's Herse*
With never-fading Garlands, never-dying Verse.
Ye gentle Swans, that haunt the Brooks, and Springs,
Pine with sad grief, and droop your sickly Wings:
In doleful notes the heavy loss bewail,
Such as you sing at your own Funeral,
Such as you sung when your lov'd *Orpheus* fell.
Tell it to all the Rivers, Hills, and Plains,
Tell it to all the *British* Nymphs and Swains,
And bid them too the dismal tydings spread
Of *Bion's* fate, of *England's Orpheus* dead,
Come all ye Muses, *come, adorn the Shepherd's Herse*
With never-fading Garlands, never-dying Verse.
No more, alas! no more that lovely Swain
Charms with his tuneful Pipe the wondring Plain:
Ceast are those Lays, ceast are those sprightly airs,
That woo'd our Souls into our ravish'd Ears:
For which the list'ning streams forgot to run,
And Trees lean'd their attentive branches down:
While the glad Hills, loth the sweet sounds to lose,
Lengthen'd in Echoes every heav'nly close.
Down to the melancholy Shades he's gone,
And there to *Lethe's* Banks reports his moan:
Nothing is heard upon the Mountains now
But pensive Herds that for their Master low:
Stragling and comfortless about they rove,
Unmindful of their Pasture, and their Love.
Come all ye Muses, *come, adorn the Shepherd's Herse*
With never-fading Garlands, never-dying Verse.

For thee, dear Swain, for thee, his much lov'd Son,
Does *Phœbus* Clouds of mourning black put on:
For thee the *Satyrs* and the rustick *Fauns*
Sigh and lament through all the Woods and Lawns
For thee the *Fairies* grieve, and cease to dance
In sportful Rings by night upon the Plains:
The water *Nymphs* alike thy absence mourn,
And all their Springs to tears and sorrow turn:
Sad *Eccho* too does in deep silence moan,
Since thou art mute, since thou art speechless grown:
She finds nought worth her pains to imitate,
Now thy sweet breath's stopt by untimely fate:
Trees drop their Leaves to dress thy Funeral,
And all their Fruit before its *Autumn* fall:
Each Flower fades, and hangs its wither'd head,
And scorns to thrive, or live, now thou art dead:
Their bleating Flocks no more their Udders fill,
The painful Bees neglect their wonted toil:
Alas! what boots it now their Hives to store
With the rich spoils of every plunder'd Flower,
When thou, that wast all sweetness, art no more?
Come, all ye Muses, *come, adorn the Shepherd's Herse*
With never-fading Garlands, never-dying Verse.
Ne'r did the Dolphins on the lonely Shore
In such loud plaints utter their grief before:
Never in such sad Notes did *Philomel*
To the relenting Rocks her sorrow tell:
Ne'r on the Beech did poor *Alcyone*
So weep, when she her floating Lover saw:
Nor that dead Lover, to a Sea-fowl turn'd,
Upon those Waves, where he was drown'd, so mourn'd:
Nor did the Bird of *Memnon* with such grief
Bedew those Ashes, which late gave him life:
As they did now with vying grief bewail,
As they did all lament dear *Bion's* fall.
Come all ye Muses, *come, adorn the Shepherd's Herse*
With never-fading Garlands, never-dying Verse.
In every Wood, on every Tree, and Bush
The Lark, the Linnet, Nightingale, and Thrush,

And all the feather'd Choir, that us'd to throng
In list'ning Flocks to learn his well-tun'd Song;
Now each in the sad Confort bear a part,
And with kind Notes repay their Teachers Art:
Ye Turtles too (I charge you) here assist,
Let not your murmurs in the crowd be mist:
To the dear Swain do not ungrateful prove,
That taught you how to sing, and how to love.
   Come all ye Muses, *come, adorn the Shepherd's Herse*
   With never-fading Garlands, never-dying Verse,
Whom hast thou left behind thee, skilful Swain,
That dares aspire to reach thy matchless strain?
Who is there after thee, that dares pretend
Rashly to take thy warbling Pipe in hand?
Thy Notes remain yet fresh in every ear,
And give us all delight, and all despair:
Pleas'd *Eccho* still does on them meditate,
And to the whistling Reeds their sounds repeat.
Pan only e're can equal thee in Song,
That task does only to great *Pan* belong:
But *Pan* himself perhaps will fear to try,
Will fear perhaps to be out-done by thee.
   Come all ye Muses, *come, adorn the Shepherd's Herse*
   With never-fading Garlands, never-dying Verse.
Fair *Galatea* too laments thy death,
Laments the ceasing of thy tuneful breath:
Oft she, kind Nymph, resorted heretofore
To hear thy artful measures from the shore:
Not harsh like the rude *Cyclops* were thy lays,
Whose grating sounds did her soft ears displease:
Such was the force of thy enchanting tongue,
That she for ever could have heard thy Song,
And chid the hours, that did so swiftly run,
And thought the Sun too hasty to go down,
Now does that lovely *Nereid* for thy sake
The Sea, and all her fellow Nymphs forsake:
Pensive upon the Beach, she sits alone,
And kindly tends the Flocks from which thou'rt gone.
   Come all ye Muses, *come, adorn the Shepherd's Herse*
   With never-fading Garlands, never-dying Verse.

With thee, sweet *Bion*, all the grace of Song,
And all the *Muses* boasted Art is gone:
Mute is thy Voice, which could all hearts command,
Whose pow'r no Shepherdess could e're withstand:
All the soft weeping *Loves* about thee moan,
At once their Mothers darling, and their own:
Dearer wast thou to *Venus* than her *Loves*,
Than her charm'd Girdle, than her faithful Doves,
Than the last gasping Kisses, which in death
Adonis gave, and with them gave his breath.
This, *Thames*, ah! this is now the second loss,
For which in tears thy weeping Current flows:
Spencer, the Muses glory, went before,
He pass'd long since to the *Elysian* shore:
For him (they say) for him, thy dear-lov'd Son,
Thy Waves did long in sobbing murmurs groan,
Long fill'd the Sea with their complaint, and moan:
But now, alas! thou do'st afresh bewail,
Another Son does now thy sorrow call:
To part with either thou alike wast loth,
Both dear to Thee, dear to the Fountains both:
He largely drank the Rills of sacred *Cham*,
And this no less of *Isis* nobler stream:
He sung of Hero's, and of hardy Knights
Far-fam'd in Battels, and renown'd Exploits:
This meddled not with bloudy Fights, and Wars,
Pan was his Song, and Shepherds harmless jars,
Loves peaceful combats, and its gentle cares.
Love ever was the subject of his Lays,
And his soft Lays did *Venus* ever please.
Come all ye Muses, *come, adorn the Shepherd's Herse*
With never-fading Garlands, never-dying Verse.
Thou, sacred *Bion*, art lamented more
Than all our tuneful Bards, that dy'd before:
Old *Chaucer*, who first taught the use of Verse,
No longer has the tribute of our tears:
Milton, whose Muse with such a daring flight
Led out the warring *Seraphims* to fight:
Blest *Cowley* too, who on the banks of *Cham*
So sweetly sigh'd his wrongs, and told his flame:

And *He*, whose Song rais'd *Cooper's* Hill so high,
As made its glory with *Parnassus* vie:
And soft *Orinda*, whose bright shining name
Stands next great *Sappho's* in the ranks of fame:
All now unwept, and unrelented pass,
And in our grief no longer share a place:
Bion alone does all our tears engross,
Our tears are all too few for *Bion's* loss.
Come all ye Muses, *come, adorn the Shepherd's Herse*
With never-fading Garlands, never-dying Verse.
Thee all the Herdsmen mourn in gentlest Lays,
And rival one another in thy praise:
In spreading Letters they engrave thy Name
On every Bark, that's worthy of the fame:
Thy Name is warbled forth by every tongue,
Thy Name the Burthen of each Shepherd's Song:
Waller, the sweet'st of living Bards, prepares
For thee his tender'st, and his mournfull'st airs,[1]
And I, the meanest of the British Swains,
Amongst the rest offer these humble strains:
If I am reckon'd not unblest in Song,
'Tis what I ow to thy all-teaching tongue:
Some of thy Art, some of thy tuneful breath
Thou didst by Will to worthless me bequeath:
Others thy Flocks, thy Lands, thy Riches have,
To me thou didst thy Pipe, and Skill vouchsafe.
Come all ye Muses, *come, adorn the Shepherd's Herse*
With never-fading Garlands, never-dying Verse.
Alas! by what ill Fate, to man unkind,
Were we to so severe a lot design'd?
The meanest Flowers which the Gardens yield,
The vilest Weeds that flourish in the Field,
Which must e're long lie dead in Winter's Snow,
Shall spring again, again more vigorous grow:
Yon Sun, and this bright glory of the day,
Which night is hasting now to snatch away,
Shall rise anew more shining and more gay:
But wretched we must harder measure find,

[1] The only lines by Waller referring to Rochester are an epigram on the elegies and the lines to Anne Wharton (No. 14b).

The great'st, the brav'st, the witti'st of mankind,
When Death has once put out their light, in vain
Ever expect the dawn of Life again:
In the dark Grave insensible they lie,
And there sleep out endless Eternity.
There thou to silence ever art confin'd,
While less deserving Swains are left behind:
So please the Fates to deal with us below,
They cull out thee, and let dull *Mævius* go:
Mævius still lives; still let him live for me,
He, and his Pipe shall ne'r my envy be:
None e're that heard thy sweet, thy Artful Tongue,
Will grate their ears with his rough untun'd Song.
Come, all ye Muses, *come, adorn the Shepherd's Herse*
With never-fading Garlands, never-dying Verse.
A fierce Disease, sent by ungentle Death,
Snatch'd *Bion* hence, and stop'd his hallow'd breath:
A fatal damp put out that heav'nly fire,
That sacred heat which did his breast inspire.
Ah! what malignant ill could boast that pow'r,
Which his sweet voice's Magick could not cure?
Ah cruel Fate! how could'st thou chuse but spare?
How could'st thou exercise thy rigour here?
Would thou hadst thrown thy Dart at worthless me,
And let this dear, this valued life go free:
Better ten thousand meaner Swains had dy'd,
Than this best work of Nature been destroy'd.
Come, all ye Muses, *come, adorn the Shepherd's Herse*
With never-fading Garlands, never-dying Verse.
Ah! would kind Death alike had sent me hence;
But grief shall do the work, and save its pains:
Grief shall accomplish my desired doom,
And soon dispatch me to *Elysium*:
There, *Bion*, would I be, there gladly know,
How with thy voice thou charm'st the shades below.
Sing, Shepherd, sing one of thy strains divine,
Such as may melt the fierce *Elysian* Queen:
She once her self was pleas'd with tuneful strains,
And sung, and danc'd on the *Sicilian* Plains:
Fear not, thy Song should unsuccessful prove,

Fear not, but 'twill the pitying Goddess move:
She once was won by *Orpheus'* heav'nly Lays,
And gave his fair *Eurydice* release.
And thine as pow'rful (question not, dear Swain)
Shall bring thee back to these glad Hills again.
Ev'n I my self, did I at all excel,
Would try the utmost of my voice and skill,
Would try to move the rigid King of Hell.

13. An Elegy by Aphra Behn and Commendatory Verses on it

1680

Aphra Behn (1640–89), had an adventurous and distinguished career. Her childhood and youth was spent in Surinam, and after marrying a rich merchant of Dutch extraction in 1663, she found herself, on his death in 1665, obliged to earn her own living first in government secret service work in Holland and afterwards by writing for the stage. She was noted for her wit and vivacity and was popular as a playwright. Her admiration for Rochester seems genuine. The commendatory verses by Anne Wharton, which follow, in turn received a reply from Aphra Behn. Anne Wharton (c. 1632–85), was a relative of Rochester. Her father, Sir Henry Lee of Ditchley, Oxfordshire, was his first cousin. She married the first Marquis of Wharton.

---

a) Aphra Behn, On the Death of the late Earl of Rochester:

Mourn, Mourn, ye Muses, all your loss deplore,
The Young, the Noble *Strephon* is no more.
Yes, yes, he fled quick as departing Light,
And ne're shall rise from Death's eternal Night,

So rich a Prize the *Stygian* Gods ne're bore,
Such Wit, such Beauty, never grac'd their Shore.
He was but lent this duller World t'improve
In all the charms of Poetry, and Love;
Both were his gift, which freely he bestow'd,
And like a God, dealt to the wond'ring Crowd.
Scorning the little Vanity of Fame,
Spight of himself attain'd a Glorious name.
But oh! in vain was all his peevish Pride,
The Sun as soon might his vast Lustre hide,
As piercing, pointed, and more lasting bright,
As suffering no vicissitudes of Night.
  Mourn, Mourn, ye Muses, all your loss deplore,
  The Young, the Noble *Strephon* is no more.

Now uninspir'd upon your Banks we lye,
Unless when we wou'd mourn his Elegie;
His name's a Genius that wou'd Wit dispense,
And give the Theme a Soul, the Words a Sense.
But all fine thought that Ravisht when it spoke,
With the soft Youth eternal leave has took;
Uncommon Wit that did the soul o'recome,
Is buried all in *Strephon's* Worship'd Tomb;
Satyr has lost its Art, its Sting is gone,
The Fop and Cully now may be undone;[1]
That dear instructing Rage is now allay'd,
And no sharp Pen dares tell 'em how they've stray'd;
Bold as a God was ev'ry lash he took,
But kind and gentle the chastising stroke.
  Mourn, Mourn, ye Youths, whom Fortune has
    betray'd,
  The last Reproacher of your Vice is dead.

Mourn, all ye Beauties, put your *Cyprus* on,
The truest Swain that e're Ador'd you's gone;
Think how he lov'd, and writ, and sigh'd, and spoke,
Recall his Meen, his Fashion, and his Look.
By what dear Arts the Soul he did surprize,
Soft as his Voice, and charming as his Eyes,

[1] i.e. no longer portrayed.

Bring Garlands all of never-dying Flow'rs,
Bedew'd with everlasting falling Show'rs;
Fix your fair eyes upon your victim'd Slave,
Sent Gay and Young to his untimely Grave.
See where the Noble Swain Extended lies,
Too sad a Triumph of your Victories;
Adorn'd with all the Graces Heav'n e're lent,
All that was Great, Soft, Lovely, Excellent
You've laid into his early Monument.
  Mourn, Mourn, ye Beauties, your sad loss deplore,
  The Young, the Charming *Strephon* is no more.

Mourn, all ye little Gods of Love, whose Darts
Have lost their wonted power of piercing hearts;
Lay by the gilded Quiver and the Bow,
The useless Toys can do no Mischief now,
Those Eyes that all your Arrow's points inspir'd,
Those Lights that gave ye fire are now retir'd,
Cold as his Tomb, pale as your Mother's Doves;
Bewail him then oh all ye little Loves,
For you the humblest Votary have lost
That ever your Divinities could boast;
Upon your hands your weeping Heads decline,
And let your wings encompass round his Shrine;
In stead of Flow'rs your broken Arrows strow,
And at his feet lay the neglected Bow.
  Mourn, all ye little Gods, your loss deplore,
  The soft, the Charming *Strephon* is no more.

Large was his Fame, but short his Glorious Race,
Like young *Lucretius* liv'd and dy'd apace.
So early Roses fade, so over all
They cast their fragrant scents, then softly fall,
While all the scatter'd perfum'd leaves declare,
How lovely 'twas when whole, how sweet, how fair.
Had he been to the *Roman* Empire known;
When great *Augustus* fill'd the peaceful Throne;
Had he the noble wond'rous Poet seen,
And known his Genius, and survey'd his Meen,
(When Wits, and Heroes grac'd Divine abodes,)
He had increas'd the number of their Gods;

The Royal Judge had Temples rear'd to's name,
And made him as Immortal as his Fame;
In Love and Verse his *Ovid* he'ad out-done,
And all his Laurels, and his *Julia* won.
  Mourn, Mourn, unhappy World, his loss deplore,
  The great, the charming *Strephon* is no more.

(*Poems on Several Occasions* (1685), pp. 45–9)

b) Anne Wharton, To Mrs Behn on what she writ of the Earl of Rochester:

In pleasing Transport rap't, my Thoughts aspire
With humble Verse to Praise what you Admire:
Few living Poets may the Laurel claim,
Most pass thro' Death, to reach at Living Fame.
Fame, Phoenix like, still rises from a Tomb;
But bravely you this Custom have o'ercome.

You force an Homage from each Generous Heart,
Such as you always pay to just Desert.
You prais'd him Living, whom you Dead bemoan,
And now your Tears afresh his Laurel crown.
It is this Flight of yours excites my Art,
Weak as it is, to take your Muse's part,
And pay loud Thanks back from my bleeding Heart.

May you in every pleasing Grace excel,
May Bright *Apollo* in your Bosome dwell;
May yours excel the Matchless *Sappho's* Name;
May you have all her Wit, without her Shame:
Tho' she to Honour gave a fatal Wound,
Employ your Hand to raise it from the ground.
Right its wrong'd Cause with your Inticing Strain,
Its ruin'd Temples try to build again.

Scorn meaner Theams, declining low desire,
And bid your Muse maintain a Vestal Fire.
If you do this, what Glory will insue,
To all our Sex, to Poesie, and you?
Write on, and may your Numbers ever flow,
Soft as the Wishes that I make for you.

(*The Temple of Death* (1695), pp. 242–4)

c) Aphra Behn, To Mrs W[harton]. 'On her Excellent Verses (Writ in Praise of Some I had made on the Earl of Rochester) Written in a Fit of Sickness':

Enough kind Heaven! to purpose I have liv'd,
And all my Sighs and Languishments surviv'd.
My Stars in vain their sullen influence have shed,
Round my till now Unlucky Head:
I pardon all the Silent Hours I've griev'd,
My Weary Nights, and Melancholy Days;
When no Kind Power my Pain Reliev'd,
I lose you all, ye sad Remembrancers,
I lose you all in New-born Joys,
Joys that will dissipate my Falling Tears.
The Mighty Soul of *Rochester's* reviv'd,
Enough Kind Heaven to purpose I have liv'd.
I saw the Lovely *Phantom*, no Disguise,
Veil'd the blest Vision from my Eyes,
'Twas all o're *Rochester* that pleas'd and did surprize.
Sad as the Grave I sat by Glimmering Light,
Such as attends Departing Souls by Night.
Pensive as absent Lovers left alone,
Or my poor Dove, when his Fond Mate was gone.
Silent as Groves when only Whispering Gales,
Sigh through the Rushing Leaves,
As softly as a Bashful Shepherd Breaths,
To his Lov'd Nymph his Amorous Tales.
So dull I was, scarce Thought a Subject found,
Dull as the Light that gloom'd around;
When lo the Mighty Spirit appear'd,
All Gay, all Charming to my sight;
My Drooping Soul it Rais'd and Cheer'd,
And cast about a Dazling Light.
In every part there did appear,
The Great, the God-like *Rochester*,
His Softness all, his Sweetness everywhere.
It did advance, and with a Generous Look,
To me Addrest, to worthless me it spoke:
With the same wonted Grace my Muse it prais'd,
With the same Goodness did my Faults Correct;

And careful of the Fame himself first rais'd,
Obligingly it School'd my loose Neglect.
The soft, the moving Accents soon I knew
The gentle Voice made up of Harmony;
Through the Known Paths of my glad Soul it flew;
I knew it straight, it could no others be,
'Twas not Alied but very very he.
    So the All-Ravisht Swain that hears
    The wondrous Musick of the Sphears,
For ever does the grateful Sound retain,
    Whilst all his Oaten Pipes and Reeds,
The Rural Musick of the Groves and Meads,
Strive to divert him from the Heavenly Song in vain.
    He hates their harsh and Untun'd Lays,
Which now no more his Soul and Fancy raise.
But if one Note of the remembred Air
    He chance again to hear,
He starts, and in a transport cries,—*'Tis there!*
He knows it all by that one little taste,
And by that grateful Hint remembers all the rest.
Great, Good, and Excellent, by what new way
Shall I my humble Tribute pay,
For this vast Glory you my Muse have done,
For this great Condescension shown!
So Gods of old sometimes laid by
Their Awful Trains of Majesty,
And chang'd ev'n Heav'n a while for Groves and Plains,
And to their Fellow-Gods preferr'd the lowly Swains,
And Beds of Flow'rs would oft compare
To those of Downey Clouds, or yielding Air;
At Purling Streams would drink in homely Shells,
Put off the God, to Revel it in Woods and Shepherds Cells;
Would listen to their Rustick Songs, and show
Such Divine Goodness in Commending too,
Whilst the transported Swain the Honour pays
With humble Adoration, humble Praise.

(A. Behn, *Poems on Several Occasions* (1684), pp. 57–60)

14. Anne Wharton, Elegy and lines on Mrs Wharton's Lines

1680

This was not only the most popular of the Elegies (see Introduction p. 8), it also received commendations from the doyen of Restoration poets, Edmund Waller (1606–87), John Grubham Howe (1657–1722) and Robert Wolseley. Howe's poem is the 'sympathetic elegy' to Rochester referred to in the D.N.B. under 'John Wilmot'. Howe was a whig politician who held a number of government posts. For a note on Wolseley see No. 22. Wolseley's poem is a reply to Anne Wharton's lines in praise of his Preface to *Valentinian* (see No. 22b).

a) Deep waters silent roll; so grief like mine
Tears never can relieve, nor words define.
Stop then, stop your vain source, weak springs of grief,
Let tears flow from their eyes whom tears relieve.
They from their heads shew the light trouble there,
Could my heart weep, its sorrows 'twould declare:
Weep drops of blood, my heart, thou'st lost thy pride,
The cause of all thy hopes and fears, thy guide!
He would have led thee right in Wisdom's way,
And 'twas thy fault whene'er thou went'st astray:
And since thou stray'd'st when guided and led on,
Thou wilt be surely lost now left alone.
It is thy Elegy I write, not his;
He lives immortal and in highest bliss.
But thou art dead, alas! my heart, thou'rt dead:
He lives, that lovely soul for ever fled,
But thou 'mongst crowds on earth art buried.
Great was thy loss, which thou canst ne'er express,
Nor was th'insensible dull nation's less;
He civiliz'd the rude, and taught the young,

Made fools grow wise; such artful music hung
Upon his useful kind instructing tongue.
His lively wit was of himself a part,
Not, as in other men, the work of art;
For, though his learning like his wit was great,
Yet sure all learning came below his wit;
As God's immediate gifts are better far
Than those we borrow from our likeness here,
He was—but I want words, and ne'er can tell,
Yet this I know, he did mankind excell.
He was what no man ever was before,
Nor can indulgent nature give us more,
For, to make him, she exhausted all her store.

(*Poems by Several Hands* collected by Nahum Tate (1685), pp. 392–3)

b) Edmund Waller, 'Of an Elegy made by Mrs Wharton on the Earl of Rochester':

Thus mourn the Muses on the Hearse,
Not strowing Tears, but lasting Verse;
Which so preserves the Heroe's Name,
They make him live again in Fame.
Chloris in lines so like his own,
Gives him so just and high Renown,
That she the afflicted World relieves,
And shows that still in her he lives.
Her Wit as graceful, great, and good,
Ally'd in Genius, as in Blood;
His loss supply'd, now all our Fears
Are, that the Nymph shou'd wast in Tears.
Then fairest *Chloris* comfort take,
For his, your own, and for our Sake;
Lest his fair Soul that lives in you,
Should from the World for ever go.

(*Examen Miscellaneum* (1702), pp. 20–1)

c) John Grubham Howe, On Mrs Wharton's Elegy:

Thus, of his dear *Euridice* depriv'd,
In Numbers soft the faithful Orpheus griev'd,
Thus charm'd the World, while he his Pains reliev'd.

To hear his Lyre the Beasts and Forests strove;
But yours alone can Men, and Angels move,
Can teach those how to write, these how to love.

You only cou'd deserve so good a Friend,
And to be thus lamented by your Pen,
Was only due to th'wittyest, best of Men.

His Soul to Heav'n he willingly resign'd,
But kindly left within your Matchless Mind
A double Portion of his Wit behind.

Equal to this is the Return you give,
Lofty as Clouds, which did his Soul receive;
His well-sung Name does in your Poem live.

(*Examen Miscellaneum* (1702), pp. 19–20)

d) Robert Wolseley, lines from 'To Mrs Wharton':

Cease *England*, thy late loss so high to rate,
Here learn thy mighty sorrow to abate,
By her instructive gentle Song half reconcil'd to fate.

Your tender moan, you tuneful *Nine*[1] give o'er,
Lament your darling *Bion's*[2] death no more.
In her lov'd Lays his better part survives,
He dyes not all, while soft *Urania* lives
Her Heaven has warm'd, with the same pleasing fires,
In her like noble blood, like noble thoughts inspires.
His perishing goods to others let him leave,
To Her his deathless Pen he did bequeave;[3]
And if my humble Muse, whose luckless strain
Was us'd alone of Beauty to complain,
And sing in melancholy notes love's unregarded pain,

Rais'd by that theme, above her usual height
Cou'd clear his fame, or do his virtue right,

[1] The nine muses.
[2] 'The Earl of Rochester, her Uncle' [marginal note].
[3] These lines seem to be plagiarized from Oldham's Elegy (see No. 12), where Rochester is also referred to as 'Bion'.

How well do's she the trifling debt acquit,
She whose resembling Genius shews her fit
To be his sole Executrix in wit.

(*Lycidus: or The Lover in Fashion* [by Aphra Behn] *together with a Miscellany of New Poems* (1688), pp. 100–1)

15. Anonymous, 'An Elegie Upon the Death, and in Commemoration of the Truly Honourable and Truly Learned, John Lord Wilmot, Earl of Rochester'

1680

This is an anonymous broadside headed 'Memento Mori', London, 1680. There are copies in the British Museum and Bodleian libraries. The former copy has 'Aug. 5' written in ink on it.

Alas! what dark benighting Clouds or shade
Of Gloomy Fate has this Invasion made
On the bright Confines of far shining day,
And there Eclips'd the light refulgent Ray
Of Sacred Honour, and transplendent Worth,
Which Wisdom still from thence was beaming forth?
But can it be that he's so quickly gone,
Rapt from the Earth so soon the Muses Son,
Who from the evening World such Lawrels won,
As with Eternal Green must wreath his brow,
Till Time shall be no more, and Fate shall bow?
Fame cannot be unjust to him she bore,
And with him on her Silver wings did soare
Higher than *Pegasus* durst ever rise,

His Name engraving in the starry skies.
Great Rochester, *Minerva's* darling wit,
Inspir'd by her, the famous Heroe writ
Such Mysteries as puzzle'd [*sic*] dull Mankind
The meaning of those deep Profounds to find:
And having long paus'd on the Mystick Theam,
Like the Magicians upon *Pharoah's* dream,
They did confess that they had sought in vain,
Till the renowned Author did explain
The weighty Syllogisms. For none could bring
More loyal attestations for their King.
Truely Heroick, more than can be told;
Indu'd with vertues far exceeding gold,
Or all the precious Oriental Jems
The bounding Ocean holds, that *India* hems.
Flow, brynie Orbs; weep, *Britains* Isles for him,
Till in salt tears thou like to *Delos* swim.
For can such Sapience unregarded set?
Or can ungrateful Man his worth forget,
Whose Candid soul in a sublimer sphere
Divinest Attributes deserves to share?
Should his great *Requiems* now be left unsung,
No doubt the golden Lyres by Angels strung,
In doleful Numbers from the high rais'd Pole,
On which the glittering Orbs of Heaven do roul,
Would nightly from Seraphick Hierarchs sound,
To wake the drousie world through Earth's vast round,
The great Idea's of his far-strech'd fame,
And Sapience Angelical proclaime.
With Conduct and with Courage was he fill'd,
Those great Foundations on which Empires build.
In War renown'd, at home for Peace besought:
For with his Pen as well as Sword he fought:[1]
Equally dreadful[2] to correct the proud,
And send Chimera's to their Mother-Cloud.
Though great by Birth, yet condescendent still
To all that sought him with compliant Will.

[1] There were other opinions about Rochester's courage. This line is possibly an allusion to Carr Scroope's Epigram, see No. 5.

[2] i.e. awe-inspiring.

Meek in himself, true Honour's brighter eye,
The only Badge of true Nobility.
For Pride in Greatness gets Contempt and Scorn;
Which dwells in Baseness rais'd, not Nobly born,
Heroick Virtues shin'd in him so bright,
That they oft daz'd the sharpest Eagles sight
Of prying Envy, which is only fed
On Honours Ruines, when 'tis Captive led.
'Tis sure, the fates were cruel to supplant
The Man, whom now so much this Isle must want;
Yet wanting him, in loss for ever lye;
Too good for Earth, now rap'd above the Sky,
Where Hallelujahs he Triumphant sings,
Born up aloft on high Cherubean wings,
To eccho Praises to the King of Kings:
Whilst o're the bright Empyrean fields he strays,
Crown'd with a Wreath of never-fading Bays;
Admir'd by the Angelick Orders there,
Whose beaming Faces are Eternal fair;
And yet from his diviner Soul did gain
A pleasing sense of Joy which they sustain
In endless Bliss, and coeternal Praise:
There let him dwell time boundless without Days.

Epitaph

Here lies the Muses' Darling, and the Son
Of great Apollo, who such praises won
Upon this Mole-hill Globe, that Heav'n thought fit
He rais'd on high should in bright Mansions sit,
And safely thence upon the world look down,
Whilst ever-radiant Wreaths his Temples Crown.
The loss is ours; from Earth Heav'n won the Prize:
His body's here, but Soul above the Skies.

16. An elegy 'On the Death of the Earl of Rochester', by 'an unknown Hand'

1680

What words, what sense, what Night-piece can
  express
The World's Obscurity and Emptiness?
Since *Rochester* withdrew his Vital Beams
From the great *chaos*; fam'd for high Extreams
The Hero's Talent, or in Good or Ill,
Dull Mediocrity misjüdging still.
Seraphic Lord! whom Heav'n for wonders meant,
The earliest Wit, and the most sudden Saint.
What tho the Vulgar may traduce thy ways,
And strive to rob thee of thy Moral Praise?
If, with thy Rival *Solomon's* intent,
Thou sin'dst a little for Experiment;
Or to maintain a Paradox, which none
Had Wit to answer but thy self alone;
Thy Soul flew higher; that strict sacred tye
With thy Creator, time was to discry.
Thus pregnant Prophets us'd uncommon ways,
Play'd their wild pranks and made the Vulgar gaze.
Till their great Message came to be declar'd:
They sin in Types, that sin so unprepar'd.
An unexpected change attracts all Eyes,
They needs must conquer that can well surprise.
Now Lechers whom the Pox cou'd ne'r convert,
Know where to fix a restless rambling heart.
Drunkards whose Souls, not their sick Maws
  love Drink,
Confound their Glasses, and begin to think.
The Atheist now has nothing left to say,
His Arguments were lent for sport not prey.

Like Guns to Clowns, or weapons to rash Boys,
Resum'd again for Mischief, or for noise.
The Spark cries out now e're he is aware,
(Making an Oath a Prologue to a Prayer)
ROCHESTER said 'twas true! it must be so!
He had no Dispensation from Below.
Thy dying words, (than thousands of Harangues,
Urg'd with grimaces, fortifi'd with Bangs
On dreadful Pulpit) have made more recant,
Than Plague, or War, or Penitential want;
A Declaration so well tim'd, has gain'd
More Proselytes than e're thy wildness feign'd;
Mad Debochees, whom thou didst but allure
With pleasant Baits, and tempt 'em to their cure.
Satan rejoyc'd to see thee take his part,
His Malice not so prosperous as thy Art.
He took thee for his Pilot to convey
Those easie souls he spirited away.
But to his great Confusion saw thee shift
Thy swelling Sails, to take another drift,
With an Illustrious Train, imputed his,
To the bright Region of eternal Bliss.
So have I seen a prudent General Act,
Whom Fate had forc'd with Rebels to contract
A hated League, Fight, Vote, Adhere, Obey,
Own the vile Cause as zealously as they;
Suppress the Loyal side, and pull all down,
With unresisted Force, that propt the Crown.
But when he found out the propitious hour,
To quit his Masque, and own his Prince's Power;
Boldly asserted his great Sovereign's Cause,
And brought three Kingdoms to his Master's Laws.

(*Poems on Several Occasions* (1684), pp. 136–9)

17. Thomas Flatman, 'On the Death of My Lord Rochester: Pastoral'

1680

Poems and Songs, the third edition (1682), pp. 146–7.

Thomas Flatman, 1637–88, for many years a fellow of New College, Oxford, had a reputation both as poet and painter. Rochester describes Flatman's muse as 'jaded' in *An Allusion to Horace*. A Latin translation of this poem was published in *Poems of Affairs of State* (1703), i. 253.

As on his death-bed gasping *Strephon*[1] lay,
Strephon the wonder of the Plains,
The noblest of th'*Arcadian* Swains,
Strephon the Bold, the Witty, and the Gay:
With many a sigh, and many a tear he said,
Remember me ye Shepherds, when I'm dead.

Ye trifling Glories of this world, Adieu,
And vain applauses of the Age:
For when we quit this Earthly Stage,
Believe me Shepherds, for I tell you true,
Those pleasures which from virtuous deeds we have,
Procure the sweetest slumbers in the Grave.

Then since your fatal Hour must surely come,
Surely your heads lie low as mine,
Your bright Meridian Sun decline;
Beseech the mighty *Pan* to guard you home:
If to *Elyzium* you would happy fly,
Live not like *Strephon*, but like *Strephon die*.

[1] Rochester's usual poetic soubriquet.

18. Samuel Woodford: 'An Ode to the Memory of the Right Honourable John Lord Wilmot Earl of Rochester'

1680

Prinz, *Rochesteriana* (Leipzig, 1926), pp. 59–71.

Samuel Woodford (1636–1700) was a friend of Thomas Flatman. He was ordained priest in 1669. His most notable contribution to poetry was his *Paraphrase upon the Psalms*, 1667.

I

Longer I cannot hold, and yet a Feare
I know not what, misgives me least my Song
To fields enur'd and woods, and th'artlesse throng
    Of Swayns and heard-groomes, pressing neare
Harsh notes, like those of their own pipes to heare
(Notes only worthy so unpurg'd an eare,
And through severer studys discontinued long)
Forreign to what its numbers do intend
A contrary effect should apprehend
And make me where an Honour is designd, offend.
I feare, but yet will sing; and if the Muse,
Ungratefully her noblest help refuse
Ah too ungratefull Muse! whose uncharm'd Wand
For all the Labour and the Paine
We Rhymers in her mines sustayn
Betrayes us ever to an empty veine.
The Oare exhausted, and the bed damm'd up with Sand!
    Without her help I will assay
The softest strokes of Cowleys sacred lyre
    And on its chordes such measures play
    She shall the tunefull Verse admire,
And envy those great thoughts their loftyer sounds inspire.

II

He through rough wayes, envys, distrusts, and doubt,
Sent out to search by Heavn's design
The happy Land of Poesy Divine
(Like Cowley none so fit to serch it out
Who led by an Immortall hand
Did all the tracks of Verse best understand)
Sought and discoverd farr the Happy Land.
But long he wandred first, and erring oft did stray
Often and long both miss't and chang'd his Way
And was so oft with Paynted shewes deceiv'd to stay
(Alas! whom have not paynted shewes deceiv'd
Tho happy they who have their errors griev'd
And the true road at last retriev'd!)
Even Cowley ready was to say
Now here, now there the undiscover'd Country lay.
But had he so return'd greater or more
What had he done than those who went before
Save home to come no Wiser, riffled only lesse than they.

III

Greater he did and more
Than all, who ever went, than himself ever did before
And when an ill report was brought
By other spyes upon the land he sought
(Nay by himself till better taught)
Such laurels and such crowns produc't
The Countrys growth, as Great triumphers us'd
To guard their Heads, when baser Gold as Proofless was refus'd.
Such was Heavn's will.—but in its larg foresight
Having prepar'd for us some better thing
Not fitt for Him to bring
Wholy to light
And be without us perfect in His own great right,
Something there still remaynd behind
Something by Cowley happyly begun
To be in after ages done
Which mighty *ROCHESTER* in his Vast mind

The mighty *ROCHESTER* alone
Who all his Father-Poëts has outgon
In his last vieue from Pisgahs Sacred top design'd.
And as he saw the land before him ly
Th' Whole Land in Blessed Ecstasy
(When Heav'n would not permitt
That He should enter it)
Which Noble *ROCHESTER* in legacy
Dying bequeath'd the Sons of Witt
Tell it, my Verse, for thou mayst tell
Mystrys wch none beside Thee dare reveale
Mysterys thou envious wouldst be thought shouldst thou
conceale.

IV

For the Past errors of a various Life
Where too vayne Love with vayner Honour were at strife
(Monsters, which ever on the Stage
Polluted have the Happyest Age
And fill'd it with False notions and a false beliefe)
Where Verse debaucht as Umpire stood
Defying Heav'n, and all that's Good
By Witt obscene, which King, or Kaesar never understoode
Since what is passt and gon
Tho it in tyme may be forgott
But done once ne're can be not done,
Or a fayre blank present, or draw a blott
And in the empty Space, or darker spott
His Father Virtues' grave, and his last greater owne.
But where (alas!) canst thou begin
Where end but with Thy Countrys sin!
(Ah! wretchlesse Country that, whose vices
Of virtuous men can only set the prices!
Whose Rebellion best must show
The Fathers glorys, and the Sons its Witt
To late Posterity transmitt!)
Rootes deadly both, and for such trees of life unfitt
Whose leaves for med'cin and for shaddow grow
But Witt, tho counted best o' th' two
Than Sorcery worst, and wch meets hell below.

V

For Witt, when to itself 'tis left
And nor by Vertue, nor Religion, trayn'd
Of them undisciplind, by Folly unchaynd
Is like a Man—of his reason quyte bereft
A mad-man prest to help defend a Fort
To whom nor Conduct nor Advise dos sort
Rage and his Fury to hold in uneath
He on his Captayn dos his Sword unsheath
Arrows and Fire bronds hurls and death
And says Am I not in Sport?
So the Bold Horse dos into Battel presse
His neck with thunder cloath'd, his mane with flame
Smoake through his nose-thrills breaking like two Seas
Dasht on our Solent Needles[1] (worthy name)
For Countrys sake here to reherse
And give an higher Figure to my humble Verse
With adverse force of Wind and Tyde they rolling come
They souse, they dash, they break, the very rock
Groanes and to trembles seemes, at the rough choque
Its head with drisling cloud, ye under sea all spredd with fome
So snorts he, so around
Flinging and playing on his chamfred bitt,
(Ryder beware how thou dost sitt.)
With spume he flecks the ground
And fretts, and pawes, and bounds and seemes with rage to swallow it.
Against the rattling quiver, sheild, and speare
Mocking at feare
His naked unarm'd breast dos beare
And when he dos the Trumpet heare
And military Fyfe
Snuffs and afarr off dos the battle smell
And in he rushes meslê,
And knowes not that it is for his life.

[1] The Sharp high rocks called the *Needles*, standing in the entrance of the Narrow Seas between ye Wight and Hants. [Author's note]

VI

Fly! Fly, my Verse, if Thou art wise,
Put all thy wings on and encrease thy speed
For never hadst thou equall need
And to secure the prize
Be thyne owne choyce thy flight, thy guidance Destinys.
Wilmott[1] so fled (*Wilmott*, whose noble Son
Makes all his Fathers virtues be his Own
Illumind with a brighter ray
And double claym to them in thy verse dos lay)
So Wilmott fled on *Worcesters* dismall day
When courage was by numbers overpow'rd
And, (Fates grim terrors to display)
Prosprous Rebellion shar'd the Prey
Whilst Heav'n (tho then few thought so) on ye Victors lour'd.
Few thought so then, and it was well
They did not, for it might
Have hazarded that sacred Light
Of our unblesst, unhappy Israel
Which once there quencht, (and who can tell
Whether our Sinns from blackest Hell
Might not have call'd it up by cursed spell?)
Had follow'd been by an Eternall night.
A night whose shaddow was so thick
Twenty yeares on our Goshen close did stick
With such horror and affright
Egypts for three days felt, was to it bright.

VII

Yet in it 'scapt the Dearest Head
By Angels guarded, and by Angels ledd
Heav'ns blessing on their Memory
Who the bold stratagem first counselled
Which harder was for Royall Majesty
By thousand deaths encompass'd to effect than dy
And to regain by flight both life and Victory.

[1] Henry Wilmot, first Earl of Rochester, the poet's father, who fought for Charles II at the Battle of Worcester.

Before the *KING* his loyall servants passt
        Wilmott among the rest
Who most were trusted and who lov'd him best
        The *KING* himself came last
As if in theirs his safety, not in His their hopes were plac'd.
And all the while their faynting spirits to cheere
        In so great lustre did appeare
        With such glory on his browes
        So even and so calm repose
Convinc't they were that Heav'n had other ways
Than what they saw, wch it self only knowes
    By peacefull Art and safe Delays
    The Trophys of th'Opprest to rayse
And make ye Oaken Girland farr exceede the Bayes.
    Till having many a Fortune try'd
    And many a close disguise put on
    That Heavnly Majesty to hide
        Which through them all was known
        And but by Miracle
        From others to conceale
    Was only not Impossible
    To th' sea at last they come and find
Amidst its Furys Faythlesse Floods and Wind.
Lesse certein Death, more certeyn Fayth than they had left
    behind.

VIII

'*CHARLES* and his Fortunes to the other shore
See that thou beare!'—Our seas great Sovereign sayd;
To th' sea he sayd it, and the sea obey'd
    Its Sovereigns voice, twice-heard before
And thither in its arms the sacred Treasure bore.
Obey it Thou, whom all things else obey,
Divinity of Verse, and as thou mayst
Recall him and his Coronation Day
    (Tho to all else but thee tis past)
Still present make, or let it ever last.
    Let *Wilmotts Son* then in thy Song
    From whom thou roved hast too long

The next great Figure of thy Numbers make,
    And for thy ransom'd Countrys sake
The fayrest beauty's of thy Skill partake!
    Tis done—And (Lo!) how to our time
    He leads the solemn Pomp along
With all the Harmonys of Witt and Rhime
And a free Muse wch ever will be young!
Great sense, choyce words, bold Images
    And what might serve to expresse
The loftyest subject, in the most becoming dresse.
    Ah! that it had been so employd!
And that or *Nothing*, or than Nothing worse,
Reason debas't, affronted Heav'ns last curse,
Fulsome Atheism, wherwith the age is cloyd,
    (Rank seed, rank soyle, wch every yeare
    The same ungratefull crop dos beare)
Relligion rallyed, Vertue, and Mankind,
Had not been all the Theames, the noblest pen would find.

IX

    Unworthy state of Verse! how low
    How servile art thou grown and meane
    Who wert of Old a Mighty Queen
And hadst all knees before Thy Throne to bow!
When thy whole buisinesse Worship was and Prayse
And Virtue only did to Thee Altars rayse
And all thy Robes were Arts, and Arms were all thy Bayes!
But now by every hedg than veyld dost sitt
    By every hedg dost sitt Thee down
Thy Open Quiver dos all arrowes fitt
And every little Flutter of the Town
Claymes thee the Common Prostitute of his Scurrile Witt.
Nay, treachrously thy best Friends with Thee deale
    And in pretence thy Wounds to heale
Wider have made them and inflicted more
And made thee what Thou scarce wert fear'd before
The reall Grievance of the Comon-Weale.
    In One All Mischeifes.—As when Fire
    (And still with other thy mock names

Of spirit and Salt, thou hast thy Flames,
Jargon of Verse, wch only Fopps admire.)
As Fire from th'Holy Temple ta'ne
Where it burnt nought but sacrifice
And only with accepted Smoaks did rise
When to a Mine tis putt, and hidden sulphurous Veine
Its forces unable to contayne
Up flyes the Bastion, with it up there fly
Men, Stores, Arms, Carriage, Artillary;
Shreiks, clamour, and a confus'd cry
Enough the boldest courage to amaze
From every part is heard; at gaze
The trembling Firers stand, around
Nothing but death in its grislyest shapes is found
And stayns with blood the sky, and strewes with limbs the ground.

X

Verse is that Mine, and early thus was Sprung
When once perverted from its first design
Eternall Lands, wch in its Hymns were sung
And did more beauteous in those fetters shine
When leaving Virtuous men and Virtues guide
The Schole and Camp, It all its Arts applyd
To th'Stage, and learnt those Follys, wch it did deride.
At Daunce and Ball did serve, and Playes
Whole nights in Revells spent, in Stewes whole days
By Satyr, Libell, and Lampoon
Anticks and Apes attended on
With Farce for Witt, and Grimace some, and some wth none.
Till having Lusts and Wines excesses try'd
And satiated at length, not satisfyd,
'Gainst God it did its last effort mayntayn
And upward threw that blood, Heav'n on its head did rayne.
Weep! Weep my song the daring hand
Which threw it and was deeply (ah too deeply) staynd
By youthfull heat and th' Ages Vice trappand.
Thy teares he calls for, who his own thus spent
Spent them for this without disparagment

To his Courage, Learning, Witt, or yeares
    The Great, the Noble *ROCHESTERS*.
Mix, till with his they make a flood, thy teares!
And thus at last persue his just intent.
    Perchance Thou mayst successfull prove
Those Follys, and that Madness to remove
Which dying he in Others mournd, did in Himself reprove.

XI

Madness and Follys, wch how ere begun
Were not by *ROCHESTER* sustaynd alone
Tho He almost alone, the burden bore
(Beside the monstrous pack, wch was his own)
Of all that by or Malice, or Illnature late was done.
Well were it that they would at last give o're—
    But still as they were wont before
With Farwells, Droll, and Shredds of Verse
They vex his Happy Ghost, and miserably disguise his Herse.
Yet Farwells such as those He never took
Nor would a Wise man howsoever mov'd
    Witnesse Ye Heav'ns, wch on did look
And all he sayd then, all he did, approv'd.
(Worthy the Place, the Company and Choice
        To wch hee is remov'd)
And thence with part of his Celestiall Fire
Lesse tunefull Soules with rapturous Flames inspire.
Inspire me Heav'n of tunefull Souls the least
    Inspire me as Thou knowst it best
For Thyne own Honour, and the Mans I sing
    (Now more than man, a spirit Divine
    By ways unsearchable made Thyne)
And heights wch none can reach by mortall Wing
Down on thy Sacred Doves blest pinnions bring!
Angels pure joys, triumphs wherwith they meet
Repenting Sinners, and their coming greet
With such a trayn and such a Cavalcade
    Of thy choyce Flower the whole Parade
        For One returnd agen
As ne're in thy triumphal Gates were seen
        For ninety nine just men.

XII

'Ah Mighty God!' with Zeale he spake and Feare
Sacred Revenge and Holy Griefe
And Shame, that all ye marks did beare
Of true Repentance and a Sound Belief.
'Ah God!' The Humble *ROCHESTER* cry'd out
'How misrably I was deceiv'd
Thy Spirit how oft, how strangely have I griev'd
And when at first thy Care I did but doubt
Grown obstinate thy very Being misbeliev'd.
But I'm convinc't now and thy Power adore
Nor Thee, nor Providence will question more
Only my self for such curs'd thoughts abhorr.
No! No! my God, Thou knowst I doubt it not
And that these late Confessions neither Payne
Nor a meane Spirit, as the misled feign
Extorted have, lesse are they fumes of a Distempred Brain,
But what both they and I too long forgott
(Ah! That we should so long forgett
Things wch in vieue are dayly sett)
The Dictates of that truth, whose power
Nor King, nor Wine, nor Women can controll
Nor what lesse move a Ratiunall Discursive Soule
Opinions changing every houre
Yet these their Guides are, who leave Thee
Disputes, Doubts, blind uncerteinty
Of reall Future feares wch may, Fond hopes, wch may not bee.'

XIII

'Eternall truth! How wondrous are thy ways,
Who ever liv'st, art ever strong
Free from Injustice and from wrong
And trophys to Thy self dost from Thyne Enemys rayse!
With Thee theres no acceptance of rewards
Or persons; Innocence is all Thy Guards
And all men blesse thy Works, all Verse resounds thy Prayse.
Thine Sacred Virgin, whose is majesty
The strength the Kingdom, Power and Youth

Of every Age, the Present, Past, and what shall be,
    (Bless'd be the God of truth!)
But Falshood in Thy stead, wee have made to reign
Its Thrones Supporter Pride, and Ignorance its trayn.
Of things not understood we boldly spake
And all the Lawes of truth and Nature brake
And Reasons self for Reasons shaddow did forsake.
Yet leave me, God I but this once will speake
Words wch Thy Majesty shall not offend
Against my self, the chayns wch Thou didst breake
    I'll rattle, and thus self condemn'd
Prisner of hope, the judgment of Thy barr attend.
Guilt and Thy Mercy give this Confidence
Guilt wch I here acknowledg tho tis late
Of crimes no Death but his can expiate
Whom oft I tortur'd, murderd oft by th' Great Offence.
JESU my God, by me thrice Crucify'd and more
    With shames Thou ne're endur'dst before
JESU my judg, Lo! how I mercy crave!
The greatest Mercy, wch Thou hast in store
For greatest Sinners *JESU* I implore
O! tho my God to judg, My *JESUS* be to save.'

XIV

    He spake; and then with cherfull Face
But humble Mind that Sentence to prevent
Which must the Willing and Unwilling passe
With his own hands his Witts great Offspring rent
And peice-meale into th' Flame their sever'd portions sent.
Till all consum'd, with all the Images
Of Jealousy, wch he to himself had made
    The Great, the Middle and the lesse
Rolls, pictures, parchments and of th' Riming trade
    Th' whole Garniture Obscene and stock
    Clapping to his breast the *Sacred Book.*
    'How do I love Thee now?' he sayd
'Great Guide of Life, and like thy Author true
The Power the Wisdom of ye Deity
    Always ye same yet always new

And of th' Invisible the cleare Discovery!
No Lesbian Rule of Manners or of Witt
But what all Ages, dos all Countrys fitt
And to whose Laws even Verse its Empire must submitt!
Queen of Pure minds, Empresse of thoughts sublime
    Thoughts wch the meanest Verse refine
And stamp the Nobler with a Character Divine
Since I to Thee no spoyles can Dedicate
    Of a just Enemy duely slayne,
    My life, of right Proscrib'd, to obtayn
What first I spoyld thee of, I yield again,
And my self at Thy Altar low prostrate
The Greatest Spoyler a just Victime consecrate.'
—Scarce done, His shining head a cloud did hide,
From whence a Voice as of lowd Thunder came
'Now Gloryfy'd again is th' Eternall Name
  Rochester in the *LAMBS* fresh blood new dy'd
All robed in white sings Lauds to him whom he denyd.'

Vivet

19. Samuel Holland, An Elegy on Rochester

1680

'An Elegie Humbly offered to the Memory of that Matchless Wit, and Unparallel'd Example of Sincere Penitency, the Right Honorable John Earl of Rochester, who most Piously exchanged Earthly Honour for Never-fading Glory the 26th Day of July, 1680'.

Printed for the Author [Broadside] (1680).

No more, wild *Atheists*! No more Deny
That blessed *Hope* which makes us glad to Dye;
Dispute no more the Truth of that Great Day
Shall free dead Mankind from their gloomy Clay.
See here an Argument stops all your *Lies*
The Mighty *Rochester* a *Convert* Dies,
He fell a Poet, but a Saint shall Rise.
Then help us all ye Pow'rs of Verse, and flow
Into his Praise all that Himself could do:
For who can write without him? or dares try
To speak his Worth? Unless his Ghost were nigh;
Where, when our Flames do languish we retire
To his Great *Genius*, and thence take new Fire.
Whose lofty Numbers gently slid away
Like Chrystal waters, smooth and deep as They;
Though some low Men by others *Verse* are Rais'd
(*Fools* living that would, dead, be Prais'd:)
To Celebrate his *Marble* he needs none,
His Name out-lives both *Epitaph* and *Stone*.
Excess of *Wit* alone his Fame did spoil,
So Lamps extinguish't are by too much Oil;
And since he's gone, we grov'ling Trifles Crawl
About the World, which but confirms his Fall;

As when retiring *Sol* blinds us with Night,
Each petty Star peeps forth to brag stoln Light.
Yet not his *Muse* do we so much admire,
As those rare sparks of true *Celestial Fire*
That warm'd his Breast when Nature's Heats decay'd,
And *Death-cold Horrors* did each Limb Invade:
Then did a sudden *Beam* of *Light Divine*
Inspire his Soul, his Faculties Refine,
And from *Pernassus* [*sic*] drew his fixed Eye
To Pigsah-Mount [*sic*], and saving Calvary;
The Bubbling *Froth* that wanton *Fancy* rais'd
(Which for *Extravagance* was only *Prais'd*)
Is soon beat down by this more *Glorious Flame*,
Whence straight a *Noble* true *Elixir* came;
This *Solomon* for *Wit* and *Pleasures* too
Bids *Vanity* of *Vanities* adieu.
And having tasted all the *sweets* are Hurl'd
O're Youthful minds by a *deluding* World;
Begins to Descant on *Eternal Themes*,
And then saw *Visions*, that before dream'd *Dreams*:
He finds Religion is no forged Law
For cunning *Knaves* to keep dull *Fools* in Awe;[1]
That *Future State*, and the Dread *Judgment Day*,
And *Heav'n* and *Hell* (what e're our Drols may say)
Are serious things. Nor did this *Knowledge* scare
Or fright him to wild Desarts of *Despair*;
But gently wrought, to shew 'twas from above
Th' instructive Breathings of the *Holy Dove*;
Taught him with humble *Faith* and *Hope* to fly
For Balm to *Gilead*, and on Christ relye.
Now with redoubled *Sighs* and Floods of *Tears*,
He chides the *Follies* of his mispent years:
Himself his *looser Lines* to Flames bequeaths,[2]
And *Hobs's Creed* with Detestation leaves;
Warns all our *Youthful Nobles*, lets them know
True *Honour* can from *Vertue* only flow:
That *Piety* will give a lasting Crown

[1] Perhaps a reference to Rochester's translation from Seneca's *Troades* (Pinto, xxxix).
[2] See Parsons' *Funeral Sermon* (1680) pp. 28–9.

When their *Gay Titles* All must tumble down,
And dark *Oblivion* worldly *Grandeur* Drown.
To hear him thus on Solemn *Death-Bed* Preach,
Did more than Forty *Languid Sermons* Teach.
The *Angels* clapt their Wings on that blest Day
Envy'd unworthy *Earth* his longer stay,
And so in *Triumph* bore his *Soul* away.

The Epitaph

Under this Tomb we do Interr
The Ashes of Great Rochester;
Whose pointed Wit (his worst of Crimes)
So Justly lasht our Foppish Times;
Let none too Rigorous Censures fix
Great Errors with great Parts will mix;
How broad soe're his Faults be shown,
His Penitence as large was known.
    Forbear then!—and let you and I
    By him, at least, learn how to Dye.

20. From the anonymous *Metamorphoses*

c. 1684

Poems on Affairs of State (1703), ii. 159.

This anti-Catholic poem seems to have been written sometime between the execution of Algernon Sidney, 1683 (mentioned in the poem), and the accession of James II in 1685. The reference to plots in line 2 is primarily to the Rye House plot, 1683, a largely fictitious event in which it was claimed the King was to have been assassinated. It was generally taken to have been inspired by Catholics.

Had the late fam'd Lord Rochester surviv'd,
We'd been inform'd who all our Plots contriv'd.
Authors and Actors we had long since seen,
In sharpest Satyrs they'd recorded been,
Tho' Captain, Doctor, Lord, Duke, King or Queen:
His bold and daring Muse had soar'd on high,
And brought down true Intelligence from the Sky,
He oft the Court has of its Vices told,
While Priests pretend they dare not be so bold . . .

21. Three Prologues to *Valentinian*

1684

Valentinian, a Tragedy (1685).

Rochester's Valentinian was first acted, with great success, in 1684 and printed with the following prologues in 1685. The three prologues were provided for the three successive nights of the opening run. The play is an adaptation of John Fletcher's tragedy of the same name.

a) Aphra Behn: Prologue spoken by Mrs Cook the First Day:

With that assurance we to day address,
As standard Beauties, certain of Success.
With careless Pride at once they charm and vex,
And scorn the little Censures of their Sex.
Sure of the unregarded Spoyl, despise
The needless Affectation of the Eyes,
The softening Languishment that faintly warms,
But trust alone to their resistless Charms.
So we secur'd by undisputed Wit,
Disdain the damning Malice of the Pit,
Nor need false Arts to set great Nature off,
Or studied Tricks to force the Clap and Laugh.
Ye Wou'd-be-Criticks, you are all undone,
For here's no Theam for you to work upon.
Faith seem to talk to *Jenny*, I advise,
Of who likes who, and how Love's Markets rise.
Try these hard Times how to abate the Price;
Tell her how cheap were Damsels on the Ice.
'Mongst City-Wives, and Daughters that came there,
How far a Guinny went at *Blanket-Fair*.[1]

[1] 'The Fair on the *Thames* so called.' [Marginal note]. This was during the very severe winter of 1683–4.

Thus you may find some good Excuse for failing
Of your beloved Exercise of Railing.
That when Friend cryes—How did the Play succeed?
Deme, I hardly minded—what they did.
We shall not your Ill-nature please to day,
With some fond Scribbler's new uncertain Play,
Loose as vain Youth, and tedious as dull Age,
Or Love and Honour that o're-runs the Stage.
Fam'd and substantial Authors give this Treat,
And 'twill be solemn, Noble all and Great.
Wit, sacred Wit, is all the bus'ness here;
Great *Fletcher*, and the greater *Rochester*.
Now name the hardy Man one fault dares find,
In the vast Work of two such Heroes joyn'd.
None but Great *Strephon's* soft and pow'rful Wit
Durst undertake to mend what *Fletcher* writ.
Different their heav'nly Notes; yet both agree
To make an everlasting Harmony.
Listen, ye Virgins to his charming Song,
Eternal Musick dwelt upon his Tongue.
The Gods of Love and Wit inspir'd his Pen,
And Love and Beauty was his glorious Theam.

Now, Ladies, you may celebrate his Name,
Without a scandal on your spotless Fame.
With Praise his dear lov'd Memory pursue,
And pay his Death, what to his Life was due.

b) Anonymous, Prologue to *Valentinian* spoken by Mrs Cook the Second Day:

'Tis not your easiness to give Applause,
This long hid Jewel into publick draws
Our matchless Author, who to Wit gave Rules,
Scorns Praise, that has been prostitute to Fools.
To factious favour, the sole Prop and Fence
Of Hackney-Scriblers, he quits all Pretence,
And for their Flatteries brings you Truth and Sence.
Things we our selves confess to be unfit
For such side-Boxes, and for such a Pit.
To the fair Sex some Complement were due,

Did they not slight themselves in liking you;
How can they here for Judges be thought fit,
Who daily your soft Nonsence take for Wit;
Do on your ill-bred Noise for Humour doat,
And choose the Man by the embroider'd Coat?
Our Author lov'd the youthful and the fair,
But even in those their Follies could not spare;
Bid them discreetly use their present store,
Be Friends to Pleasure, when they please no more;
Desir'd the Ladies of maturer Ages,
If some remaining Spark their Hearts enrages,
At home to quench their Embers with their Pages.
Pert, patch'd, and painted, there to spend their days;
Not crowd the fronts of Boxes at new Plays:
Advis'd young sighing Fools to be more pressing,
And Fops of Forty to give over dressing.
By this he got the Envy of the Age,
No Fury's like a libell'd Blockhead's Rage,
Hence some despis'd him for his want of Wit,[1]
And others said he too obscenely writ.
Dull Niceness, envious of Mankind's Delight,
Abortive Pang of Vanity and Spite!
It shows a Master's Hand, 'twas *Virgil's* Praise,
Things low and abject to adorn and raise.[2]
The Sun on Dunghils shining is as bright,
As when his Beams the fairest Flowers invite,
But all weak Eyes are hurt by too much Light.
Let then these *Owls* against the *Eagle* preach,
And blame those Flights which they want Wing to reach.
Like *Falstaffe* let 'em conquer Heroes dead,
And praise *Greek* Poets they cou'd never read.
Criticks should personal Quarrels lay aside,
The poet from the Enemy divide.
'Twas Charity that made our Author write,
For your Instruction 'tis we Act to night;
For sure no Age was ever known before,
Wanting an *Æcius* and *Lucina* more.

[1] This is clearly a reference to Mulgrave's *Essay upon Satire* (see No. 7a).

[2] This point is made in Wolseley's Preface to *Valentinian* (see No. 22a) and this Prologue may be by him; the idea is, however, a commonplace one.

c) Anonymous, Prologue intended for *Valentinian*, to be spoken by Mrs Barrey:

Now would you have me rail, swell, and look big,
Like rampant *Tory* over couchant *Whig*.
As spit-fire Bullies swagger, swear, and roar,
And brandish Bilbo, when the Fray is o're.
Must we huff on when we're oppos'd by none?
But Poets are most fierce on those wh'are down.
Shall I jeer Popish Plots that once did fright us,
And with most bitter Bobs taunt little *Titus*?
Or with sharp Style, on sneaking *Trimmers* fall,
Who civilly themselves *Prudential* call?
Yet Witlings to true Wits as soon may rise,
As a prudential Man can ere be wise.
No, even the worst of all yet I will spare,
The nauseous Floater, changeable as Air,
A nasty thing, which on the surface rides,
Backward and forward with all turns of Tides.
An Audience I will not so coursely use;
'Tis the lewd way of every common *Muse*.
Let *Grubstreet*-Pens such mean Diversion find,
But we have Subjects of a nobler kind.
We of legitimate Poets sing the praise,
No kin to th' spurious Issue of these days.
But such as with desert their Laurels gain'd,
And by true Wit immortal Names obtain'd.
Two like Wit-*Consuls* rul'd the former Age,[1]
With Love, and Honour grac'd that flourishing Stage,
And t'every Passion did the Mind engage.
They sweetness first into our Language brought,
They all the Secrets of man's Nature sought,
And lasting Wonders they have in conjunction wrought.

Now joyns a third, a *Genius* as sublime
As ever flourish'd in *Rome's* happiest time.
As sharply could he wound, as sweetly engage,
As soft his Love, and as divine his Rage.

[1] Shakespeare and Fletcher presumably, with Jonson generally thought of as the major figures of the earlier drama.

He charm'd the tenderest Virgins to delight,
And with his Style did fiercest Blockheads fright.
Some Beauties here I see—
Though now demure, have felt his pow'rful Charms,
And languish'd in the circle of his Arms.
But for Ye Fops, his Satyr reach'd ye all,
Under his Lash your whole vast Herd did fall.
Oh fatal loss! that mighty Spirit's gone!
Alas! his too great heat went out too soon!
So fatal is it vastly to excel;
Thus young, thus mourn'd, his lov'd *Lucretius* fell.

And now ye little Sparks who infest the Pit,
Learn all the Reverence due to Sacred Wit.
Disturb not with your empty noise each Bench,
Nor break your bawdy Jests to th' *Orange-Wench*;
Nor in that Scene of Fops, the Gallery,
Vent your No-wit, and spurious Raillery:
That noisie Place, where meet all sort of Tools,
Your huge fat Lovers, and consumptive Fools,
Half Wits, and Gamesters, and gay Fops, whose Tasks
Are daily to invade the dangerous Masks;
And ye little Brood of Poetasters,
Amend and learn to write from these your Masters.

22. Robert Wolseley, Preface to *Valentinian*

1685

Valentinian, a Tragedy as 'tis Alter'd by the Late Earl of Rochester, together with a Preface by one of his Friends (1685).

This essay is primarily intended as a defence of Rochester's lyrics against Mulgrave's attack on them in his *Essay upon Poetry* (No. 7b). Robert Wolseley (1649–97) was a minor poet and wit and, in William III's reign, diplomat and duellist. (For an example of his verse see No. 14d.)

a) I am desir'd to let the World know, that my late Lord Rochester intended to have alter'd and corrected this Play much more than it is, before it had come abroad, and to have mended not only those Scenes of *Fletcher* which remain, but his own too, and the Model of the Plot it self. If therefore the Reader do not find it every where to answer the great Reputation of the Author; if he think the Plot too thin, or any of the Scenes too long, 'tis hop'd he will be so just to remember, that he looks upon an unfinish'd Piece, and what faults soever of this or any other kind some may pretend to see, who cannot yet forgive my Lord the having had more Wit than themselves, we have all the reason imaginable to conclude from the correctness of his other Poetry, that had he liv'd to put the last Hand to this, he wou'd have left true Criticks and impartial Judges no business but to admire, especially if we consider how much he has mended the old Play by that little he has done to it, for he had but just drawn it into a regular Form, and laid the Plane of what he further design'd, when his Countrey and his Friends had the irreparable misfortune to loose him. But as the loosest Negligence of a great Genius is infinitely preferable to that *obscura diligentia*, of which *Terence* speaks,[1] the obscure diligence and labour'd Ornaments of little Pretenders; and as the rudest Drawings of famous Hands have been always more esteem'd (especially among the knowing) than the most perfect Pieces of ordinary Painters, the Publishers of *Valentinian* cou'd

[1] Terence, *Andria*, Prologue 1. 21.

not but believe the World wou'd thank 'em for any thing that was of my Lord *Rochester's* manner, tho' it might want some of those nicer Beauties, those Grace-strokes and finishing Touches, which are so remarkable both in his former and latter Writings: and yet as imperfect as *Valentinian* is left, I am of opinion his Enemies will not meet with that occasion in it for their Ill-nature, which perhaps they expect; for besides that my Lord has made it a Play, which he did not find it, the chief business of it (as *Fletcher* had contriv'd it) ending with the *Fourth Act*, and a new Design, which has no kind of relation to the other, is introduc'd in the *Fifth*, contrary to a Fundamental Rule of the Stage; I say besides that 'tis now adorn'd with that necessary Beauty of a Play, the Unity of Action, and judiciously heighten'd and reform'd through the whole conduct of the Plot from what it was, those Scenes which my Lord has added, have a gracefulness in the Cast, a justness in the Sence, and a nobleness in the Genius, altogether like himself, which (to do my Lord but a bare Right) is far beyond that of most men who write now, and equal even to the Fancy of *Fletcher*, which I think no man's can exceed, there is a chearfulness in it that is every where entertaining, and a Mettle that never tires. But as my Lord in the suiting of his Style to that of *Fletcher*, (which he here seems to have endeavour'd, that the Play might look more of a Piece) cannot with any justice be deny'd the Glory of having reach'd his most admir'd Heights, and to have match'd him in his Fancy, which was his chief Excellence, so it must be also confess'd, that my Lord's constant living at Court, and the Conversation of Persons of Quality, to which from his greenest Youth both his Birth and his Choice had accustom'd him, gave him some great Advantages above this so much and so justly applauded Author, I mean a nicer knowledge both of Men and Manners, an Air of good Breeding, and a Gentleman-like easiness in all he writ, to which *Fletcher's* obscure Education, and the mean Company he kept, had made him wholly a Stranger. If it were at all proper to pursue a Comparison, where there is so little Resemblence, tho' *Fletcher* might be allow'd some Preference in the skill of a Play-Wright, (a thing my Lord had not much study'd) in the contrivance and working up of a passionate Scene, yet my Lord had so many other far more eminent Virtues to lay in the contrary Scale, as must necessarily weigh down the Ballance; for sure there has not liv'd in many Ages (if ever) so extraordinary, and I think I may add so useful a Person, as most *Englishmen* know my Lord to have been, whether we consider the constant good Sence, and the agreeable Mirth of his ordinary Conversation, or the vast Reach and Compass of his Invention, and the wonderful Depths of his retir'd Thoughts, the uncommon Graces of his Fashion, or the inimitable Turns of his Wit, the becoming gentleness, the bewitching softness of his Civility, or the force and fitness of his Satyre; for as he was both the Delight and the Wonder of Men, the Love and the Dotage of Women, so he was a continual Curb to Impertinence and the publick Censor of Folly. Never did Man stay in his Company un-entertain'd, or leave it un-instructed; never was his Understanding biass'd, or his Pleasantness forc'd; never did he laugh in the wrong place, or prostitute his Sence to serve his Luxury; never did he stab into the Wounds of fallen Virtue, with a base and cowardly Insult, or smooth the Face of prosperous Villany, with the Paint and Washes of a mercenary Wit; never did he spare a Fop for being rich, or flatter a Knave for being great. As most men had an Ambition (thinking it an indisputable Title to Wit) to be in the number of his Friends, so few were his Enemies, but such as did not know him, or such as hated him for what others lov'd him, and never did he go among Strangers but he gain'd Admirers, if not Friends, and commonly of such who had been before prejudic'd against him. Never was his Talk thought too much, or his Visit too long; Enjoyment did but increase Appetite, and the more men had of his Company, the less willing they were to part with it. He had a Wit that cou'd make even his Spleen and his Ill-humour pleasant to his Friends, and the publick chiding of his Servants, which wou'd have been Ill-breeding and intolerable in any other man, became not only civil and inoffensive, but agreeable and entertaining in him: A Wit that cou'd please the most morose, perswade the most obstinate, and soften the most obdurate: A Wit whose Edge cou'd ease by cutting, and whose Point cou'd tickle while it prob'd. A Wit that us'd to nip in the very Bud the growing Fopperies of the Times, and keep down those Weeds and Suckers of Humanity; nor was it an Enemy to such only as are troublesom to men of sence in Conversation, but to those also (of a far worse Nature) that are destructive of publick Good, and pernicious to the common Interest of Mankind; that Vein of Knavery that has of late years run through all Orders and Degrees of men among us, spreading it self like a pestilential Poyson through the great and lesser Arteries of our seeming strong-built Leviathan, damping and corrupting the Blood, and choaking the very vital Spirits of the Kingdom.

I might here take occasion to point out in particular, and lash (as they deserve) those daily-increasing Vices and long uncorrected Follies, which are our present Grievances: the Subject is but too fruitful, and the Usefulness too apparent, nor cou'd I ever purchase Reputation at a cheaper rate; nothing is more easie than to pull off the thin Veil, and bare the vileness of those odious Practices, which some who are ready at any time to *run with a Multitude to do mischief*, applaud for the highest Virtue and Merit; nothing requires less skill, than to baffle and expose to universal Contempt those slight and trivial Notions, which others who seem *given over to believe a Lye*, cry up for Master-pieces of Wit and Reason; to name 'em for Arguments is to ridicule 'em, and but to state 'em right is to confute 'em. But common prudence will teach a man not to hurt himself, while he vainly endeavours the good of others; for as there never was any Time or Countrey that wanted Satyre so much, that cou'd bear it so little as ours, so the men I wou'd reform are a sort of harden'd irreclaimable Blockheads, whose Understandings seem perfect *Solids*, as dead to Wit, and as insensible of Reason, as if there Souls and their Bodies (according to *Hobbes's* Philosophy) were both made of the same stuff, and equally impenetrable; so ty'd to their little Prejudices, and so wilful in their Blindness, that were they in a Storm at Sea, that threaten'd every moment those *Lives and Fortunes* of which they are sometimes so unnecessarily prodigal, it wou'd be impossible to make 'em own, there were a breath of Wind stirring, unless it suited with their Humours, or was to the purpose of their Folly. With them Seeing in some cases is not Believing, and the most perfect sence they have (if it cross their Inclination) must pass for an *Irish Evidence*. I shall leave therefore to their own Conduct and Destiny this forlorn Hope of Ignorance and Stupidity, and return to what I was saying of my Lord *Rochester*.

He had a Wit that was accompanied with an unaffected greatness of Mind, and a natural Love to Justice and Truth; a Wit that was in perpetual War with Knavery, and ever attacking those kind of Vices most, whose malignity was like to be most diffusive, such as tended more immediately to the prejudice of publick Bodies, and were of a common Nusance to the happiness of humane kind. Never was his Pen drawn but on the side of good Sence, and usually imploy'd like the Arms of the ancient Heroes, to stop the progress of arbitrary Oppression, and beat down the Bruitishness of head-strong Will; to do his King and Countrey justice upon such publick State-Thieves, as would beggar a Kingdom to enrich themselves, who abusing the Confidence, and undeserving the Favour of a gracious Prince, will not be asham'd to maintain the cheating of their Master, by the robbing and starving of their fellow-Servants, and under the best Form of Government in the World blush not to live upon the spoyl of others, till by their impudent Violations of Right, they grow like Beasts of Prey, *Hostes humani Generis.*[1] These were the Vermin whom (to his eternal Honour) his Pen was continually pricking and goading. A Pen, if not so happy in the Success, as generous in the Aim, as either the Sword of *Theseus*, or the Club of *Hercules*, nor was it less sharp than that, or less weighty than this. If he did not take so much care of himself as he ought, he had the Humanity however to wish well to others, and I think I may truly affirm, he did the World as much good by a right application of Satyre, as he hurt himself by a wrong pursuit of Pleasure.

I must not here forget, that a considerable time before his last Sickness, his Wit began to take a more serious Bent, and to frame and fashion it self to publick Business; he begun to inform himself of the Wisdom of our Laws, and the excellent Constitution of the *English* Government, and to speak in the House of Peers with general approbation; he was inquisitive after all kind of Histories, that concern'd *England*, both ancient and modern, and set himself to read the Journals of Parliament Proceedings. In effect, he seem'd to study nothing more, than which way to make that great Understanding God had given him, most useful to his Countrey, and I am confident, had he liv'd, his riper Age wou'd have serv'd it, as much as his Youth had diverted it. Add to this, the generousness of his Temper, and the affability of his good Sence; the willingness he still show'd to raise the oppress'd, and the pleasure he took to humble the proud; the constant readiness of his Parts, and that great presence of Mind, that never let him want a fit and pertinent Answer to the most sudden and unexpected Question, (a Talent as useful as 'tis rare) the admirable skill he was Master of, to countermine the Plots of his Enemies, and break through the Traps that were laid for him, to work himself out of the entanglement of unlucky Accidents, and repair the Indiscretions of his Youth, by the Quickness and fineness of his Wit; the strang facility he had to talk to all Capacities in their own Dialect, and make himself good Company to all kind of People at all times; so that if we wou'd find a Soul to resemble that beautiful Portraiture of Man, with which *Lucretius* (according to his sublime manner of Description) complements his Friend *Memmius*, when he says that *Venus*, the Goddess of Beauty, and second Cause of all things, had form'd him to excel (and that upon all occasions) in every necessary Grace and Virtue; I say, if we wou'd justifie this charming Picture, and clear it from flattery even to humane Nature, we must set it by my late

[1] Enemies of the human race.

Lord Rochester; of him it may be truly said in the fullest sence of the words,

> *Quem Tu, Dea, tempore in omni,*
> *Omnibus ornatum voluisti excellere rebus.*[1]

What last, and most of all, deserves admiration in my Lord, was his Poetry, which alone is Subject enough for perpetual Panegyrick. But the Character of it is so generally known; it has so eminently distinguish'd it self from that of other men, by a thousand irresistible Beauties; every Body is so well acquainted with it, by the effect it has had upon 'em, that to trace and single out the several Graces may seem a Task as superfluous, as to describe to a Lover the Lines and Features of his Mistress's Face. 'Tis sufficient to observe, that his Poetry, like himself, was all Original, and has a stamp so particular, so unlike any thing that has been writ before, that as it disdain'd all servile imitation, and copying from others, so neither is it capable (in my opinion) of being copy'd, any more than the manner of his Discourse could be copy'd; the Excellencies are too many and too masterly; on the other side the Faults are few, and those inconsiderable; their Eyes must be better than ordinary, who can see the minute spots with which so bright a Jewel is stain'd, or rather set off, for those it has are of the kind which *Horace* says, can never offend:

> *Quas aut incuria fudit,*
> *Aut humana parum cavit Natura*[2]

Such little Negligences as Humanity cannot be exempt from, and such as perhaps were necessary to make his Lines run natural and easie; for as nothing is more disagreeable either in Verse or Prose than a slovenly loosness of Style, so on the other hand too nice a correctness will be apt to deaden the Life, and make the Piece too stiff; between these two Extreams is the just Character of my *Lord Rochester's* Poetry to be found, nor do I know any thing that the severest Critick, who will be impartial, can object, unless he will say (as some have done) that there is not altogether so much strength and closeness in my Lord's Style, as in that of one of his Friends, a Person of great Quality and Worth, whom I think it not proper to name, because he has never yet publickly own'd any of his Writings, tho' none have been more generally or more justly

[1] 'A man that you, oh Goddess, have wished to see adorned with excellence in everything for all time' (Lucretius, *De Rerum Natura*, i. 26–7).

[2] 'Which either carelessness has produced or human nature has been too negligent about.' Horace, *Ars Poetica*, ll. 352–3.

admir'd;[1] but if my Lord's Sence be not always so strong and full (for often it is) as that of this Honourable Person his Friend, yet in revenge the Spirit that diffuses it self through the Whole, and warms and animates every Part, the newness of his Thought, the liveliness of his Expression, the purity of his Phrase, and the delicacy of his Turn is admirable; if he does not say so much in so little Compass, yet he says always enough to please; what he wants in Force is supply'd in Grace, and where he has not this strength and fulness of Sence, that is so much his Friend's particular Talent, he has Touches that are more affecting, so that when we do not find it, we do not miss it. To conclude this Point, his Poetry has every where a Tincture of that unaccountable Charm in his Fashion and Conversation, that peculiar Becomingness in all he said and did, that drew the Eyes and won the Hearts of all who came near him.

The Reader may perhaps judge a Discourse of this nature very unnecessary; I am apt to believe, no unprejudic'd man, who has read my *Lord Rochester's* Writings, will think they can need a Defence, or that any of his Enemies shou'd be so forsaken both of common Justice and common Sence, so blind in their Vanity, and so un-skilful in their Malice, as to tax him with any failing in Wit; He whose Name was the very Mark it pass'd by, and who seem'd to have in his Keeping the *Privy-Seal* of Sence; and yet some such there are, who, having no way to be remarkable above the ordinary Level of Mankind, but by being singular, will needs assault him on this his strongest side, and give occasion for more than has been yet said in his favour; a sort of men, who have been always so in Love with themselves, as never to be able to see any merit or hear any praise but their own, looking on what is paid elsewhere (how due soever) as so much stollen from them, and mistaking their own Talents as much as they undervalue other men's, are perpetually doing that most which least becomes 'em; in spite of the friendly Admonitions of daily Satyre, and the Remonstrances of almost all the Town, tir'd with the Persecution, they persist in an untoward spiritless Vein of Rhiming, being perhaps too considerable (in their own opinions) to design the pleasing any Body but themselves, and so far certainly they are in the Right, in that they do not aim at what they can never effect; Men who have got the *Form* of Poetry without the *Power*, and by a laborious Insipidness, a polish'd Dulness, seem not design'd to't as a Diversion, but condemn'd to't as a Penance for some yet unexpiated Sin of their forefathers: Men who like old Lovers are

[1] Charles Sackville, 6th Earl of Dorset.

curst with a strong Inclination and weak Abilities, to whom nothing is more unlucky, than an opportunity to satisfie their unnatural Longings; fatal to them is the Favour of their Muse, especially if (because they have ill Meens and ugly Faces) they set up for *Satyres*; when most they wou'd serve the Lust of their Spite, they do but betray the Impotence of their Wit; but they despair to put off that sorry stock they have, till by under-rating other men's they have starv'd the Market, by disgracing Commodities of an intrinsick Worth and staple Price, they hope to recommend their Gawze and Tinsel. In the number of these *Well-wishers* to Verse and men that are *towards Wit*, we may reckon (and that without doing him any Wrong) the conceal'd Author of the late *Essay upon Poetry*,[1] who has in Print made a most unjust, and (to his power) a most malicious Reflexion upon my *Lord Rochester*'s since his death, a Reflexion not more ungenerous in the time and manner of publishing it, than absurd in the sence and matter, as I shall presently make appear, for having always profess'd to be my Lord's Friend, I cannot but think my self oblig'd upon this occasion to vindicate his Memory from so undeserv'd a Libel. Had my Lord been living, I am of the opinion we had never seen either the *Reflexion* or the *Essay*. This Author (whoever he is, or how fond soever he may be of his own Parts) cou'd not but know himself as unfit to play a Prize in Satyre with my late *Lord Rochester*, as feeble *Troilus* was heretofore to fight single with *Achilles*, and therefore probably wou'd not have provok'd a man, who cou'd have beat him to the ground with one stroke of his Pen, and have for ever crush'd his creeping Wit; Or had he had Bravery enough to attack my Lord while he was alive, he wou'd certainly have had Honour enough to let him alone when he was dead; but as he cou'd not but be sensible, any false Criticism upon my Lord's Poetry during his Life, must needs turn to the Critick's shame, so neither cou'd he hope while my Lord liv'd an Indempnity for the dulness of his own; it wou'd have been to no purpose then, to pick up Scraps of *Bossu, Rapin, Boileau, Mr. Dryden's* Prefaces, and Table-Talk, (for every one of these have a large share in his *Essay*), and send 'em into the World for a new *Art of Poetry*, especially after he had defac'd the native Beauty of their thoughts, by new casting 'em in the Mould of a flat, unmusical Verse, and put out all the spirit by the coldness and deadness of his Expression; my Lord wou'd never have suffer'd such a Coyner and Debaser of other men's Bullion, to take upon him the Authority of a Say-Master, nor his light alloy'd Mettle to pass upon the Town for sterling; he, who by his great

[1] John Sheffield, Earl of Mulgrave, see No. 7b.

Mastery in Satyre seem'd to be particularly trusted with the Justice of *Apollo*, did not use to let the purloiners of Wit retail their stollen Goods to the People, without bringing 'em to open shame, nor *Quacks* and *Mountebanks* in Poetry, furnish'd with nothing but a few borrow'd *Recipes*, to put on the Face and Gravity, and appear in publick with the pride and positiveness of Doctors; the vainest Pretenders in his time, the most confident *Essayers*, cow'd and aw'd under the known force of a sence so superiour to their own, were glad at any rate to keep their empty Heads out of Observation, as the Fowl of a whole Countrey creep into the Bushes, when an Eagle hangs hovering above 'em. If ever they attempted to make Verses, 'twas with the same secrecy that others make Love, and none were troubled with the sight of 'em, but those who had the ill fortune to be their particular Friends; however they might sometimes lye under the suspicion of Poetry, they took care there shou'd never be Evidence enough to convict 'em, and happy did they then think themselves, if in parting with their vain hope of passing for Wits, they cou'd escape being mark'd out for Fops; 'tis true, some few remain'd incorrigible even then (as always there will be some whom no kind of sence how forcible soever can make any Impression upon) but for the most part, Ignorance begun to wear the Mask of Modesty, which is certainly her most becoming Dress, and men were contented to be no wiser than God had made 'em; at least those who wanted Wit, did not contrive (as the manner now is) to make their dulness remarkable, by exposing to the World their painful and fruitless Endeavours after it, but were willing to be valued for some other Talent (perhaps more beneficial) which Nature in her equitable distribution of things had given 'em instead of it. Thus was Vanity kept within some tolerable Bounds, while my *Lord Rochester* liv'd, by the general Dread of a Pen so severe and impartial. But his Death has prov'd a Jubilee to the little Witlings of the Town, by which they have got Indulgence for a thousand Fopperies, more mischievous and more senceless than were ever yet imported from *France*, and as much empty Rhime as they are capable of committing as long as they live; nor have they spar'd to use this *Poetical Licence* to the utmost extent of men's patience: Never was there known so many Versifyers, and so few Poets; every Ass that's Romantick believes he's inspir'd, and none have been so forward to teach others as those who cannot write themselves; every man is ready to be a Judge, but few will be at the trouble to understand, and none are more blind to the faults of their own Poetry, than those who are so sharp-sighted in other men's; Every Fop that falls in Love, thinks he has a Right to make Songs, and all kind of People that are gifted with the least knowledge of *Latin* and *Greek*, pretend to translate; the most reverenc'd Authors of Antiquity, have not been able to escape the Conceitedness of *Essayers*, nor *Hudibras*[1] himself, that admirable Original, his little Apers, tho' so artless are their Imitations, so unlike and so liveless are their Copies, that 'twere impossible to guess after what Hands they drew, if there Vanity did not take care to inform us in the Title-Page.

For Satyre, that most needful part of our Poetry, it has of late been more abus'd, and is grown more degenerate than any other; most commonly like a Sword in the hands of a Mad-man, it runs a Tilt at all manner of Persons without any sort of distinction or reason, and so ill-guided is this furious Career, that the Thrusts are most aim'd, where the Enemy is best arm'd. Women's Reputations (of what Quality or Conduct soever) have been reckon'd as lawful Game as Watchmen's Heads, and 'tis thought as glorious a piece of Gallantry by some of our modern Sparks, to libel a Woman of Honour, as to kill a Constable who is doing his duty; Justice is not in their Natures, and all kind of useful knowledge lyes out of the way of their Breeding; Slander therefore is their Wit, and Dresse is their Learning; Pleasure their Principle, and Interest their God. But how infamous, insipid, or ignorant soever the Authors themselves are, their Satyres want not sting, for upon no better Evidence than those poetical Fables and palpable Forgeries, the poor Ladies, whose little Plots they pretend to discover, are either made Prisoners in their own Houses, or banish'd into the Countrey during Life; tho' so ill-colour'd generally is the Spite, and so utterly void of all common probability are the brutal Censures, that stuff up their licentious Lampoons, that 'tis not easie to determine, which of the two deserve most to be laugh'd at, the *Fantastical Foplings* that write 'em, or the *Cautious Coxcombs* that believe 'em. But what is yet more wonderful, this Practice is applauded and carry'd on by those only, who esteem the gaining of handsom Women the greatest Felicity the Nature of man is capable of, make it the Burden of all their empty Talk, and the Businesse of their Lives; now this sole design of theirs these able Gentlemen endeavour to bring about, by doing what they can upon all occasions to fright and indeed force the whole Sex from any Commerce with men, and make all Access to 'em difficult, which is just as wise as if a man that lov'd *Setting*, as soon as he had found his Game, instead

[1] Samuel Butler's *Hudibras*, the three parts of which appeared in 1663, 1664 and 1678 respectively, was immensely popular and frequently imitated.

of observing the Wind, and preparing his Nets, shou'd hoop and hollow, and throw Stones at 'em.

This is one Branch of our present Satyre, which has much of the Nature, and more of the Wit of *Jack Pudding's* Buffoon'ry, for as he, tho' he flings Dirt at every body, is angry with no body, so do these Bully-Writers perpetually assault People from whom they never receiv'd the least Provocation, and murder their good Names in cold Blood. The other is of a more serious Cast, but withal 'tis more malicious; and falling in with the baseness of a corrupt Age, does infinitely more mischief; this is made to wound where it ought to defend, and cover where it shou'd expose, to contradict the very first Elements of Morality, and bid defiance to the unalterable Essence of things, by calling *Good Evil, and Evil Good*. Heroes have been hung up *in Effigie* who deserv'd Statues, while the worst of men have been *cens'd* with the Praises of demi-Gods; Betrayers of their Trust, and little servers of Turns have been idoliz'd, while Patriots of an unstain'd Honour, and unreproachable conduct, who were in truth the *Dei Tutelares*[1] of their distracted Countrey, have been openly blasphem'd with an impudent and witlesse Scurrility; in a word, those chiefly have been the Authors of Satyres, who ought to be the Subject, and 'tis become much more scandalous to be thought to write the best, than to be put into the most abusive.

But (as I was saying) among these *Wou'd be* Poets of the Times, who have scarce any one Talent proper for the Calling, none is more eminent than the Author of the fore-nam'd *Essay*, who while he pretends, without the least colour of Authority, either from Art or Nature, to be the Muse's Legislator, deserves not the Office of their Cryer; with so hoarse and so untunable a Voice has he republish'd the poetical Laws, not of his own, but of their true Representatives' framing; however he hopes to distinguish himself from the crowd of common Writers, by a proud and spiteful Attempt upon the Reputation of my late *Lord Rochester*, whose one Example is worth all his Precepts. But 'tis time to examine what he objects, and see if there be any Wit in his Anger; the Maxim he lays down for the foundation of his Satyre is, *That Bawdry cannot be Wit*; his words are these (Page the 6th of his *Essay*),

> Bawdry bare-fac'd, that poor Pretence to Wit,
> Such nauseous Songs, Etc.[2]

This is new Doctrine among men of Sence, but an old thread-bare

[1] Tutelary gods. [2] Mulgrave, *Essay upon Poetry*, ll. 81–2.

Saying among unthinking half-witted People, who judge without examining and talk without meaning. I'le answer for him, he did not learn this of any of the Authors I mention'd before, to whom he has been so much oblig'd for most of the other Parts of his *Essay*; it never yet came into any man's Head, who pretended to be a Critick, except this *Essayer's*, that the Wit of a Poet was to be measur'd by the worth of his Subject, and that when this was bad, that must be so too; the manner of treating his Subject has been hitherto thought the true Test, for as an ill Poet will depresse and disgrace the highest, so a good one will raise and dignifie the lowest;[1] some of the most masterly Strokes in *Virgil* are his Descriptions of the Employment of Bees, the Jealousie of Bulls, the Lust of Horses and Boars, the cutting down of a Tree, the Working of Ants, and the Swimming and Hissing of Snakes, things little and unlovely in themselves, but noble and beautiful in the Pictures he gives us of 'em. True Genius, like the *Anima Mundi*, which some of the Ancients believ'd, will enter into the hardest and dryest thing, enrich the most barren Soyl, and inform the meanest and most uncomely matter; nothing within the vast Immensity of Nature, is so devoid of Grace, or so remote from Sence, but will obey the Formings of his plastick Heat, and feel the Operations of his vivifying Power, which, when it pleases, can enliven the deadest Lump, beautifie the vilest Dirt, and sweeten the most offensive Filth; this is a Spirit that blows where it lists, and like the Philosopher's Stone, converts into it self whatsoever it touches; Nay, the baser, the emptier, the obscurer, the fouler, and the less susceptible of Ornament the Subject appears to be, the more is the Poet's Praise, who can infuse dignity and breath beauty upon it, who can hide all the natural deformities in the fashion of his Dresse, supply all the wants with his own plenty, and by a poetical Daemonianism, possesse it with the spirit of good sence and gracefulnesse, or who (as *Horace* says of *Homer*)[2] can fetch Light out of Smoak, Roses out of Dunghils, and give a kind of Life to the Inanimate, by the force of that divine and supernatural Virtue, which (if we will believe *Ovid*) is the Gift of all who are truely Poets:

Est Deus in Nobis, agitante calescimus illo,
sedibus ætheriis Spiritus ille venit.[3]

[1] This is a critical commonplace of the period, and Virgil's *Georgics*, as here, were frequently used to illustrate the point: cf. Second Prologue to *Valentinian*, No. 21b.

[2] Horace, *Ars Poetica* I. 143.

[3] 'There is a god in us and we are warmed by its stimulation, that spirit comes from celestial places.' (Ovid, *Fasti*, vi. 5 and *Ars Amatoria*, iii. 549–50).

There are no two things in the World that have a nearer affinity and resemblance than poetry and Painting; the Parallel between 'em runs throughout; every Body knows the old Adage, That Poetry is *Pictura loquens*, and Painting is *Poema silens*;[1] that paints with Words, and this speaks by Colours; nay, the very Definition of the one, (as I shall show in the pursuit of this Argument) will agree to the other; the Art in both is the same, only the Tools it works with are different. To apply this now to the present purpose; as, in the examining of a Picture, the Question is not what is drawn, but how the Draught is design'd, and the colouring laid, 'tis not at all material, whether the Object, that is set before us, be in it self amiable or deform'd, but whether the Painter has well or ill imitated that Part of Nature which he pretends to copy; so in the judging of a Poem or Verses of any kind, the Subject is no otherwise consider'd, than as it serves to prove the truth, and justifie the force of the Description; for as *Mr. Dryden* has rightly observ'd in the Preface to his *Tyrannick Love, There is as much of Art and as near an Imitation of Nature in a Lazar as in a Venus.*[2] If the Shapings be just, and the Trimming proper, no matter for the coarsenesse of the Stuffe; in all true Poetry, let the Subject or Matter of the Poem be in it self never so great, or so good, 'tis still the Fashion that makes the Value, as in the selling of Filigren, men reckon more for the Work than for the Silver. Were the *Essayer* as well read in *Latin* Authors as he seems to be in *French*; or if his Learning cou'd carry him no further, (as I much suspect by his Style) wou'd he have vouchsaf'd but to look on a Translation of *Horace's Art of Poetry*, before he had put out his own, he might have sav'd himself the shame of so fundamental a mistake as this crude Objection is guilty of; where plain common sence fail'd him, *Horace* wou'd have inform'd him, that Poets and Painters have been always allow'd to represent whatever they wou'd:

Pictoribus atque Poetis,
Quidlibet audendi semper fuit æqua potestas.[3]

I know *Horace* brings in this as an Objection to what he is discoursing, but he speaks of it at the same time as a general Maxim, and owns it himself for an undoubted Truth, for the very next Verse is,

Scimus, & hanc veniam petimusque damusque vicissim.[4]

[1] Plutarch, *De Gloria Atheniensium* 3 and *De Audiendis Poetis* 3.

[2] Dryden, Preface to *Tyrannic Love*, ed. Scott, iii. 377.

[3] 'Painters and poets have always had an equal right to venture on anything.' (*Ars Poetica*, 9–10).

[4] 'We know this, and we seek this indulgence and in our turn grant it.' *ibid.*

He only restrains it at last with one Exception, which, they say confirms a Rule:

Sed non ut placidis coeant immitia, non ut
Serpentes avibus geminentur, tigribus agni.[1]

The sence of which is, I grant (says He) that Poets and Painters have an equal right to design and draw what they please, provided their Draughts and their Models be fram'd and govern'd by the nature of things; they must not joyn Serpents with Doves, nor Tygers with Lambs; that is, they must not couple Contraries, and show impossible Chimaeras. This is all the Caution *Horace* gives either to Poets or Painters; he exempts nothing that is natural from the imitation of Art, nor does he set anything out of the reach of Fancy, that is within the bounds of Truth. I know very well that some natural Objects are not in themselves pleasant, nor others fit to be expos'd to publick View, but Decency is one thing, and Poetry and Painting, or the skill of Drawing and Describing, is another. I have been told, that in the late Auction at Whitehall,[2] among other Pieces was set up the Picture of a Man fleaing, with one Arm quite unskin'd, of which tho' every body dislik'd the sight, yet did no body therefore discommend the Painting. But to come closer to the *Essayer's* Cavil, there has not been a very famous Painter in the World, who has not made either Pictures or Drawings of Men or Women in Postures and with Parts obscene, not one of any Note, but like my *Lord Rochester* he has been guilty of *barefac'd Bawdry*. What does he think of the *Hercules* of *Pierino del Vaga,* the *Venus* and the *Cupid* of *Annibal Caraccio*, the *Leda* of *Parmegiano*, the *Diana* and the *Andromeda* of *Titian*, the sleeping *Venus* of *Corregio*, the *Paris* of *Raphael Urbin*, and the *Leda* of *Michael Angelo*? Will he say that these great Master-pieces of Genius and Skill, that have been Ornaments for the Closets of Princes, are *poor Pretences* to Painting, because they are obscene? Or (to presse this Argument a little further) will he condemn all the old Statues, that are yet remaining in the World (for the Parallel holds here too, and his Rule reaches even them) the Labour of so many differently excelling Hands, and the Wonder of so many years, because most of 'em are not only naked but obscene Figures? Particularly, wou'd he for this Reason deface the *Hercules* that is now at *Rome* in the Palace of *Farnese*, a Work more valuable than the Capitol? Can we hope no Quarter for that fam'd *Apollo*, and that so much prais'd *Laocoon*,

[1] 'But not so far that wild should mate with tame or serpents unite with birds or lambs with tigers.' *ibid.*

[2] The sale of Charles I's pictures after his execution.

which are plac'd in the Garden of the *Vatican*? Will he not pardon the two *Alexanders*, that are in white Marble upon Monte Cavallo, one done by Praxiteles, and the other by *Phidias*; the *Meleager* (that Miracle of Art) in the Palace of *Pichini*; the *Mars*, the *Orpheus*, the *Bacchus*, and the dying *Seneca*, in the Palace of *Burghese*, with many others (too numerous to name) that have stood so long the shame and the despair of modern, and the Glory of ancient Artists; who imploy'd as much skill, and thought it as necessary to perfect and make apparent the obscene Parts as any other whatever? Must then these venerable Relicks of Antiquity, that have escap'd the Barbarousness of *Goths* and *Vandals*, fall a Sacrifice at last to the grosser and lesse pardonable Ignorance of a whimsical Reformer? Wou'd he have men pound 'em to dust to humour his Caprice, or must we say that *Nudities* are *poor Pretences* to Sculpture? We may say it indeed with as much truth and justice as he can say that my *Lord Rochester's* Songs are *nauseous*, or that his other obscene Verses are *a poor Pretence to Wit*; for none of the ancient Statuaries, none of those admir'd Painters whom I have nam'd, were greater Masters in their kind, than my Lord was in his; none of 'em cou'd take the Air of Nature truer; none of 'em knew how to show indecent and ill-favour'd Objects, after a more agreeable and delightful manner, nor have any of 'em grac'd their obscene Representations with a bolder strength, or a fuller Life. But lastly, (to bring this Discourse yet more home to him, and give Instances even in Poetry it self) what opinion has he of *Juvenal, Martial, Petronius Arbiter, Catullus, Tibullus, Ovid,* nay and *Horace* too, whose Sence is often obscene, and sometimes their very Words? which I mention the rather, because he seems to lay a great Weight upon the *Barefac'dness* of my *Lord Rochester's Bawdry*, and the downright obsceneness of his Expression, I say, what Sentence will he pass on these so long lasting, and ever honour'd Names? Are these men *poor Pretenders* to Wit? Or is the *Essayer* a *poor Pretender* to Criticism? Shall we think their poetry, that has pass'd the Test of so many Ages, or his Judgement faulty? especially when we find our Understandings still own the truth of their instructive sence, and all our Passions feel the Charm of their Versification; when we find the kindest propensions of Nature, and all the sensibility of our Souls, waking at the Call of that celestial Musick, our Cares laid asleep, and even our Pains intermitted by the unaccountable Magick of their powerful Descriptions. Shall we now take his word, that such kind of Painting is not Wit, contrary to the opinion of all good Criticks, that have ever been, and refuse to be pleas'd because he's out of humour? Shall we believe him (as the *Papists* do their

Priests) contrary to all the possible Evidence of Reason, and trust him against all the certainty of Sence? Shall we lay aside the Prescriptions of *Aristotle, Longinus,* and *Horace,* contrary to the Experience of near *2000* years, and practise hereafter by his new Dispensatory? Will he set up his own Authority against that of all Antiquity, and oppose his single Fancy, to the unanimous Judgement of Mankind? 'Twill be great, no doubt, and becoming the absoluteness of so famous a Dictator, who is giving Laws to Invention, setting out the Boundaries of Sence, and teaching the World to understand.

I confess, Bawdry alone, that is, obscene Words thrown out at random like Bullies' Oaths, without Design, Order, or Application, is as *poor a Pretence* to Wit, as 'tis to good Manners, or as Pride and Ill-nature without either Genius or Learning, is to the writing of *poetical Essays.* But he cannot be suppos'd to charge any of my *Lord Rochester's* Verses with such Barrenness as this; the notorious Evidence of Fact, and the contrary Testimony of a whole Nation, wou'd fly too full in his Face; No, the chief Crime (as I intimated before) is the *Barefac'd-ness* of their *Bawdry,* which the *Essayer's* great *Bashfulness* is not able to suffer; to put an end therefore to the Dispute, and because I believe nothing has so long shelter'd the lamentable weakness of his ignorant Censure from common Apprehensions but the doubtful and unsettled signification of this Term, *Wit,* I shall bring it to the scrutiny of a Definition, (which is the only sure way to decide the matter) and not-withstanding all that has been hitherto discours'd, if it can bear that Test, I shall be so far from reproaching him with the newness of his Notion, that I will be one of the first to thank him for the discovery. I take Wit then in Poetry, or poetical Wit (for that is the Wit here in Question) to be nothing else but a *true and lively expression of Nature.* By *Nature* I do not only mean all sorts of material Objects, and every species of Substance whatsoever, but also general Notions and abstracted Truths, such as exist only in the Minds of men and in the property and relation of things one to another, in short, whatever has a Being of any kind; the other Terms of the Definition are (I think) so plain, as not to need Explication; *true* this expression of Nature must be, that it may gain our Reason, and *lively* that it may affect our Passions: upon the whole matter, to draw and describe things that either are not in Nature, or things that are otherwise than they are, or to represent 'em heavily (as the *Essayer* does) and colour 'em dully, this is the only false Wit, and the vicious Poetry; on the other side, to make a very like Picture of anything that really exists, is the perfection as well of Poetry as Painting, where by the way the Reader may take notice, that one Definition will serve both, and also include the Art of Sculpture, which has the same general End, and is guided by the same general Rules with the other two. For the rest, if the *Essayer* dislike the Definition, which I have here propos'd, when he makes his particular Exceptions to it, I shall further clear it, and show that there is nothing either in the ancient or modern Wit, but what is comprehended within it; or if he thinks he can give a juster himself, when what he shall offer, appears to be so, I am so perfectly well satisfy'd of the goodness of my Cause, he will find me always ready to joyn issue with him, either upon that or any other. In the mean time let us compare his Criticism with this, and see how out of Countenance and how simply 'twill then look; it runs thus; *Bawdry barefac'd* (says he) *is a poor Pretence to Wit,* that is, *Bawdry barefac'd is a poor Pretence to a true and lively Expression of Nature.*

Risum teneatis, Amici?[1]

No reader can be so dull as not presently to perceive the *barefac'd* Contradiction, and see the transparent folly of this Assertion; there needs now no long Train of Discourse, nor any far-fetch'd Arguments to refute it; 'tis a piece of self-evident Nonsence, (I can give it no other Name without miscalling it) and Blunder at first sight; for why an obscene Action may not be describ'd, or an obscene Imagination express'd, *truly* and *lively*, or why either of 'em is not capable of the Graces of correct Versification, as well as any other thing, is for ever unintelligible.

But because some may be apt to suspect, how little ground soever they have for it, that I have fram'd this Definition on purpose to make the *Essayer's* Notion ridiculous; if he believes his Cause will fare the better for being remov'd into another Court, I am not only willing to gratifie him in this Particular, but shall carry it to be try'd even there where the Judge is his Friend; I shall afresh examine his Criticism by a Definition of Wit, which *Mr. Dryden* has given us, whose Judgement in anything that relates to Poetry, I suppose he will not dispute, and whose Arbitration (if we may measure his Confidence in him by his Obligations to him) he has no manner of Reason to decline. The Definition I mean is in the Preface to his Opera, call'd the *State of Innocence*; the words are these—*Wit* (says *Mr. Dryden*) *is a Propriety of Thoughts and Words—Or Thoughts and Words elegantly adapted to the*

[1] 'Could you hold back your laughter my friends?' (Horace, *Ars Poetica*, I, 5).

Subject.[1] The Judicious Reader will easily observe that this Definition, tho' it differ in sound, is much the same in sence with mine; what Mr. Dryden calls *Propriety*, I have call'd *true Expression*, and that *elegantly adapted* in the explication of his, answers directly to what I intend by *lively* in mine; so that had I remember'd that (which I did not) before I form'd my own, I shou'd not have troubled my self to make another. But let us now joyn the *Essayer's* Criticism, and *Mr. Dryden's* Definition together, and try what a new species of Absurdity this unnatural Mixture will produce; we must then read it thus—*Bawdry barefac'd is a poor Pretence to a Propriety of Thoughts and Words.*—He that can make sence of this Proposition, may go far to solve the grossest Impossibilities in Transubstantiation, and reconcile all the Antipathies in Nature. *Bawdry barefac'd*, whatever defect it has, cannot want Propriety; this is the very fault that uses to be objected to it, by such nice Gentlemen as the *Essayer*, viz. that the Thoughts and Words are too proper and too expressive of what they wou'd have understood, so that according to this Definition, there is nothing in the World that comes nearer the nature of Wit than *Bawdry barefac'd*.

I hope no Body will so quite mistake the design of this Discourse as to think that I have been all this while pleading the cause of *Bawdry*, as a thing in it self (and upon all occasions) allowable and fit; this was never in my thoughts, and far from my meaning, nor is it any part of the Question between the *Essayer* and me; He brands not *Bawdry* for being indecent and immoral, but for being unwitty; so unlucky a hand he has at Criticism, when he trusts to his own Understanding, and being himself but a Stranger upon *Parnassus*, will needs pretend to show others the way; he says indeed that *Bawdry* in Songs and every where else is unfit, but his Reason is, not because it contradicts universally-receiv'd Custom, and wounds common Civility, or because it may offend Age, and corrupt Youth, but because (as he imagines) 'tis a *poor Pretence to Wit* and *palls* instead of *raising Appetite*, that is, in plain *English*, he dislikes it, because it does no hurt; all that I have undertaken therefore, or am oblig'd to defend, is the *Wit* of my *Lord Rochester's* obscene Writings, not the *Manners*; for even Wit it self, as it may be sometimes unseasonable and impertinent, so at other times it may be also libertine, unjust, ungrateful, and every way immoral, yet still 'tis Wit, and we may then say of it as the *Civilians* do of uncanonical Marriages, *Quod Fieri non debet factum valet*,[2] of this nature is my *Lord Rochester's* obscene

[1] Dryden, 'Preface' to *The State of Innocence*, ed. Scott, v, 124.

[2] 'That what ought not to have happened has nevertheless become valid.'

Poetry, which tho' it be much the best that ever was seen of the Kind, and Wit without the least Allay either of Flatnesse or Fustian, must yet be reckon'd among the Extravagancies of his Youth, and the carelesse Gayeties of his Pen, when he was carry'd away with the precipitancy of that *Liber spiritus*, as *Petronius* calls it,[1] the too great fervour of his universal Genius, and the overfruitfulness of an unbounded Fancy. But tho' his obscene Poetry cannot be directly justified, in point of Decency, it may however be a little excus'd, and where it cannot challenge Approbation, it may perhaps deserve Pardon, if we consider not only when 'twas writ, but also to whom 'twas address'd; for as those Painters I mention'd before, tho' they liv'd in Popish Countreys, did not, I suppose, intend their obscene Pieces for the service of the Church, or to be set up at the Market-Cross, but probably for the secret Apartments of some particular Persons, who cou'd look unscandaliz'd on a skilful Imitation of any thing that was natural, with the freedom and the reflexion of Philosophers, so neither did my *Lord Rochester* design those Songs the *Essayer* is so offended with, to be sung for *Anthems* in the *King's-Chappel*, any more than he did his other obscene Writings (however they may have been since abus'd) for the Cabinets of Ladies, or the Closets of Divines, or for any publick or common Entertainment whatever, but for the private Diversion of those happy Few, whom he us'd to charm with his Company and honour with his Friendship.

As to the *Essayer's* calling my Lord's Songs *nauseous*, besides what has been already answer'd, he cannot but know that my Lord writ a great number, without the least obscenenesse in 'em, which are not only far better than any he is capable of making, (for to say no more of 'em were to praise 'em poorly) but so correct, and yet so natural, so easily wrought and so justly finish'd, with that elegant Aptnesse in the Words, and that unordinary Beauty in the Thoughts, as no other man ever did or can exceed.

His last Exception to my Lord's Poetry, is that the grosse Obscenenesse of it *palls* instead of *raising Appetite*, where he finds fault with that only thing, that (were his Exception just) wou'd excuse it to much the major part of Mankind; for that which chiefly makes Bawdry in so ill Repute, is because it has been always believ'd an Incentive to such Desires, as Divines tell us, shou'd rather be curb'd than encourag'd, and apt to bring Thoughts into peoples Heads, which ought not, and perhaps otherwise never wou'd come there; now, if barefac'd Bawdry has this particular property, that it does not hint these forbidden Thoughts,

[1] 'Free Spirit', Petronius, *Satyricon*, 118.

nor stir those unlawful Desires, but on the contrary flattens and stifles 'em, 'tis much more innocent, and consequently fitter to be us'd, or at least to be pardon'd, than any other. But he's beside the Cushion again, and as wide here of the Mark he aims at, as he was before; there are indeed scarce more Lines than Mistakes in this half Paragraph, that concerns my *Lord Rochester*; he cannot see (it seems) at all but by other men's Eyes, for he stumbles at every Step, when he ventures to walk without his Guides. However, let us take a view of this his legitimate Sence in his own Dresse; the lines are these:

> But obscene Words, too grosse to move Desire,
> Like heaps of Fuel do but choak the Fire,
> The Author's Name has undeserved Praise,
> Who pall'd the Appetite he meant to raise.[1]

In the first place, What does that *ed* in *undeserved* do there? I know no businesse it has, unlesse it be to crutch a lame Verse, and each out a scanty Sence, for the Word that is now us'd is *undeserv'd*. I shou'd not take notice of so trivial a thing as this, but that I have to do with a Giver of Rules, and a magisterial Correcter of other men, tho' upon observing of such little Niceties, does all the Musick of Numbers depend; but the Refinement of our Versification is a sort of Criticism, which the *Essayer* (if we may judge of his Knowledge by his Practice) seems yet to learn, for never was there such a Pack of stiff ill-sounding Rhimes put together as his *Essay* is stuff'd with; to add therefore to his other Collections, let him remember hereafter, that Verses have Feet given 'em, either to walk, graceful and smooth, and sometimes with Majesty and State, like *Virgil's*, or to run, light and easie, like *Ovid's*, not to stand stock-still, like *Dr. Donne's*, or to hobble like indigested Prose; that the counting of the Syllables is the least part of the Poet's Work, in the turning either of a soft or a sonorous Line; that the *eds* went away with the *for-to's* and the *untils*, in that general Rout, that fell on the whole Body of the *thereons*, the *thereins*, and the *therebys*, when those useful *Expletives*, the *althos* and the *untos*, and those most convenient *Synalaephas, 'midst, 'mongst, 'gainst,* and *'twixt*, were every one cut off; which dismal slaughter was follow'd with the utter extirpation of the ancient House of the *hereofs* and the *therefroms*, &c. Nor is this Reformation the arbitrary Fancy of a few, who wou'd impose their own private Opinions and Practice upon the rest of their Countreymen, but grounded on the Authority of *Horace*, who tells us in his Epistle *de Arte Poetica*, That

[1] *Essay upon Poetry*, ll. 86–9.

present Use is the final Judge of Language.[1] (the Verse is too well known to need quoting) and on the common Reason of Mankind, which forbids us those antiquated Words and obsolete Idioms of Speech, whose Worth time has worn out, how well soever they may seem to stop a Gap in Verse, and suit our shapelesse immature Conceptions; for what is grown pedantick and unbecoming when 'tis spoke, will not have a jot the better grace for being writ down.

In the next place, To what purpose does he keep such a pudder here about *moving Desire* and *raising Appetite*? Does he think that all kind of obscene Poetry is design'd to *raise Appetite*? Does he not know that obscene Satyre (of which nature are most of my *Lord Rochester's* obscene Writings, and particularly several of his Songs) has a quite different end, and is so far from being intended to raise, that the whole force of it is generally turn'd to restrain *Appetite*, and keep it within due Bounds, to reprove the unjust Designs, and check the Excesses of that lawlesse Tyrant? If therefore some of my *Lord Rochester's* Songs shou'd misse a Mark, which they neither did, nor ought to aim at, I believe no body but the *Essayer* will think it a Fault. But to strike at the root of his Objection, what does he mean by saying, That obscene Words are *too grosse to move Desire*? he might say with as much sence that pious Words are too good to move Devotion; 'tis impossible that any Words shou'd come too near the nature of the things they are to represent, when the design is to touch our Passions by that representation, for if there be an attraction of any sort in the nature of the things, the more truly they are describ'd to us, the more is that attractive virtue drawn forth, and made to exert it self; so that what he calls *grossenesse*, is here the chief power, the main weight and stamp of the Poet's Expression, by which a just and full Notion of what he wou'd have us apprehend, is more clearly and more forcibly impress'd upon the Imagination; Propriety being (as I have already show'd) the very Essence of Wit, and the only possible way to win the Understanding and engage the Affections of a rational Creature. 'Tis true (as I hinted once before) obscene Words us'd unnecessarily, and with as little pertinence, as some of our modern *Enthusiasts* use godly Phrases and Scripture Expressions, when six of 'em sometimes shall signifie but one thing, (if by great chance they signifie any thing) will provoke indeed the wrong way, and nauseate instead of affecting; but if a man of Wit has the ranging and applying of the one, and a man of Learning and Judgement the other, both will operate according to their natural tendency, that is, these will incline to Virtue and those to Vice;

[1] *Ars Poetica*, 71–2.

the short and true state of the Case is this; all depends upon the Genius and Art of the Writer, for as an obscene Thought, if it be not livelily painted, will have but a small or perhaps no effect upon the Mind of the Reader, according to the proportion of flatness in the Expression, so a chast or a pious Meditation, if it has the same disadvantage, will work as little. Thus (to come to his own Allusion) Heaps of Fuel, when they are carelesly thrown on, and after a disorderly manner cramm'd together, do no doubt choak and dead a Fire, but if they are regularly laid, and artificially pil'd up, they will as much enliven and increase it, a Demonstration of which he may see every *Twenty ninth of May* in a Bonefire; 'tis not then the Heaps or Quantity of Fuel, but the unskilful placing, that puts out the Fire. We may therefore with a very little trouble turn the small Shot of his *Simile* upon him, for adding but a word or two it will speak a direct contrary sence, as thus,

> But obscene Words, if right apply'd, raise and inflame Desire,
> As Heaps of Fuel, plac'd with skill, make and maintain the Fire.

For a further Proof of this, when his squeamish Fit is over, I wou'd recommend to his Perusal, *Aloisia Sigea*,[1] or if that be too hard for him because 'tis writ in Latin, let him read *L'Escole des Filles*,[2] and if the obscene Words and Descriptions he will meet with there, do not raise his Appetite, the World will be apt to conclude it, not only very dull, but absolutely dead and as bad as his Poetry is, his Reader will be better entertain'd than his Mistress.

If I were now of a humour to please my self with finding other men's Faults, it were no hard matter to make the *Essayer* give my *Lord Rochester* his Revenge. I shou'd then ask him from what Ballad he took that Heroical height of Expression, and that noble Turn of a Verse, which we find in the first page of his *Essay*,

> —None there are
> That can the least with Poetry compare[3]

How long *Cadance* and *Foibles* have been *English* words? Or whether despairing to get any Credit by his Wit, he speaks *French*, like the *Kings of Brentford, to show his Breeding*? Why he who in Page the *4th* thinks it so easie to rob the Ancients, will stoop so low, as in most of the following, to borrow from the Moderns? Why he suffers a *Muse*, who

[1] A pornographic work, probably by Nicolas Chorier (1609–92).
[2] A French pornographic work published in 1655.
[3] *Essay upon Poetry*, II. 3–4.

has so sowr a Countenance and so ungraceful a Fashion as his, to play the Wag, and be such a merry Grig, as she sometimes aims to appear? Or in plain terms, what is the meaning of all that forc'd insipid Raillery, that fills his *18th* Page, for 'tis not more dull than 'tis unintelligible? I shou'd also desire to be inform'd, by what new *Grammar* he construes the six last Lines of his *7th* Page? And when we may hope to know from him, what the Consequence will be, if in an *Elegy*

> A just Coherence be not made
> Between each Thought, &c.,[1]

For he has left it at present, as *Mr. Bayes* did his Plot, for the Reader to find out of himself, if he will; and some have been guessing that 'tis much the same as when in an *Essay* the like *Coherence* is not observ'd. Lastly, how comes his *Eagle* in Page the *11th*, which we expected by the pompous preparation wou'd presently have mounted out of sight, to fly so like a *Buzzard* and flounce like a *Fish*? But 'tis no great Wonder, I confesse, that an *Eagle*, who seems afraid to get upon her Wings, and warily *considers the Perils of her Case* in so doing, which by the way is a Phrase fitter for an *Affidavit* than a *Poem*, and as natural an Image, as if he had describ'd a Man afraid to walk; but, I say, 'tis not at all strange, that such a cautious *Eagle*, who is so distrustful of her Wings, shou'd keep so near the Ground in her *Flight*.

'Tis as easie as 'twou'd perhaps be pleasant, to enlarge this *poetical Catechism*, for there is yet good store of Materials left; but this little may suffice at present to give the World a Taste of the *Essayer's* Abilities, and how fit he is to correct my *Lord Rochester*, or to teach us; for I find this *Preface* is already run out beyond the ordinary Length of such Discourses, nor was it at all intended (this being not worth the trouble) to blast a Wit, which will die of it self in a little time, but to do Right to that which is likely to live as long as our *Language*, and defend a Man, whose Person I was ever naturally inclin'd to love, and whose Friendship I shall upon all occasions be proud to own; a Man, whose Wit wou'd never have wanted the assistance of mine, nor a much better, either to recommend or justifie it, were not that Part of his Writings the *Essayer* has censur'd, of such an unhappy Kind, as few will examine; otherwise, as to what concerns the Poetry of 'em, they are their own best Encomium and Defence, no Body being able to say so much for 'em as they do for themselves. To conclude, Whatever Faults my *Lord Rochester* might have, I am confident the *Essayer* is the only Person in

[1] *Essay upon Poetry*, II. 106–7.

the Kingdom who wou'd have gone about to look for 'em in his *Wit*; the Applause of that was so universal, and the manner so agreeable, none ever dislik'd it, but those who fear'd it, none ever decry'd it, but those who envied it.

b) Anne Wharton, 'To Mr Wolseley on his Preface to Valentinian, by a Lady of Quality':

To you, the generous task belongs alone
To clear the injur'd and instruct the Town:
Where, but in you is found a mind so brave
To stretch the bounds of Love beyond the grave?
Anger may last, but friendships quickly dy,
For anxious thoughts are longer-liv'd than joy.
Yet those, whom active fancies have misled
So far as to assault the mighty dead;
Now, taught by your reproofes a noble shame,
Will strive by surer ways to raise their fame.
But from our sex what praise do you deserve?
We by your help may all our rights preserve,
While others rob the Deities they serve,
For never sacriledge cou'd greater be
Than to steal Honour from a Deitie.
Such are the paths to fame, in which you tread,
You bafle envy, while you nobly aide
The helpless living and more helpless dead.

(*Lycidus: or the Lover in Fashion* [by Aphra Behn] *together with a Miscellany of New Poems*, 1688, pp. 95–6)

23. William Winstanley on Rochester

1686

The Lives of the Most Famous English Poets (1686).

William Winstanley (*c.* 1628–*c.* 1690), was a Grub Street writer who dealt in a variety of literary kinds from biography to doggerel verse.

This Earl for Poetical Wit, was accounted the chief of his time; his Numbers flowing with so smooth and accute a Strain, that had they been all confined within the bounds of Modesty, we might well affirm they were unparallel'd; yet was not his Muse altogether so loose but that with his Mirth he mixed Seriousness, and had a knack at once to tickle the Fancy, and inform the Judgment.[1]

[1] As an example Winstanley quotes the poem 'In Defence of Satyr' (Pinto, lxxiii) which is in fact by Sir Carr Scroope.

24. Matthew Prior, two References to Rochester

1687

Poems on Several Occasions (1707).

Matthew Prior (1664–1721), diplomat and wit, to some extent continued the tradition of wit of the Restoration poets into the eighteenth century. In his earlier poems, like those represented here, he not surprisingly shows sympathy for the gentlemen wits and a corresponding lack of sympathy for professional writers like Dryden. Prior was a protégé of Rochester's friend, the sixth Earl of Dorset. In the extract from the *Satyr on the Poets* Prior is giving examples of the difficulty of earning a living out of poetry.

---

a) From *Satyr on the Poets* (ll. 145–54):

Sidley indeed and *Rochester* might Write,
For their own Credit, and their Friends' Delight,
Shewing how far they cou'd the rest out-do,
As in their Fortunes, so their Writings too;
But shou'd Drudge *Dryden* this Example take,
And *Absoloms* for empty Glory make,
He'd soon perceive his Income scarce enough,
To feed his Nostrils with Inspiring Snuff,
Starving for Meat, nor surfeiting on Praise,
He'd find his Brain as barren as his Bays.

b) From *Epistle to Lord* [*Dorset*] (ll. 7–15):

That You write so that since great Strephon's[1] death
No daring brow claims ev'n the second wreath:
Yet these Perfections, were my thoughts declar'd,
Nor ask that praise, nor merit that reward,
As that one good, which ev'n Your Foes confess
(If any such there can be) You possess:
A real Judgment, and a Solid Mind
Expert to use these blessings in their kind,
As Prudence dictates, and as God design'd.

[1] Rochester.

25. Tom Durfey: 'A Lash at Atheists'

1690

New Poems (1690), pp. 54–8.

Tom Durfey (1653–1723), was one of the most popular and successful of the Grub Street writers of his day and in Charles II's reign a hanger-on of the Court Wits. The following poem is a typical example of the way Rochester came to assume legendary status.

'A Lash at Atheists: The Poet speaking, as the Ghost of a Quondam Libertine, suppos'd to be the late E[arl] of R[ochester] reflects on that part of Seneca's Troas beginning at *Post Mortem nihil est* . . .'[1]

Incumbred with vile Flesh, to Earth inclin'd,
Prophane *Tragedian*, once I wore thy Mind,
Born on the Wings of Soaring Wit so high,
I thought my Soul no farther pitch could fly
Than the gay Regions of Philosophy.
The hot-brain'd Stag' rite[2] in my Breast did reign,
And Sacred Prophets preach'd the Truth in vain,
Nourish'd by Logick Arts so well I knew
To vent false Reason and disguise the true:
Around my Beams the Athiests of the Times,
Like Attoms, danc'd and wanton'd in my Crimes,

[1] Durfey quotes five lines from Act II of Seneca's tragedy the Troades, which Rochester had himself translated as follows:

After Death Nothing is, and nothing Death;
The utmost Limits of a gasp of Breath.
Let the ambitious Zealot lay aside
His hopes of Heav'n; (whose Faith is but his Pride)
Let Slavish Souls lay by their Fear,
Nor be concern'd which way or where
After this life they shall be hurl'd.

[2] Aristotle.

Strong Vice Opinion of my Wisdom bred,
Which round the World, those false Apostles led,
Whilst scandal hourly I on Vertue threw,
Nor would be witty, unless wicked too;
All thy pernicious Tenets then I own'd,
And Wit prophane with circling Bays I crown'd,
Proud of short-sighted Reason, my design
Was still to blast the Mysteries Divine;
Defame Religion with unhallow'd wit,
And ridicule the Laws of Sacred Writ:
But Oh, you foolish, fond, and apish Crew,
Ye learned Idiots that my Tracts pursue,
Ye crawling Worms that bask in the Sun's Ray,
And yet the Sun's great Maker disobey.
Pernicious Snakes that by Celestial Fire,
Reliev'd from frozen Ignorance, conspire
Against your God, and think frail Eyes can see
Through the Arcana of the Trinity,
Reflect how false your Notions are, by me.
And thou, poor Heathen, that hadst wit to write,
Yet not the Truth, hadst Eyes, and yet no sight,
That wert in th' dawn of our Redemption driven
Through moral Mists to grope the way to Heaven,
Thou that with one poor glimpse of Reason blest,
Given only as distinction from the Beast;
Prophanely dar'st affirm there nothing is
Beyond the Grave, of Misery or Bliss:
But that the Soul and Body, like a Tree,
Rest undisturb'd in Earth's Obscurity.
With me art now severely undeceiv'd
In those dam'd Tenets which we once believ'd,
Yet not believ'd, for in each vile Harrangue
The Atheist speaks he feels a secret Pang:
Poor tortur'd Conscience peeps through his disguise,
And tells the noisie hot-brain'd Fool he lyes;
Thus Man more Sordid than a Brute must be,
That plagu'd with the Salt Itch of Sophistry,
Forfeits his Soul, prophanes all Sacred Laws,
For the vain blast of Popular Applause.
Had Reverend *Hobbs* this Revelation mark'd

Before his dubious leap into the dark;
Had he found Faith, before false Sence approv'd,
Moses, instead of *Aristotle* lov'd,
Eternal Vengeance had not found him then,
Nor gorg'd him with his own *Leviathan*;
Like him, or worse, once madly did I Rave
Till I had got one Foot into the Grave:
But there, as if Eternal Power had pleas'd
To shew in me that Wonders were not ceas'd;
My Guardian Angel snatch'd my Soul from Night
To the clear Paths of Everlasting Light:
Then banish'd Wisdom reassum'd my Brain,
Religious Reason took her Seat agen;
I sigh'd, and trembled at the horrid view
Of my past Crimes, and scarcely could renew
Forgotten Prayer, so little good I knew,
Till heavenly Mercy down like *Manna* fell,
And true Repentance lifted me from Hell:
Thus Sickness which my Mourning Friends condole
When Art could not restore my Body whole,
Prov'd the Divine Physitian of my Soul.
How deeply then my long lost Reason pris'd
The Balmy Scriptures I so late despis'd!
How poorly Tinsel rob'd Philosophy
Appear'd when Rich Divinity was by!
And how th' Evangelists and Prophets shone
'Mongst Heathen Poets, that my Heart had won.
Gone was my doubt, the Resurrection plain,
And if there be a Fool, so vile, so vain,
That in his Head that Scruple does retain:
Let him but think what first Created Man,
Then let him be an Atheist if he can.

26. Thomas Rymer on Rochester

1691

'Preface to the Reader',

Poems etc. on Several Occasions: with Valentinian, a Tragedy. Written by the Right Honourable John Late Earl of Rochester.

Thomas Rymer (*c.* 1643–1713), one of the most distinguished critics of the period, contributed this Preface anonymously to the edition of Rochester's poems published by Jacob Tonson in 1691. It is important as the first attempt at a dispassionate appraisal of Rochester's poetry, and its high praise of the poet may be taken as an indication of the critical esteem that Rochester's verse then enjoyed. The Preface was first ascribed to Rymer in a reprint of this edition in 1714.

AMONGST THE ANCIENTS, *Horace* deservedly bears the Name from 'em all, for Occasional *Poems.* Many of which were addressed to *Pollio, Mecœnas,* and *Augustus,* the greatest Men, and the best Judges, and all his Poetry over-look'd by them. This made him of the Temper not to part with a Piece over hastily; but to bring his Matter to a Review, to cool a little, and think twice before it went out of his Hands.

On the contrary, My Lord *Rochester* was loose from all Discipline of that kind. He found no Body of Quality or Severity so much above himself, to Challenge a Deference, or to Check the ordinary Licenses of Youth, and impose on him the Obligation to copy over again, what on any Occasion had not been so exquisitely design'd.

Nor did he live long enough for Maturity and cool Reflections. He was born (as, in his Life, Dr. *Burnet* tells us) in 1648. and died 1680. At which Age of 32 Years, *Horace* had done no wonders, nor had attain'd to that *Curiosa Fœlicitas,*[1] which so fairly distinguish'd him afterwards.

[1] Careful felicity.

Neither had *Virgil* himself, at that Age, ventur'd out of the Woods, or attempted any thing beyond the *Roundelays* and Conversation of *Dàmon* and *Amaryllis*.

Nor indeed, when my Lord came to appear in the World, was *Poetry*, at Court, under any good Aspect, unless it was notably flourish'd with Ribaldry and Debauch: which could not but prove of fatal Consequence to a Wit of his Gentleness and Complaisance.

Far be it from me to insinuate any thing like a Comparison with the Ancients. Only we may observe that no Style or Turn of Thought came in his way that he was not ready to improve. Something of *Ovid* he render'd into *English*, which is almost a Verbal Translation that matches the Original. He has Paraphras'd something of *Lucretius* and *Seneca;* and in his Verses on the *Cup*, he gives us *Anacreon* with the same Air and Gaiety: what is added falls in so proper and so easie, one might question whether My Lord *Rochester* imitates *Anacreon*, or *Anacreon* humours My Lord *Rochester*.

The *Satyr upon Man* is commonly taken to be a Translation from *Boileau*. The *French* have ordinarily compar'd their *Ronsards* and their *Malherbes* with *Virgil* and *Horace*; *Boileau* understands better. He has gone farthest to purge out that Chaff and Trifling so familiar in the *French Poetry*, and to settle a Traffick of good Sence amongst them. It may not be amiss to see some Lines of *Boileau* and of My Lord *Rochester* together, on the same Subject.

A Monsieur M—

Docteur de *Sorb.*

De tous les Animaux qui s'elevent dans l'Air,
Qui marchent sur la Terre, ou nagent dans la Mer,
De Paris, au Perou, du Japon jusqu'à Rome,
Le plus sot animal, à mon avis, c'est l'homme.
Quoi, dira-t-on d'abord, un ver, une fourmi,
Un insecte rampant qui ne vit qu'à demi,
Un taureau qui rumine, une cheure qui broute,
Ont l'Esprit mieux tournè que n'a l'homme? oûi sans doute.
Ce discours te surprend, Docteur, je l'apperçoi:
L'Homme de la Nature est le Chef & le Roy:
Bois, Prez, Champs, Animaux, tout est pour son usage;
Et lui seul a, dis-tu, la raison en partage.
Il est vrai, de tout temps la raison fut son lot,
Mais delà je conclus que l'homme est le plus Sot.

In English,

By Mr. Oldham.

Of all the Creatures in the world that be,
Beast, Fish, or Fowl, that go, or swim, or fly,
Throughout the Globe from London, to Japan,
The arrant'st Fool in my Opinion's Man.
What (strait I'm taken up) an Ant, a Fly,
A tiny Mite which we can hardly see
Without a Perspective, a silly Ass,
Or freakish Ape? dare you affirm that these
Have greater Sence than Man? Ay, questionless.
Doctor, I find you're shock'd at this discourse;
Man is, you cry, Lord of the Universe;
For him was this fair Frame of Nature made,
And all the Creatures for his Use and Aid;
To him alone of all the Living kind,
Has bounteous Heav'n the reas'ning Gift assign'd.
True, Sir, that Reason always was his Lot;
But thence I argue Man the greater Sot.

By my Lord *Rochester*, thus,

Were I (who, to my Cost, already am,
One of those strange, prodigious Creatures, Man)
A spirit, free to chuse for my own share,
What sort of Flesh and Blood I pleas'd to wear,
I'd be a Dog, a Monkey, or a Bear,
Or any thing, but that vain Animal,
Who is so proud of being Rational.

It might vex a patient Reader, shou'd I go about very minutely to shew the Difference here betwixt these two Authors; 'tis sufficient to set them together. My Lord *Rochester* gives us another Cast of Thought, another Turn of Expression, a strength, a Spirit, and Manly Vigour, which the *French* are utter strangers to. Whatever Giant *Boileau* may be in his own Country, He seems little more than a Man of Straw with my Lord *Rochester*.[1]

What the former had expounded in a long-winded Circumference of Fourteen Lines, is here most happily express'd within half the Compass. What work might that single Couplet [*A Spirit free*, &c.] make

[1] For praise of this passage see Ezra Pound, *ABC of Reading* (1934) p. 133.

for one that loves to dilate? some able Commentator wou'd hammer out of it all *Plato*, *St. Origen*, and *Virgil* too, in to the Bargain.

Whatsoever he imitated or Translated, was Loss to him. He had a Treasure of his own; a Mine not to be exhausted. His own Oar and Thoughts were rich and fine: his own Stamp and Expression more neat and beautiful than any he cou'd borrow or fetch from abroad.

No Imitation cou'd bound or prescribe whither his Flights should carry him: were the Subject light, you find him a Philosopher, grave and profound, to wonder: Were the Subject lumpish and heavy, then wou'd his Mercury dissolve all into Gaity and Diversion. You wou'd take his *Monkey* for a Man of *Metaphysicks*: and his *Gondibert* he sends with all that Grimace to *demolish Windows*, or do some, the like *Important Mischief*.[1]

But, after all, what must be done for the Fair Sex? They confess[2] a delicious Garden, but are told that *Venus* has her share in the Ornamental part and Imagery. They are afraid of some *Cupid*, that levels at the next tender Dame that stands fair in the way; and must not expect a *Diana* or *Hippolytus* on every Pedestal.

For this matter the *Publisher* assures us, he has been diligent out of Measure, and has taken exceeding Care that every Block of Offence shou'd be removed.

So that this Book is a Collection of such Pieces only, as may be received in a vertuous Court, and not unbecome the Cabinet of the Severest Matron.

[1] *Monkey/Gondibert*: the point that Rymer is making is that Rochester sometimes uses the trivial to make profound comments on life and to make them in an amusing manner as he does in Artemisia's comment on the fine lady playing with her monkey (*Artemisia to Cloe*, II. 137f.) while at other times he uses a pompous style for trivial ends as he does in the use of the heroic 'Gondibert' Stanza in his poem 'The Maim'd Debauchee'.

[2] i.e. disclose.

27. Anthony à Wood on Rochester

1692

The entry on Rochester from Wood's *Athenae Oxonienses* is an important source of information. Wood's life (1632–95), was spent in and around Oxford.

---

a) From *Athenae Oxonienses*:

John Wilmot Earl of *Rochester*, Viscount *Athlone* in *Ireland*, and Baron of *Adderbury* in *Oxfordshire*, was born at *Dichley* near *Wodstock* in the said County, . . . April 1648,[1] educated in Grammar learning in the Free-school at *Burford*, under a noted Master called *John Martin*, became a Nobleman of *Wadham* College under the tuition of *Phineas Bury* Fellow, and inspection of Mr. *Blandford* the Warden, *an.* 1659, actually created Master of Arts in Convocation, with several other noble persons, *an.* 1661; at which time, he, and none else, was admitted very affectionately into the fraternity by a kiss on the left cheek from the Chancellour of the University (*Clarendon*) who then sate in the supreme chair to honour that Assembly. Afterwards he travelled into *France* and *Italy*, and at his return frequented the Court (which not only debauched him but made him a perfect *Hobbist*) and was at length made one of the Gentlemen of the Bedchamber to his Majesty King Charles II and Controller of *Wodstock* Park, in the place of Sir William *Fleetwood* deceased. He was a person of most rare parts, and his natural talent was excellent, much improved by learning and industry, being thoroughly acquainted with all classick Authors, both Greek and Latine; a thing very rare (if not peculiar to him) among those of his quality.[2] He knew also how to use them, not as other Poets have done, to transcribe and

[1] This is an error, he was born in April 1647.

[2] Thomas Hearne, however, who knew Rochester's earliest tutor Giffard, has a different opinion of Rochester's learning 'Mr. Giffard says that my Lord understood very little or no Greek, and that he had but little Latin, and that therefore 'tis a great mistake in making him (as Burnett and Wood have done) so great a Master of Classick Learning', *Remarks and Collections*, ed. C. E. Doble (1889), iii. 263. See also Burnet's *Life*, No. 10.

steal from, but rather to better and improve, them by his fancy.[1] But the eager tendency and violent impulses of his natural temper, unhappily inclining him to the excesses of Pleasure and Mirth; which, with the pleasantness of his unimitable humour, did so far engage the affections of the Dissolute towards him, that to make him delightfully ventrous and frolicksome to the utmost degrees of riotous extravagancy, they for some years heightened his spirits (enflamed by wine) into one almost uninterrupted fit of wantonness and intemperance. Some time before his death, were several copies of his verses printed (beside what went in MS. from hand to hand) among which were,

A Satyr against Mankind—Printed in one sheet in fol. in *June* 1679. Answer'd in another sheet in the next month by one Mr. *Griffith* a Minister.[2] *Andr. Marvell*, who was a good Judge of wit, did use to say that *Rochester was the only man in England that had the true vein of Satyr*.[3]

On Nothing; a Poem.—Printed on one side of a sheet of paper in 2 columes. But notwithstanding the strict charge which the Earl of Rochester gave on his death-bed to those persons, in whose custody his papers were, *to burn all his prophane and rude Writings*,[4] as being only fit to promote Vice and Immorality, by which he had so highly offended the Omnipotent, and sham'd and blasphem'd that holy Religion into which he had been baptized; yet no sooner was his breath out of his body, but some person, or persons, who had made a collection of most of his Poetry in Manuscript, did, meerly for lucre sake, (as 'twas conceived) publish them under this title.

Poems on several occasions.[5] *Antwerp* (alias *London*) 1680. oct. Among which, as those before-mention'd are numbred, so many of his composure are omitted, and there is no doubt but that other men's Poems are mixed among them. They are full of obscenity and prophaneness, and are more fit (tho' excellent in their kind) to be read by Bedlamites, than pretenders to vertue and modesty: and what are not so, are libellous and satyrical. Among them is a Poem entit. *A Ramble into St. James's Park*, p. 14, which I guess is the same with that which is meant and challenged in the preface to the Poems of *Alexander Radcliff* of *Greys* inn entit. *The Ramble, an anti-heroick Poem, together with some terrestial Hymns, and carnal Ejaculations* Lond. 1682 oct. as the true composure of

1 Wood gets this passage from Parson's funeral sermon on Rochester, see No. 9.

2 In several of the collections of the time this answer is said to be by 'Dr. Pockock'.

3 Wood obviously got this from John Aubrey (see No. 29), who supplied him with much unacknowledged information.

4 Reported in Parsons' *Sermon*, pp. 28–9.

5 An edition of this has been reprinted in facsimile by James Thorpe, Princeton, 1950.

the said *Radcliff*, but being falsly and imperfectly published under the Earl's name, is said there to be enlarged two thirds, above what it was, when before in print.[1] The Reader is to know also that a most wretched and obscene and scandalously infamous Play, not wholly compleated, passed some hands privately in MS, under the name of *Sodom*, and fathered upon the Earl (as most of this kind were, right or wrong, which came out at any time, after he had once obtained the name of an excellent smooth, but withall a most lewd Poet) as the true author of it; but if that copy of verses inserted among his printed Poems before-mention'd, in pag. 129. wrote upon the author of the play call'd *Sodom* be really his, then questionless the writing of this vile piece is not to be laid to his charge; unless we should suppose him to have turned the keeness and sharpness of his piercing satyr (for such is this) upon himself.[2] He hath also written,

A Letter to Dr. Gilb. Burnet, written on his Death-bed. Lond. 1680 in one sh. in fol.[3] And that he was the author of it, the Doctor himself acknowledgeth in the *History of Some Passages of the Life and Death of John Earl of Rochester.* About the same time also was published a sheet in fol. entit. *The two noble Converts; or the Earl of Marlborough and the Earl of Rochester, their dying Requests to the Atheists and Debauchees of this Age:* but this was feigned and meerly written by a scribler to get a little money. In *Nov.* 1684 was a play of John Fletcher's published entit. *Valentinian: a Tragedy as 'tis altered by the late Earl of Rochester, and acted at the Theater-Royal.* Lond. 1685. qu. To which is put, by a nameless writer,[4] a large Preface concerning the Author and his Writings, wherein among too many things, and high-flown surfeiting *Encomiums*, that are by him given of the said Count, is this, . . . 'For 'tis sure there has not lived in many ages (if ever) so extraordinary, and I think I may add, so useful a person, as most English men know my Lord to have been . . .'[5] etc.—To pass by other characters, which the said *Anonymus* too fondly mentions of the Count, I shall proceed and tell you that he hath also written,

Poems etc. on several Occasions: with Valentinian a Tragedy Lond. 1691 Oct. They were published in the latter end of Feb. 1690, but the large

[1] Wood has confused two quite separate poems *The Ramble in St James's Park* which is by Rochester, and Alexander Radcliff's *The Ramble.*

[2] Rochester probably wrote neither the poem nor the play.

[3] Published in the first edition of Burnet's *Life of Rochester*, 1680.

[4] Robert Wolseley, see No. 22a.

[5] Wood quotes a paragraph from Wolseley's preface down to the sentence beginning 'Never was his pen drawn but on the side of good sense . . .' see p. 140 above.

Preface before-mention'd is there omitted. These poems, which are different from those that came out in 1680, have before them an admirable Pastoral on the death of the Earl of Rochester, in imitation of the Greek of *Moschus*, made by Oldham . . . .[1] At length, after a short, but pleasant, life, this noble and beautiful Count paid his last debt to nature in the *Ranger's Lodge* in *Wodstock-Park*, very early in the morning of the 26th of *July* in sixteen hundred and eighty.

(*Athenae Oxonienses* (1691–2), ii. 488–490)

b) From *the Life and Times*;

In this vault also lies buried John earl of Rochester . . . This John made a great noise in the world for his noted and professed atheisme, his lampoons and other frivolous stuffe; and a great noise after his death for his penitent departure.

(*The Life and Times of Anthony Wood . . . described by Himself*, ed. Andrew Clark, 5 vols. (Oxford 1892), ii. 492)

[1] Wood here lists a number of miscellanies where Rochester's poems are to be found. For Oldham's pastoral see No. 12.

28. Tom Brown on Rochester's Satire

c. 1692

'A Short Essay on English Satire' *Works* (1707), i. 34–8.

Tom Brown (1663–1704), 'the prince of Grub Street', consistently defended the witty attitudes of Charles II's reign against the soberer attitudes of the 1690s. The part of the Essay printed here is preceded by a short discussion of classical satire. The essay is dated 1692 by Boyce, *Tom Brown of Facetious Memory* (1939), p. 57 n. 2.

Poetry has had its *Crisis* in these Nations, as well as in other Countries. It was during the reign of king *Charles II* that Learning in general flourish'd, and the Muses, like other fair Ladies, met with the civillest sort of Entertainment. The Immoralities the *English* learn'd from the court of *France*, during the unhappy Exile of that Prince, and the luxurious Idleness which succeeded the long fatigues of our Civil Wars, frequently gave Birth to Lampoons and Satires; but as the first of these were perfectly Malicious, and the last pointed too much at great Men, lashing the Persons more than the Vices; they escaped the Censure of Posterity, and are interr'd in the Tombs of Forgetfulness. Those *Embrio's* of Satire were succeeded by three great Wits, all Contemporaries, with little difference in their Age, and great Similitude in their Writings. Satire was the principal Talent of them all: In which way of Writing, my Lord *Rochester* and my Lord *Dorset* exceeded all the Modern Poets, and perchance were not inferior to the best of the Antients. *Oldham* indeed has not imitated *Juvenal* so well as my lord *Rochester* has Paraphrased upon *Boileau*: But then, as there is no comparison betwixt *Boileau* and *Juvenal*; so there's no conclusion to be made from my lord *Rochester*'s exceeding his Original, and Mr. *Oldham*'s not coming up to the Genius, Beauty and Fire, of his *Roman* example.

These three are the greatest *Satirists* of the *English*, and have their several Beauties distinct and a-part from each other. My Lords *Rochester* and *Dorset* had all the advantages of a generous Education; the greatness of their Genius was improv'd by the Acquisitions of Art; and their Natural Parts were Cultivated by the Care of the ablest Masters. *Oldham* ow'd every thing to himself, nothing to his Birth, but little to the Precepts of *Pedants*, and seems, as it were, Predestinated to the Service of the Muses, and the ridiculing that Class of Men, who, of all Persons, least deserve to draw the Appellation of their Order from the Sacred Name of *Jesus*.[1] His Conceptions were Noble, infinitely Bold, full of Fire and Vivacity; he seldom was Flat, and generally spoke to the purpose; he always was an Enemy to Vice, and encouraged the Good and Virtuous. Yet, on the other Hand, it must be confess'd, that the same Author was always in a Passion; that he was inclinable to Rail at every thing; that both his Thoughts were too Furious, and his Stile too bold to be Correct, or to partake of those Beauties which even his great Master *Juvenal* did not think unworthy his Care. His Curses were Cruel, and sometimes stretch'd to that degree that his Verses could be term'd no longer *Satire*, but rather the hot Expressions of some witty Madman. *Satire* is design'd to expose Vice and encourage Virtue; he Obeyed but half of that solid Maxim. 'Tis true, he Expos'd and Rail'd at Vice; but then his pursuing both the Theme and Persons too far, obliged the Criminal he expos'd to believe that the sharpness of his Satire proceeded rather from some Personal disgust, than any aversion to Vice and Immorality in general. Instead of Correcting the Manners of the Age, he fermented the Passions of the Vicious, and render'd their Minds only capable of such Sentiments as Revenge and Fury suggested. *Juvenal* himself taught Mr. *Oldham* the way; and was in some measure guilty of the fault which is Universally objected against his Scholar; but then it must be urg'd on the *Roman's* behalf, that he liv'd and writ in the time of *Domitian*, the most scandalous Emperor and most infamous of Men. There's no occasion to mention his cruel Treatment of the *Christians*. *Juvenal* was a *Pagan* author, and neglected the ill usage of the *Nazarenes*; he had no other regard in the Fire of his Writings, than to reform a Luxurious, Bloody Court, a cowardly Senate, and a Despicable Populace. These were the proper Engines and Subjects of a Tyrant; the Immorality and Baseness of the *Roman* Empire might justly exact the heaviest Censures; and if *Juvenal* sometimes forgets his Morals and Philosophy, it must be attributed to the Reasons I have mention'd; but Mr. *Oldham* could not alledge such pretensions for that ungovernable heat which appears in all his Poetry, nor indeed can the Court of King *Charles* be compared to that of *Rome*; tho', it must be own'd,

[1] A reference to Oldham's *Satires upon the Jesuits*.

there happen'd, but too often, sufficient Arguments for Satire, whilst he sate upon the Throne. Whether Mr. *Oldham* would have Corrected his Writings, if he had attained to a longer date of Years, and seen the Turns and Changes of Fortune, which happen'd soon after his Death, is uncertain; yet this Character ought to be allow'd his Memory, (and, I believe, Mr. *Dennis*, who hath Judiciously Criticised upon his Passion of *Byblis*,[1] will admit) that he was Born a Poet, had a Genius very Bold and Sublime; that his Thoughts were generally very Noble; that his Heat was Masculine, and always pointed against Vice; that he was one of the best Translators, had a Vein rich enough of his own without borrowing from the Labour of others; and that if Fortune had permitted him time, and those opportunities which some Poets of greater Quality enjoy'd, he had not only equal'd them, but been superior to all that went before him. The Earls of *Rochester* and *Dorset* had the happiness to address themselves to the Muses, favour'd by a noble Extraction, and blest abundantly with the Goods of Fortune. Their Natural parts wanted very little from Study, or the Precepts of the Dead; and the Vivacity of their Wit might have prefer'd them to the eminent Station they possess'd, if Providence had not been so propitious to them in their Birth. Yet, tho' the Quality of these two Great Men, their Inclination to Poetry in general, and Satire in particular, was much the same, their Learning and great Capacities not much unlike, yet there was a wonderful difference in their Humours and Morals. My lord *Rochester* was always witty, and always very ill-Natur'd; he never troubled himself much about correcting the Vice, unless it disturb'd him in his Pleasure, (for reforming the Age was none of his Province) he generally took care to expose the Person, and that in such a manner, as usually begat more Crimes in those that were the Subjects of his Satires, than he corrected faults. His Wit was often Profane, and he neither spar'd Prince nor God, from whom he receiv'd both the greatest Abilities, a splendid Title, and a magnificent Fortune. My lord *Dorset* was as much his Equal in Learning and Sense, as he was inferior to him in Ill-Nature and Invectives; his Natural Sweetness led him to speak better of Mankind, as my Lord *Rochester* spake always worse than they deserv'd; and as my lord *Dorset's* Morals and Integrity, his Candor and his Honour, were infinitely beyond his Rival's, so his performance in Satire was no less. And this may be added to his Character, that his Writings contain'd as severe reprehensions as any others, either of the Antients or Moderns; but had the Air of Court, and a particular rich-

[1] See *The Critical Works of John Dennis*, ed. Hooker, i. 4–5.

ness of Expression, if possible, even beyond my lord *Rochester's*; and what was yet more Wonderful, is, that he was able to exert so vigorous a Satire, when his Compassion for Mankind, and Consideration of Learned Men, render'd him the most Generous Patron of the Muses, and the most certain Friend of good men in Distress.

> *For Pointed* Satire, *I would* Buckhurst *chuse;*
> *The best good Man with the worst Natur'd* Muse.[1]

This was my Lord *Rochester's* Character of his Lordship, and all the World knows my Lord *Rochester* never flatter'd any Person. I shan't add any further Remarks upon a Gentleman, whose Worth, Learning and Judgment, all will allow, that have any of these distinguishing Qualities of their own; who was as much beyond the Celebrated *Mæcenas* of the *Romans* in Learning, and the Favour of the Muses, as that Favourite exceeded him in the advantages of Riches and good Fortune.

29. John Aubrey's *Brief Life of Rochester*

before 1697

Aubrey's Brief Lives, ed. Andrew Clark, 2 vols. (1898), ii. 304.

The *Brief Lives* of John Aubrey (1626–97), were written between 1669 and 1696 but were not published until 1813 and then in an incomplete form.

John, Earl of Rochester:—he went to schoole at (Burford); was of Wadham College, Oxford; I suppose had been in France.

About eighteen, he stole his lady, (Elizabeth) Malet, a daughter and heir, a great fortune; for which I remember I sawe him a prisoner in the Tower about 1662.

[1] Rochester, *An Allusion to Horace*, 59–60.

His youthly spirit and oppulent fortune did sometimes make him doe extravagant actions, but in the country he was generally civill enough. He was wont to say that when he came to Brentford the devill entred into him and never left him till he came into the country again to Alderbury or Woodstock.

He was raunger of Woodstock-parke and lived often at the lodge at the west end, a very delightfull place and noble prospect westwards. Here his lordship had severall lascivious pictures drawen.

His lordship read all manner of bookes. Mr. Andrew Marvell, who was a good judge of witt, was wont to say that he was the best English satyrist and had the right veine. 'Twas pitty death tooke him off so soon.

In his last sicknesse he was exceedingly paenitent and wrote a lettre of his repentance to Dr. Burnet, which is printed.[1]

He sent for all his servants, even the piggard-boy, to come and heare his palinode. He dyed at Woodstock-parke, 26 July, 1680; and buried at Spilsbury in the same countie, Aug. 9 following.

His immature death putts me in mind of these verses of Propertius:—

Vere novo primoque in aetatis flore juventae,
Ceu rosa virgineo pollice carpta, jaces.[2]

[1] In Burnet's *Life of Rochester*, 1680.

[2] 'You lie in the new spring and first flower of your youth, like a rose plucked by a virgin hand.' I have not been able to trace the source of this quotation.

30. Thomas Dilke, a reference to the Maim'd Debauchee

1697

The City Lady (1697), p. 35.

The character Bevis, who makes this reference to Rochester's poem in the comedy, is described in the *Dramatis Personae* as 'an old wild Town-Spark'. Thorn-Drury in a note on the inside cover of his copy of *The Works of the Earls*, 1752 (now in the Bodleian library) refers to an edition of this play dated 1691. I have not been able to trace this.

BEVIS: My Lads and lovely Pupils, fail not to read Night and Morning that Heroick Canticle of my Lord Rochester's

As some Old Admiral etc.[1]

Ah noble Rochester! those glorious words deserve to be stamp't in Characters upon beaten Gold.

[1] Pinto, l.

31. Isaac Watts on Rochester

It is impossible to date this short poem by the great hymnist, who was born in 1674 and died in 1748. The lines were first published in the religious tract *The Repentance and Happy Death of the Celebrated Earl of Rochester*, Nottingham, 1814.

The following Lines were written by Dr Watts the name Strephon being intended for the Earl of Rochester.

Strephon of noble blood and mind,
(For ever shine his name!)
As Death approach'd, his Soul refin'd,
And gave his looser sonnets to the flame.
'Burn, burn, he cry'd, with sacred rage,
Hell is the Due of every page;
Such be its fate.'[1]—But, O indulgent Heaven!
So vile the Muse, and yet the man forgiven!
'Burn on my songs; for not the silver Thames,
Nor Tyber, with his yellow streams,
In endless currents rolling on the main
Can e'er dilute the poison, or wash out the stain.'—
So Moses by divine command,
Forbade the lep'rous house to stand;
When deep the *fatal spot* was grown:
'Break down the timber, and dig up the stone.'

[1] cf. Parsons' *Funeral Sermon* (1680), pp. 28–9.

ROCHESTER ACCLAIMED

1700–50

32. John Dennis, Some allusions to Rochester

1693–1717

The Critical Works of John Dennis, ed. E. N. Hooker (Baltimore, 1943).

John Dennis (1657–1734), was the most distinguished critic of his generation, with the possible exception of Joseph Addison. He greatly admired Milton, but also liked the witty literature of the Restoration. He was apt to look on Restoration literature as an ideal from which his contemporaries had fallen away. There are several other passages in Dennis's criticism which praise the literature of Charles II's reign and single out Rochester, similar to the extracts quoted.

a) *Preface to Miscellanies in Verse and Prose*, 1693

The late Lord Rochester, who was very well acquainted with *Boileau*, and who defer'd very much to his Judgment, did not at all believe that the censure of *Boileau*[1] extended to *Butler*: For if he had, he would never have follow'd his fashion in several of his masterly Copies. Nor would a noble Wit, who is a living Honour to his Country, and the English Court, have condescended to write Burlesque, if he had not discern'd

[1] A reference to a passage in Boileau's *Art of Poetry* which Dennis had shortly before quoted and then translated as follows:

'Whatever you write, let a Gentleman's manner appear in it; The lowest stile of the man who knows how to write, will still have a noble Air with it. But rightly to observe this rule, you must be sure to decline Burlesque, which not long since insolently appear'd in contempt of Reason, and pleas'd at the expence of good Sense: it pleas'd indeed a while, but pleas'd only as it was a fantastick novelty: It debas'd the dignity of Verse by its trivial Points, and taught *Parnassus* a *Billingsgate* Dialect.'

that there was in *Butler's* manner something extreamly fine, as well as something extreamly sensible in very many of his Thoughts. (Hooker, i. 8).

b) *The Epistle Dedicatory to the Advancement and Reformation of Modern Poetry*, 1701

For 'tis known to all the World, that your Lordship[1] declared against the Obscenity which was shamefully crept into *English* Poetry; at a Time when not only that way of Writing, but the Verses which you particularly hinted at, were in the very Height of their Reputation.[2] But the Success was answerable to the Nobleness of your Lordship's Attempt; those Verses have gradually declin'd ever since in their Reputation, and nothing of that Nature will now be suffer'd by any but the Rabble.

(Hooker, i. 198)

c) *Preface to Remarks upon Mr Pope's Translation of Homer*, 1717

. . . Mr Settle, who is now the *City* Poet, was formerly a Poet of the *Court*. And at what Time was he so? Why, in the Reign of King Charles II when that *Court* was more Gallant, and more Polite, than ever the *English Court* perhaps had been before: When there were at Court the present and the late Duke of Buckingham, the late Earl of Dorset, Wilmot, Lord *Rochester*, famous for his Wit and Poetry, Sir Charles Sedley, Mr Savil, Mr Buckley, and several others.

(Hooker, ii. 118.)

[1] John Sheffield, Earl of Mulgrave, to whom the *Epistle* is dedicated.
[2] A reference to Mulgrave's attack on Rochester in the *Essay upon Poetry*, see No. 7b.

33. Pierre Bayle, a reference to Rochester

1702

Dictionnaire Historique et Philosophique, 2nd ed. (Rotterdam, 1702), iii. 3145.

Pierre Bayle's famous *Dictionnaire Historique et Philosophique* was first published in Rotterdam in 1697. It was published in an English translation in 1710 where a shorter version of the following note appears.

John Wilmot, Count of Rochester, born April 1638 [for 1648], died a penitent in 1680. A man distinguished by his wit and by compositions full of pungency and gaiety and one of those atheists who live according to their principles, for he submersed himself in the most frightening excesses of drunkenness and lewdness.

34. An anonymous essay on Rochester

1707

The Miscellaneous Works of the Right Hon. the late Earls of Rochester and Roscommon (1707). Sigg. A8^{v}, B6^{r}–7^{v}.

This essay was first published as 'The Memoirs of the Life and Character of the late Earl of Rochester, in a letter to the Duchess of Mazarine. By Mons. St Evremont' in Bragge's edition of the poems of Rochester and Roscommon (1707). It was not however, published in Evremond's *Works* (1704), and in the edition of his *Works* (1714) the translator, Des Maizeaux, specifically disclaims it with the words: 'I must not forget to inform the Publick that the Memoirs of the Life of the Earl of Rochester in a letter to the Duchess of Mazarin . . . were not written by Mons. de St. Evremond.'

His talent of Satire was admirable, and in it he spar'd none, not even the King himself, whose Weakness for some of his Mistresses he endeavour'd to cure by several Means; that is, either by winning them from him, in spite of the Indulgence and Liberality they felt from a Royal Gallant, or by severely lampooning them and him on various Occasions; which generally the King (who was a Man of Wit and Pleasure, as well as my Lord) took for the natural Sallies of his Genius, and meant as Sports of Fancy more than the Efforts of Malice. . . . It may be here expected, that I should give a Character of his Lordship's Writings, his Genius, his Temper and the like: But the first are so well defended already, that there is nothing left for me to add; and it is so difficult a Matter to paint the latter, that I am afraid to attempt it. However, since it seems the Duty of this Task I have undertaken, I shall venture to add a few Words on both.

He had a Strength of Expression, and a Happiness of Thought peculiar to himself, and seems to me, of all the Moderns, to have come nearest the Ancients in Satire, scarce excepting our *Boileau*; for tho' he be very correct, and has spar'd no Pains to dress the Satires of *Horace* in good *French*, yet it smells too much of the Lamp: Whereas, when any Thought of *Horace, Juvenal, Persius*, or *Boileau*, falls in my Lord's Verses, it is plainly his Lordship's, without any Marks of borrowing it from any other, the Spirit and Easiness of the whole being of a Piece. His looser Songs, and Pieces, too obscene for the Ladies' Eyes, have their peculiar Beauties and are indeed too dangerous to peruse; for what would have render'd them nauseous, if they had been written by a Genius less powerful, in him alarms the Fancy, and rouzes the Blood and Appetite more than all the Medicaments of *Cleopatra* . . . He had a particular Picque to *Dryden*, after his mighty Success in the Town, either because he was sensible that he deserv'd not that Applause for his Tragedies, which the mad unthinking Audience gave them, (which Corruptness of Taste was afterwards somewhat corrected by the Duke of *Buckingham's Rehearsal*)[1] or whether it was out of Indignation of having any Rival in Reputation, either as a Poet in General, or a Satyrist in particular; Satire, indeed, being one of the chief Excellencies of Dryden, as well as of my Lord Rochester.

35. Daniel Defoe, remarks on Rochester from the *Review*

1706–13

Like John Dennis, Defoe tended to see the reign of Charles II as a golden age of literature.

a) *August 31st 1706*,

All the regulated Life of a just and pious Man is Musick in the Eye of the Observer; the Eloquence of the Orator, the Lines of the Poet make Musick in the Soul; who can read *Virgil, Horace, Milton, Waller*, or *Rochester*, without touching the Strings of his Soul, and finding a Unison of the most charming Influence there?

[1] The publication of Buckingham's *Rehearsal* in 1672 preceded Rochester's quarrel with Dryden.

b) *June 8th 1708,*

But I cannot quit this Affair of Elections, before I take Notice a little of the general Behaviour of the Gentry and Persons of Quallity, in order to their Election—What is become of all our Comedians? Ah, *Rochester, Shadwel, Otway, Oldham,* where is your Genius? Certainly, no subject ever deserv'd so much to be exposed, nothing can be so fruitful in Banter, or deserved more to be ridicul'd.

c) *March 29th 1711,*

And I appeal to any Man that remembers the Days of King Charles II. when the License Tyranny Reign'd over the Press, whether that Age did not abound in Lampoons and Satyrs, that Wounded; and at last went far in Ruining the Parties they were pointed at, more than has ever been practis'd since the Liberty of the Press—And he that does not know it, must be very Ignorant of those Times, and has heard very little of *Andrew Marvel,* Sir *John Denham, Rochester, Buckhurst,* and several others, whose Wit made the Court odious to the People, beyond what had been possible if the Press had been open.

d) *March 28th 1713,*

But I cannot but make one Observation as I go, (viz) That the Lampoons of this Age differ very much from those we have seen in former Times; and tho' *at the same time,* we pretend much to have a degree of Polite Wit beyond those Days; yet nothing of that keenness of Satyr, the happy turns and brightness of Fancy appears in the Lampoons of this Age, that were seen in *Andrew Marvel,* Sir *John Denham, Rochester, Buckingham, Buckhurst, Sidley*[1] and others, *the Wits of that Day*; nay, give *Sing-Song D'Urfey* his due, even his Ballads *outdid us* exceedingly: What wretched Stuff have we seen in our publick Prints on both sides, one as well as t'other, which pass for Satyr!

[1] i.e. Sir Charles Sedley.

36. Anthony Hamilton, *Memoirs of Count Grammont*

1713

Memoirs of Count Grammont (1811), ii. 120–1.

Born 1646 in Ireland of noble Scottish family, Anthony Hamilton spent most of his life in France. The *Memoirs*, for long regarded as a French classic, is a record of the life of Hamilton's brother-in-law, the Count de Grammont, which Hamilton began writing about 1704. The passages on the Court of Charles II may stem from personal knowledge, for he was a frequent visitor to London in the period. Rochester figures largely in this section of the narrative. The first edition of the *Memoirs* was published in French, 1713, and in English, 1714.

Miss Price[1] was witty; and as her person was not very likely to attract many admirers, which, however, she was resolved to have, she was far from being coy, when occasion offered: she did not so much as make any terms: she was violent in her resentments, as well as in her attachments, which had exposed her to some inconveniencies; and she had very indiscreetly quarrelled with a young girl whom Lord Rochester admired. This connection, which till then had been secret, she had the imprudence to publish to the whole world, and thereby drew upon herself the most dangerous enemy in the universe: never did any man write with more ease, humour, spirit, and delicacy; but he was at the same time the most severe satirist.

Poor Miss Price, who had thus voluntarily provoked his resentment, was daily exposed in some new shape: there was every day some new song or other, the subject of which was her conduct, and the burden her name. How was it possible for her to bear up against these attacks,

[1] One of the Queen's maids of honour. It is impossible to decide how much of this account is fact and how much fiction.

in a court, where every person was eager to obtain the most insignificant trifle that came from the pen of Lord Rochester? The loss of her lover, and the discovery that attended it, was only wanting to complete the persecution that was raised against her.

37. The Preface to Thomas Dryar's (largely spurious) edition of *Rochester*

1718

Reproduced from J. Prinz, *John Wilmot Earl of Rochester* (Leipzig, 1927), p. 366.

There is no Occasion (except Custom) for a Preface. Whoever reads the following Lines, and has a Taste of Poetry will find the lively Genius of the Witty and Excellent Author. Neither need I make an Apology for the Book; and would not in a Prolix Preface keep the Reader from better entertaining himself in the following Sheets. 'Tis enough that they are the Earl of Rochester's, and that I have prevented their lying longer in Obscurity.

38. Giles Jacob on Rochester

1720

The Poetical Register (1719–20), ii. 230–3.

Giles Jacob (1686–1744), was a lawyer by training. He wrote voluminously on literary and legal subjects.

JOHN WILMOT, *Earl of* Rochester.

This shining Nobleman was the Son of *Henry* Earl of *Rochester*; whose Fame, for Loyalty and Valour, equall'd his Son's for his surprizing Wit and Genius. He was born at *Dichley*, near *Woodstock*, in *Oxfordshire*, in the Year 1648, and educated in *Wadham*-College, *Oxford*, under the Tuition of Dr. *Blandford*, afterwards successively Bishop of *Oxford* and *Worcester*. He was a Person of most excellent Parts and great Learning, being thorowly acquainted with all Classick Authors, both *Greek* and *Latin*. He early suck'd in those Perfections of Wit, Eloquence, and Poetry, which made him the Wonder of the Age wherein he liv'd. In all his Composures there is something peculiarly Great and New; and tho' he has lent to many, he has borrow'd of none: Nor was he deficient in his other personal Accomplishments, which were very much improv'd by his Travels; for in all the Qualifications of a Gentleman for the Court or the Country, he was universally known, and acknowledg'd to be a very great Master; but the natural Tendency of his Temper unhappily inclin'd him to Excesses of Pleasure and Wantonness. He had a strange Vivacity of Thought, and Vigour of Expression; his Style was clear and strong, and his Figures very lively, and few Men ever had a bolder Flight of Fancy, more steddily govern'd by Judgment than his Lordship. He laid out his Wit very freely in Libels and Satires, in which he had a peculiar Talent of mixing his Wit with his Malice, and fitting both with such apt words, that Men were tempted to be pleased with them. From thence his Compositions came to be easily known, few or none having such an artful way of tempering these together as he had: And his Satire he always defended, by alledging there were some Persons that could not be kept in Order, or admonish'd, but in this way. His Poetry has eminently distinguish'd it self from that of other Men, by a thousand irresistable Beauties: 'Twas all Original, like himself; the Excellencies are many and masterly, and the Faults few and inconsiderable; and those it has are of the kind, which *Horace* says, can never offend.

> —*Quas aut incuria fudit;*[1]
> *Aut humana parum cavit Natura.*

But in his Choice of Subjects, he frequently border'd on Obscenity. He would often retire into the Country, and be for some Months wholly employ'd in Study, or the Sallies of his Wit: His Studies were divided between the comical and witty Writings of the Antients and Moderns, the *Roman* Authors, Books of History and Physick; and *Boileau* among the *French*, and *Cowley* among the *English* Wits, were those he admir'd most. Nature had fitted him for great Things, and his Knowledge and Observation qualified him to have been one of the most extraordinary Men *England* has produc'd: But Death took him off in the three and thirtieth Year of his Age. He died in the Ranger's-Lodge in *Woodstock*-Park, on the 26th of *July*, 1680. of a lingring Disease (which was attended with great Marks of Repentance for his Vices and Extravagancies) and was bury'd in a Vault under the North Isle joining to *Spellesbury* Church in *Oxfordshire*. The chief of his incomparable Poems are the following:

I. *A Satire against Man*; an inimitable Piece, and the severest Satire that ever was penn'd.

II. *Horace's tenth Satire of the first Book imitated.* This Poem lashes Mr. *Dryden* and several of the top Poets of his time.

III. *A Satire upon the Times.*

IV. *Satire on the King*, for which he was banish'd the Court, and afterwards set up on *Tower-street* for an *Italian* Mountebank; which occasion'd his famous Speech of *Alexander Bendo*

V. *Tunbridge-Wells*, a Satire.

VI. *Bath Intrigues.*

VII. *The young Statesman*, a Satire.

VIII. *A Satire against Marriage.*

[1] 'Which either carelessness has produced or human nature has been too negligent about.' Horace, *Ars Poetica*, 352–3. This is quoted in Wolseley's Preface, and Jacob is obviously borrowing from Wolseley in this passage.

IX. *A Session of the Poets.* This is a comical Satire on the Dramatick Poets.

X. *The Rehearsal*, a Satire.

XI. *A Defence of Satire.* This Poem begins,

> *When* Shakespear, Johnson, Fletcher *rul'd the Stage,*
> *They took so bold a Freedom with the Age,*
> *That there was scarce a Knave or Fool in Town*
> *Of any Note, but had his Picture shown.*

And in his Answer to the Defence of Satire, written by Sir *C. S.* he has these Lines:

> *Satire is of Divine Authority,*
> *For God made one of Man, when he made Thee.*

XII. *On the Death of Mr.* Greenhill, *the famous Painter.*

XIII. *Upon Nothing*, an excellent Piece.

XIV. *The Perfect Enjoyment.*

XV. *The Disappointment.*

XVI. *The Virgin's Desire.*

XVII. *Et Cætera.*

XVIII. *To his Mistress.*

XIX. *On a false Mistress.*

XX. *An Extempore*, upon receiving a Fall at *Whitehall*-Gate, by attempting to salute the Dutchess of *Cleaveland*, as she was stepping out of her Chariot.[1]

[1] I include this list as an illustration of the muddle the Rochester canon had got into. Only items I, II, IV, V, XIII, XIV, XVIII and possibly XIX and XX would be accepted as by Rochester today. Jacob's scholarship can be judged on item XI where he lists as Rochester's a poem which he goes on to tell us was written by 'C.S.'—Carr Scroope. Item XVII is particularly intriguing.

39. A Comment on Rochester from a Life of Sedley

1721

The Works of Sir Charles Sedley (1722 [for 1721]), i. 8–9.

This life of Sir Charles Sedley, said on the title page to be 'by an eminent hand', is usually ascribed to Daniel Defoe. It borrows freely from Giles Jacob's accounts of the poets [see No. 38].

It is true, it [the writing of love poetry] was an Art too successful in those Days, to propagate[1] the Immoralities of those Times; nor did it at all assist to protect the Vertue of the Readers, whether of one Sex or another. But it must be acknowledg'd, he [Sedley] excell'd Dorset, Rochester, and those superior Poets, who, as they conceiv'd lewdly, so they wrote in plain *English*, and took no care to cover up the worst of their Thoughts in clean Linnen; which scandalous Custom, in a Word, has assisted to bury the best Performances of that Age, because blended with Prophaneness or Indecency. They are not fit to be read by People whose Religion and Modesty have not quite forsaken them; and which, had those grosser Parts been left out, would justly have pass'd for the most polite Poetry that the World ever saw.

[1] i.e. in propagating.

40. Pope and Spence on Rochester

1728–43

Joseph Spence (1699–1768) from whom the following material is quoted was made Professor of Poetry at Oxford in 1728. The *Anecdotes* for which he is now chiefly remembered are a lifetime's record of conversations with his literary acquaintances. They were first published in 1820. For Pope's view of Rochester see Introduction, pp. 14–15. The last extract is translated from a short history of the English poets written by Spence in French.

---

a) 1728?

POPE: Lord Rochester was of a very bad turn of mind, as well as debauched.

SPENCE: (From the Duke of Buckingham[1] and others that knew him.)

(*Anecdotes*, ed. J. M. Osborn (1966), i. 470)

b) 1–7 May, 1730

POPE: Oldham is a very undelicate writer. He has strong rage, but 'tis too much like Billingsgate. Lord Rochester had much more delicacy and more knowledge of mankind. [Osborn, i. 473].

c) 1734

POPE: Oldham is too rough and coarse. Rochester is the medium between him and the Earl of Dorset. Lord Dorset is the best of all those writers.

SPENCE: What, better than Rochester?

POPE: Yes; Rochester has neither so much delicacy nor exactness as Dorset. (instance: his *Satire on Man.*) [Osborn, i. 472]

d) March, 1743

POPE: He [Lord Dorset] and Lord Rochester should be considered as holiday writers—as gentlemen that diverted themselves now and then with poetry, rather than as poets.

SPENCE: (This was said kindly of them, rather to excuse their defects than to lessen their characters.) [Osborn, i. 469]

[1] Presumably John Sheffield, Earl of Mulgrave, Duke of Buckinghamshire, with whom Pope was acquainted.

e) March, 1743

POPE: Rochester has very bad versification sometimes.

SPENCE: (He instanced this from his tenth satire of Horace,[1] his full rhymes etc.) [Osborn, i. 471]

f) SPENCE, 1732–3

This period was very rich in satire. Besides the great Dryden it produced Dorset, Rochester, Oldham, Buckingham and Butler [Remarks on Butler and Buckingham's *Rehearsal* omitted]. Oldham wrote in a strong and very severe manner. Rochester was more perceptive of the characters of men; he had a more penetrating force and was more polished. (*Pope and his Contemporaries* (1949), ed. J. M. Osborn.)

41. Voltaire on Rochester

1729, 1775

Voltaire was perhaps the first major French writer to take a serious interest in English literature. The *Lettres Philosophiques*, an early work, were written during or soon after Voltaire's visit to England from mid-1726 to the beginning of 1729. They were first published in 1733 in an English translation by John Lockman and were first published in French the following year.

---

a) Letter 21, 'Of the Earl of Rochester and Mr Waller'.

The Earl of Rochester's name is universally known. Mr. de St. Evremont has made very frequent mention of him, but then he has represented this famous nobleman in no other light than as the man of pleasure, as one who was the idol of the fair; but with regard to myself, I would willingly describe in him the man of genius, the great poet. Among

[1] *An Allusion to Horace*, Pinto, lv.

other pieces which display the shining imagination his lordship only could boast, he wrote some satires on the same subjects as those our celebrated Boileau made choice of. I do not know any better method of improving the taste, than to compare the productions of such great geniuses as have exercised their talent on the same subject. Boileau declaims as follows against human reason in his satire on man.

Cependant à le voir plein de vapeurs légères,
Soi-même se bercer de ses propres chimères,
Lui seul de la nature est la base et l'appui,
Et le dixième Ciel ne tourne que pour lui.
De tous les Animaux il ist ici le Maître;
Qui pourait le nier, poursuis-tu? Moi peut-être:
Ce maître prétendu qui leur donne des loix,
Ce Roi des Animaux combien a-t-il de Rois?[1]

The Lord Rochester expresses himself, in his satire against man, in pretty near the following manner: but I must first desire you always to remember, that the versions I give you from the English poets are written with freedom and latitude; and that the restraint of our versification, and the delicacies of the French tongue, will not allow a translator to convey into it the licentious impetuosity and fire of the English numbers.

[Voltaire here translates lines 72–95 of the *Satire Against Mankind* into French.]

[1] Boileau, *Satire*. A translation of these lines by Oldham 'a little altered' are given in the text as follows:

Yet, pleas'd with idle whimsies of his brain,
And puff'd with pride, this haughty thing would fain
Be thought himself the only stay and prop
That holds the mighty frame of nature up.
The skies and stars his properties must seem,
. . . . .
Of all the creatures he's the Lord, he cries.
. . . . .
And who is there, say you, that dares deny
So own'd a truth? That may be, Sir, do I.
. . . . .
This boasted monarch of the world who awes
The creatures here, and with his nod give(s) laws:
This self-nam'd king, who thus pretends to be
The lord of all, how many lords has he?

For a comparison of Boileau's, Oldham's and Rochester's version of this satire see Rhymer, No. 26.

Whether these ideas are true or false, it is certain they are expressed with an energy and fire which form the poet. I shall be very far from attempting to examine philosophically into these verses, to lay down the pencil and take up the rule and compass on this occasion; my only design in this letter, being to display the genius of the English poets, and therefore I shall continue in the same view.

[Voltaire ends the letter with a discussion of Edmund Waller.]

(*Letters concerning the English Nation* (1733))

b) From Chapter 7 of the *Histoire de Jenni.*

. . . extreme in his dissipation, in his courage, in his ideas, in his expression, in his Epicurean philosophy, attracted to nothing unless it was extraordinary, which he very soon got tired of, having the kind of spirit which takes likeness for demonstration; wiser and more eloquent than any other young man of his period but never giving himself the trouble of going into anything deeply.

('*Histoire de Jenni*', *Works* (Paris, 1879), xxi. 551)

42. Francis Lockier on Rochester

September 1730

Joseph Spence, *Anecdotes*, ed. J. M. Osborn (1966).

Francis Lockier 1667–1740, Dean of Peterborough, was a noted litterateur.

---

a) Horace's 'Supper', Boileau's 'Festin' and Lord Rochester's 'Feast' [are] all very good. Rochester's *Satire on Man* exceeds and much elevates (instance the first lines) his pattern in Boileau.[1]

(Osborn, i. 720)

[1] The references are to Horace *Satires*, II. viii, Boileau's third satire and Rochester's *Timon*. Both *Timon* and the *Satire against Mankind* owe something to Boileau's satires.

b) Lord Rochester and Lord Dorset's two copies on Ned Howard[1] (intended to have been set before his works in ridicule) show their different tastes. One is mighty easy and natural, the other has more uncommon, beautiful, [and] quite new thought in it than any copy perhaps that ever was written.

(Osborn, i. 679)

[1] The reference seems to be to Dorset's poem beginning 'Come on, ye critics! Find one fault who dare' and to a poem beginning 'As when a bully draws his sword' which came to be attributed to Rochester but is probably by Edward Ashton; both poems are in the new Yale edition of *Poems on Affairs of State* (i. 338–40). The passage illustrates, however, a familiar comparison between Rochester's natural style and Dorset's inventiveness, for references to 'easy' Rochester cf. No. 6 and No. 22a.

GROWING DISAPPROVAL

1750–1800

43. 'Mr. Cibber' [Robert Shiels] moralizes on Rochester

1753

'Mr. Cibber', The *Lives of the Poets* (1753), ii. 269f.

The composition of the *Lives of the Poets* from which this extract is taken has until recently been a matter of some dispute. Dr. Johnson in his *Life of Hammond* says that the actor Theophilus Cibber (son of the irrepressible Colley Cibber) lent his name to the work for ten guineas but that it was written by Robert Shiels, a Scot who helped Johnson in the compilation of the Dictionary. Johnson's account is now accepted as substantially correct. Cibber apparently revised some of the *Lives*, while Johnson himself is thought to have provided some information. For a detailed account of Shiels' part in the *Lives* see David Nicol Smith's note to Sir Walter Raleigh's *Six Essays on Johnson* (1910), pp. 120–5.

It is an observation founded on experience, that the poets have, of all other men, been most addicted to the gratifications of appetite, and have pursued pleasure with more unwearied application than men of other characters. In this respect they are indeed unhappy, and have ever been more subject to pity than envy. A violent love of pleasure, if it does not destroy, yet, in a great measure, enervates all other good qualities with which a man may be endowed; and as no men have ever enjoyed higher parts from nature, than the poets, so few, from this unhappy attachment to pleasure, have effected so little good by those amazing powers. Of the truth of this observation, the nobleman, whose memoirs we are now to present to the reader, is a strong and indelible instance, for few ever had more ability, and more frequent opportunities, for promoting the interests of society, and none ever prostituted the gifts of Heaven to a more inglorious purpose. Lord Rochester was not more remarkable for the superiority of his parts, than the extraordinary debauchery of his life, and with his dissipations of pleasure, he suffered sometimes malevolent principles to govern him, and was equally odious for malice and envy, as for the boundless gratifications of his appetites.

This is, no doubt, the character of his lordship, confirmed by all who have transmitted any account of him: but if his life was supremely wicked, his death was exemplarily pious . . . [here, pp. 270–5 follows a brief biography]. Rochester had certainly a true talent for satire, and he spared neither friends nor foes, but let it loose on all without discrimination. Majesty itself was not secure from it. . . . The Restoration, or the History of the Insipids . . . contains the keenest reflexions against the political conduct, and private character of that Prince . . . [this poem is quoted here, pp. 282–91, at length; it is followed by an extended account of Rochester's escapades, Wolseley's sympathetic account of Rochester is dissented from and finally his death is recounted, pp. 291–9.] We might now enumerate his lordship's writings, of which we have already given some character; but unhappily for the world they are too generally diffused, and we think ourselves under no obligations to particularize those works which have been so fruitful of mischief to society, by promoting a general corruption of morals, and which he himself in his last moments wished he could recal, or rather that he never had composed.

44. David Hume on Rochester

1757

History of Great Britain (1757), ii. 453.

David Hume (1711–76), Scotland's greatest philosopher, was born in Edinburgh. His most important works are the *Treatise of Human Nature* (1739–40), *Enquiry concerning Human Understanding* (1748) and *Enquiry concerning the Principles of Morals* (1751).

Most of the celebrated writers of this age remain monuments of genius, perverted by indecency and bad taste. [Hume discusses Dryden here before turning to Rochester.] The very name of Rochester is offensive to modern ears; yet does his poetry discover such energy of style and such poignancy of satyre, as give ground to imagine what so fine a genius, had he fallen in a more happy age and followed better models, was capable of producing. The ancient satyrists often used great liberty in their expressions; but their freedom no more resembles the licence of Rochester than the nakedness of an Indian does that of a common prostitute.

45. Horace Walpole disapproves

1758

A Catalogue of the Royal and Noble Authors of England (Strawberry Hill, 1758), ii. 37–9.

Horace Walpole, fourth Earl of Orford (1717–97), was the son of Robert Walpole, the chief minister of George I and George II. Horace Walpole is now chiefly remembered as one of the initiators of the gothic revival and for his voluminous literary correspondence.

John Wilmot, Earl of Rochester; A man, whom the Muses were fond to inspire, and ashamed to avow, and who practised without the least reserve that secret which can make verses more read for their defects than for their merits. The art is neither commendable nor difficult. Moralists proclaim loudly that there is no wit in indecency: It is very true: Indecency is far from conferring wit; but it does not destroy it neither. Lord Rochester's poems have much more obscenity than wit, more wit than poetry, more poetry than politeness. One is amazed at hearing the age of Charles the Second called polite: Because the Presbyterians and Religionists had affected to call every thing by a Scripture-name, the new Court affected to call every thing by it's own name. That Court had no pretensions to politeness but by it's resemblance to another age, which called it's own grossness polite, the age of Aristophanes. Would a Scythian have been civilized by the Athenian stage, or a Hottentot by the Drawing room of Charles the Second? The Characters and anecdotes being forgot, the State-poems of that time are a heap of senseless ribaldry, scarcely in rhime, and more seldom in metre. When Satyrs were brought to Court, no wonder the Graces would not trust themselves there.

The writings of this *noble* and *beautiful Count*, as Anthony Wood[1] calls him, (for his Lordship's vices were among the fruits of the Restoration, and consequently not unlovely in that Biographer's eyes) in the

[1] Anthony à Wood, *Athenae Oxonienses*, ed. Clark, ii. See no. 27 above.

order they were published, at least as they are ranged by that Author were

A Satire against Mankind, printed in one sheet in folio, June 1679.

It is more than an imitation of Boileau. One Griffith a Minister wrote against it. We are told that Andrew Marvel used to say, 'That Rochester was the only Man in England that had the true vein of Satire'.[1] A very wrong judgment: Indelicacy does not spoil flattery more than it does satire.

[The remainder of Walpole's account consists of a bare list of some of the publications of Rochester's work.]

46. From the Preface to *The Poetical Works of Rochester*

1761

The Poetical Works of Rochester (1761), p. v.

This collection of largely spurious pieces is claimed in the Preface to have been saved from burning by one of Rochester's servants.

As to the Work itself, the very Name of *Rochester* is a sufficient Passport wherever the English is spoken or understood: And we doubt not but it will give the highest Delight to all those who have Youth, Fire, Wit and Discernment; nor be even distasteful to those cool Readers who have lived 'till Pleasure hath lost its Relish, and witty Things their Power to provoke Mirth, Laughter and Delectation.

[1] See No. 29 above.

47. Samuel Johnson on Rochester

1779

Lives of the English Poets, ed. G. Birkbeck Hill (1905), i. 219–26.

Dr. Johnson's essay on Rochester is discussed in the Introduction, pp. 17–19.

John Wilmot, afterwards Earl of Rochester, the son of Henry, Earl of Rochester, better known by the title of Lord Wilmot, so often mentioned in Clarendon's History, was born April 10, 1647, at Ditchley, in Oxfordshire. After a grammatical education at the school of Burford, he entered a nobleman into Wadham College in 1659, only twelve years old; and in 1661, at fourteen, was, with some other persons of high rank, made master of arts by Lord Clarendon in person.

He travelled afterwards into France and Italy; and, at his return, devoted himself to the Court. In 1665 he went to sea with Sandwich, and distinguished himself at Bergen by uncommon intrepidity; and the next summer served again on board (the ship commanded by) Sir Edward Spragge, who, in the heat of the engagement, having a message of reproof to send to one of his captains, could find no man ready to carry it but Wilmot, who, in an open boat, went and returned amidst the storm of shot.

But his reputation for bravery was not lasting: he was reproached with slinking away in street quarrels and leaving his companions to shift as they could without him; and Sheffield, Duke of Buckingham, has left a story of his refusal to fight him.

He had very early an inclination to intemperance, which he totally subdued in his travels; but when he became a courtier he unhappily addicted himself to dissolute and vitious company, by which his principles were corrupted and his manners depraved. He lost all sense of religious restraint; and, finding it not convenient to admit the authority of laws which he was resolved not to obey, sheltered his wickedness behind infidelity.

As he excelled in that noisy and licentious merriment which wine incites, his companions eagerly encouraged him in excess, and he willingly indulged it, till, as he confessed to Dr. Burnet, he was for five years together continually drunk, or so much inflamed by frequent ebriety as in no interval to be master of himself.

In this state he played many frolicks, which it is not for his honour that we should remember, and which are not now distinctly known. He often pursued low amours in mean disguises, and always acted with great exactness and dexterity the characters which he assumed.

He once erected a stage on Tower-hill, and harangued the populace as a mountebank; and, having made physick part of his study, is said to have practised it successfully.

He was so much in favour with King Charles that he was made one of the gentlemen of the bedchamber, and comptroller of Woodstock Park.

Having an active and inquisitive mind he never, except in his paroxysms of intemperance, was wholly negligent of study; he read what is considered as polite learning so much that he is mentioned by Wood as the greatest scholar of all the nobility. Sometimes he retired into the country and amused himself with writing libels, in which he did not pretend to confine himself to truth.

His favourite author in French was Boileau, and in English Cowley.

Thus in a course of drunken gaiety and gross sensuality, with intervals of study perhaps yet more criminal, with an avowed contempt of all decency and order, a total disregard to every moral, and a resolute denial of every religious obligation, he lived worthless and useless, and blazed out his youth and his health in lavish voluptuousness, till, at the age of one and thirty, he had exhausted the fund of life, and reduced himself to a state of weakness and decay.

At this time he was led to an acquaintance with Dr. Burnet, to whom he laid open with great freedom the tenour of his opinions and the course of his life, and from whom he received such conviction of the reasonableness of moral duty and the truth of Christianity as produced a total change both of his manners and opinions. The account of those salutary conferences is given by Burnet, in a book intituled *Some Passages of the Life and Death of John Earl of Rochester*, which the critick ought to read for its elegance, the philosopher for its arguments, and the saint for its piety. It were an injury to the reader to offer him an abridgement.

He died July 26, 1680, before he had completed his thirty-fourth year; and was so worn away by a long illness that life went out without a struggle.

Lord Rochester was eminent for the vigour of his colloquial wit, and remarkable for many wild pranks and sallies of extravagance. The glare of his general character diffused itself upon his writings; the compositions of a man whose name was heard so often were certain of attention, and from many readers certain of applause. This blaze of reputation is not yet quite extinguished; and his poetry still retains some splendour beyond that which genius has bestowed.

Wood and Burnet give us reason to believe that much was imputed to him which he did not write. I know not by whom the original collection was made or by what authority its genuineness was ascertained. The first edition was published in the year of his death, with an air of concealment, professing in the title page to be printed at Antwerp.

Of some of the pieces, however, there is no doubt. *The Imitation of Horace's Satire*, the *Verses to Lord Mulgrave*, the *Satire against Man*, the *Verses upon Nothing*, and perhaps some others, are, I believe, genuine, and perhaps most of those which the late collection exhibits.

As he cannot be supposed to have found leisure for any course of continued study, his pieces are commonly short, such as one fit of resolution would produce.

His songs have no particular character: they tell, like other songs, in smooth and easy language of scorn and kindness, dismission and desertion, absence and inconstancy, with the common places of artificial courtship. They are commonly smooth and easy; but have little nature, and little sentiment.

His imitation of Horace on Lucilius is not inelegant or unhappy. In the reign of Charles the Second began that adaptation, which has since been very frequent, of ancient poetry to present times; and perhaps few will be found where the parallelism is better preserved than in this. The versification is indeed sometimes careless, but it is sometimes vigorous and weighty.

The strongest effort of his Muse is his poem upon *Nothing*. He is not the first who has chosen this barren topick for the boast of his fertility.[1] There is a poem called *Nihil* in Latin by Passerat, a poet and critick of the sixteenth century in France; who, in his own epitaph, expresses his zeal for good poetry thus:

Molliter ossa quiescent
Sint modo carminibus non onerata malis.[2]

[1] It was in fact a standard subject for the exercise of rhetorical ingenuity among Renaissance poets, see Rosalie Colie's *Paradoxia Epidemica*.

[2] '(My) bones will sleep peacefully, provided they are not burdened with bad songs.'

His works are not common, and therefore I shall subjoin his verses.

In examining this performance *Nothing* must be considered as having not only a negative but a kind of positive signification; as I need not fear thieves, I have *nothing*; and *nothing* is a very powerful protector. In the first part of the sentence it is taken negatively; in the second it is taken positively, as an agent. In one of Boileau's lines it was a question, whether he should use *a rien faire* or *à ne rien faire*; and the first was preferred, because it gave rien a sense in some sort positive.[1] *Nothing* can be a subject only in its positive sense, and such a sense is given it in the first line:

> *Nothing*, thou elder brother ev'n to shade.

In this line I know not whether he does not allude to a curious book *De Umbra*, by Wowerus, which, having told the qualities of *Shade*, concludes with a poem in which are these lines:

> Jam primum terram validis circumspice claustris
> Suspensam totam, decus admirabile mundi
> Terrasque tractusque maris, camposque liquentes
> Aeris et vasti laqueata palatia coeli—
> Omnibus UMBRA prior.[2]

The positive sense is generally preserved with great skill through the whole poem, though sometimes in a subordinate sense the negative *nothing* is injudiciously mingled. Passerat confounds the two senses.

Another of his most vigorous pieces is his Lampoon on Sir Carr Scroop, who, in a poem called 'The Praise of Satire', had some lines like these:

> He who can push into a midnight fray
> His brave companion, and then run away,
> Leaving him to be murder'd in the street,
> Then put it off with some buffoon conceit;
> Him, thus dishonour'd, for a wit you own,
> And court him as top fidler of the town.[3]

This was meant of Rochester, whose 'buffoon conceit' was, I sup-

[1] *Satires*, ii, 57.

[2] 'First, then, look around the whole of the suspended globe with its strong defences, the wonderful beauty of the world, and the lands and the expanses of the sea, the liquid fields of the air, the ornamented vaulting of the palaces of the vast sky-SHADE was before all these.' (Joan. Woweri, *Dies Aestiva sive de Umbra Paegnion*, 1610, p. 130.)

[3] Johnson adds the note 'I quote from memory.' He also added at the end of this *Life* a 70-line Latin poem on nothing by Jean Passerat which Hawkins in his *Life of Johnson* says was quoted from memory.

pose, a saying often mentioned, that 'every Man would be a Coward if he durst,'[1] and drew from him those furious verses; to which Scroop made in reply an epigram, ending with these lines:

> Thou canst hurt no man's fame with thy ill word;
> Thy pen is full as harmless as thy sword.

Of the *Satire against Man* Rochester can only claim what remains when all Boileau's part is taken away.

In all his works there is sprightliness and vigour, and everywhere may be found tokens of a mind which study might have carried to excellence. What more can be expected from a life spent in ostentatious contempt of regularity, and ended before the abilities of many other men began to be displayed?

48. Joseph Warton on Rochester

1782

An Essay on the Genius and Writings of Pope, Volume the Second (1782), pp. 110–12.

Joseph Warton (1722–1800), is now chiefly remembered for his *Essay on the Genius and Writings of Pope* from which this extract is taken.

The verses on *Silence*[2] are a sensible imitation of the Earl of Rochester's on *Nothing*; which piece, together with his *Satire on Man*, from the fourth of Boileau, and the tenth Satire of Horace, are the only pieces of this profligate nobleman, which modesty or common sense will allow

[1] An illuminating series of slips on Johnson's part. This is a misquoted version of I.158 of the *Satire against Mankind*, which Johnson has purported to judge. Nor can it be the line referred to in Scroope's satire, which clearly refers to a specific occasion when Rochester was involved in a brawl. Pinto suggests that the 'buffoon conceit' is the lines 'To a Post-boy'.

[2] By Pope.

any man to read. Rochester had great energy in his thoughts and diction; and though the ancient satirists often use great liberty in their expressions, yet, as the ingenious historian observes,[1] 'their freedom no more resembles the licence of Rochester, than the nakedness of an Indian does that of a common prostitute'.

Pope in this imitation has discovered a fund of solid sense, and just observation on vice and folly, that are very remarkable in a person so extremely young as he was, at the time he composed it. I believe, on a fair comparison with Rochester's lines, it will be found that, although the turn of the Satire be copied, yet it is excelled. That Rochester should write a satire on Man, I am not surprized; it is the business of the Libertine to degrade his species, and debase the dignity of human nature, and thereby destroy the most efficacious incitements to lovely and laudable actions: but that a writer of Boileau's purity of manners should represent his kind in the dark and disagreeable colours he has done, with all the malignity of a discontented Hobbist, is a lamentable perversion of fine talents, and is a real injury to society. It is a fact worthy the attention of those who study the history of learning, that the gross licentiousness, and applauded debauchery of Charles the Second's court, proved almost as pernicious to the progress of polite literature and the fine arts that began to revive after the Grand Rebellion, as the gloomy superstition, the absurd cant, and formal hypocrisy that disgraced this nation, during the usurpation of Cromwell.

[1] David Hume *History of Great Britain*, see No. 35.

49. From Robert Anderson's *Life of Rochester*

1795

Robert Anderson, *Works of the British Poets*, London, 1795, vi 398–9.

Dr Robert Anderson's *Life of Rochester*, prefacing a selection of Rochester's poetry, was first published in Scotland in 1793. It borrows freely from Dr Johnson's *Life*, sometimes with acknowledgment.

Much has probably been imputed to him which he did not write; and the blaze of reputation which his character diffused on what he did write, if it be not extinguished, is fast wearing away; for impartial criticism warrants no distinction beyond that which genius bestows.

His songs are sprightly and easy; but have little nature and little sentiment. In his imitation of Horace on Lucilius, the parallelism between ancient and modern times is happily preserved; but the versification is careless; though it is sometimes vigorous. The poem upon *Nothing* displays an admirable fertility of invention on a barren topic. This little poem, and his tragedy of *Valentinian*, altered from Beaumont and Fletcher, and acted in 1685, shew that he was not incapable of more serious productions.

ROCHESTER IN ECLIPSE: CRITICISM

1800–50

50. An Introductory Comment

1800

From the Preface to Cooke's edition of *The Poetical Works of the Earl of Rochester* (1800), p. xii.

This Preface, reproduced in later editions, leans heavily on Johnson's *Life of Rochester* from which it quotes freely.

These brief Memoirs afford a melancholy proof of the fatal effects of genius perverted, and talents misapplied. The Earl of Rochester, from his elevated rank in life, literary endowments, and engaging qualifications, might have rendered himself an ornament to society: instead of this, the record of his transient life serves only as a memento of human frailty, and a blot to sully the page of biography.

51. An anonymous comment on Rochester

1806

Extract from an unsigned review of Thomas Moore's *Epistles, Odes and other Poems*, *Edinburgh Review* (July 1806), viii. 457.

While France has to blush for so many tomes of Poésies Erotiques we have little to answer for, but the coarse indecencies of Rochester and Dryden; and these, though sufficiently offensive to delicacy and good taste, can scarcely be regarded as dangerous. There is an antidote to the poison they contain, in the open and undisguised profligacy with which it is presented. If they are wicked, they have the honesty at least to profess wickedness. The mark of the beast is set visibly on their foreheads; and though they have the boldness to recommend vice, they want the effrontery to make her pass for virtue. In their grossest immoralities, too, they scarcely ever seem to be perfectly in earnest; and appear neither to wish nor to hope to make proselytes. They indulge their own vein of gross riot and debauchery; but they do not seek to corrupt the principles of their readers; and are contented to be reprobated as profligate, if they are admired at the same time for wit and originality.

The immorality of Mr. Moore is infinitely more insidious and malignant.

52. Thomas Park on Rochester

1806

A Note from his Edition of Horace Walpole's *A Catalogue of the Royal and Noble Authors of England* (1806), p. 224.

This lord's (Rochester's) licentious productions too forcibly warrant the sentence of outlawry that decorum and taste have passed upon them.

53. Isaac D'Israeli on Rochester's satire

1814

'Literary Quarrels from Personal Motives', *Quarrels of Authors* (1814), p. 314.

Isaac D'Israeli (1766–1848), the father of Benjamin Disraeli, was an assiduous collector of literary anecdote. His best known collection is *Curiosities of Literature* (1791–3, 1823).

. . . to give full effect to their severity,[1] poets always infuse a certain quantity of fiction. This is an artifice absolutely necessary to practise; so I collect from a great master in the arts of satire, and who once honestly avowed, that no satire could be composed, unless it was *personal*; and no personalities would sufficiently adorn a poem, without *lies*. This great satirist was Rochester. Burnet details a curious conversation between

[1] D'Israeli has just been discussing Pope's quarrel with Bentley.

himself and his lordship on this subject.[1] The bishop tells us that 'he would often go into the country, and be for some months wholly employed in study, or the sallies of his wit, chiefly directed to satire. And this he often defended to me, by saying, there were some people that could not be kept in order, or admonished but in this way.' Burnet remonstrated, and Rochester replied—'A man could not write with life, unless he were *heated by revenge*; for to make a satire without resentments, upon the notions of philosophy, was as if a man would, in cold blood, cut men's throats who had never offended him. And he said, the *lies* in these libels came often in as *ornaments*, that could not be spared without spoiling the beauty of the poem.' It is as useful to know how the materials of satire are put together; as thus the secret of pulling it to pieces more readily, may sometimes be obtained.

54. Goethe quotes the *Satire against Mankind*

1814

Goethe's Autobiography translated by R. O. Moon (1932), p. 512.

Johann Wolfgang Goethe (1749–1832) Germany's most famous poet, took a keen interest in English literature throughout his life.

The gayest and the most serious works have the same end, namely, to moderate both joy and pain by a felicitous intellectual representation. If in this light we look at the majority of the English, mostly moral didactic, poems, they will, on the average, only show us a gloomy dissatisfaction with life. Not only Young's *Night Thoughts*, where this theme is pre-eminently worked out, but also the other meditative poems wander, before one is aware of it, into this mournful region, where a task is presented to the understanding, which it is insufficient to solve, since even religion, which a man can always construct for himself, here

[1] Gilbert Burnet, *Some Passages of the Life and Death of . . . Rochester*, 1680, (No. 10).

leaves him in the lurch. Whole volumes might be compiled which could serve as a commentary to this frightful text:

> Then Old Age and Experience, hand in hand,
> Lead him to death, and make him understand,
> After a search so painful and so long,
> That all his life he has been in the wrong.[1]

55. William Hazlitt on Rochester

1818, 1824

Collected Works (1902), ed. A. R. Waller.

William Hazlitt (1778–1830), was, next to Coleridge, the best literary critic of the period.

---

a) *Lectures on the English Poets*, 1818:

Rochester's poetry is the poetry of wit combined with the love of pleasure, of thought with licentiousness. His extravagant heedless levity has a sort of passionate enthusiasm in it; his contempt for everything that others respect, almost amounts to sublimity. His poem upon Nothing is itself no trifling work. His epigrams were the bitterest, the least laboured, and the truest, that were ever written.

(v. 83)

b) Critical List of Authors from *Select British Poets*, 1824:

Rochester, as a wit, is first-rate: but his fancy is keen and caustic, not light and pleasing like Suckling or Waller. His verses cut and sparkle like diamonds.

(v. 372)

[1] *Satire against Mankind*, ii. 25–8. Goethe quotes these lines in English but does not name the author.

56. An anonymous aside on Rochester

1820

Extract from an article on 'The Countess of Pembroke's Arcadia', *Retrospective Review* (1820), ii. 35.

And, indeed, it is remarkable enough, how few of those who have astonished their contemporaries by their wit and genius, and whose name were in their own age held up to an almost idolatrous admiration, have left behind them memorials sufficient to justify their fame. . . . In the compositions of Rochester, what foundation can we find for that reputed predominancy of wit which all his contemporaries allowed him, and which seemed almost to excuse his profligacy and extenuate his vice. We look in vain, in the productions of such men, to find an adequate cause for the lavishness and superabundance of praise which was heaped on them by the devotion of their co-evals.

57. Henry Crabb Robinson on Rochester's obscenity

1820

Henry Crabb Robinson On Books and their Writers (1938), ed. E. J. Morley, i. 247.

Henry Crabb Robinson (1775–1867), friend of Lamb, Southey, Wordsworth and Coleridge, is here confuting an argument that Byron is a great poet because he reveals the depravity of human nature.

Extract from Diary for 20 September 1820: I admitted that Lord Byron's works do exhibit a most depraved and corrupt heart, but observed that he shares this merit with Voltaire, Lord Rochester, and all the obscene and profligate writers of Italy and France.

58. John Genest on Rochester's *Valentinian*

1832

Extract from *Some Account of the English Stage* (1832), i. 411–2.

This work is one of the most reliable and informative accounts of English Drama from 1660–1830.

Lord Rochester plainly saw what parts of the original ought to be omitted, and has very properly ended his play with the death of Valentinian—but he has not been fortunate in his additions, his language being very inferiour to Fletcher's. Nothing could be more a-propos than the revival of this Tragedy at this time;[1] as no Court Chaplain ever carried the doctrine of Passive obedience and Non-resistance to greater lengths than Fletcher does in the *Maid's Tragedy—The Loyal Subject—Rollo*, and this play—his father, who was Bishop of London, had probably instilled good principles into him at an early age—Lord Rochester has added some similar sentiments of his own.

59. Robert Chambers on Rochester

1836, 1844

Chambers' *History of English* claimed to be 'the only History of English which has yet been given to the world'. It was advertised as 'designed to communicate to young persons the rudiments of useful knowledge'. Robert Chambers (1802–71), is remembered as a founder of Chambers' encyclopædia. The *Cyclopædia of English Literature*, an earlier work, was compiled jointly with his friend Robert Carruthers.

---

a) Dryden had some contemporaries of considerable poetical reputation in their own day, but, with a few exceptions, now almost forgotten. It happens that four of them were Earls. The Earl of Rochester, celebrated for his profligacy and wit, displayed considerable talent without producing any one poem of distinguished merit.

(*History of English Language and Literature* (Edinburgh, 1836), p. 86)

b) His poems consist of light effusions thrown off without labour. Many of them are so very licentious as to be unfit for publication; but in one of these, he has given *in one line* a happy character of Charles II.—

A merry monarch, scandalous and poor.[2]

[1] Fletcher's play *Valentinian*, as remodelled by Rochester, seems to have been first performed in 1684.

[2] 'On King Charles', Pinto lxxii. l. 19.

His songs are sweet and musical. Rochester wrote a poem *Upon Nothing*, which is merely a string of puns and conceits. It opens, however, with a fine image. [Quotes first three lines.]

(*Cyclopaedia of English Literature* (Edinburgh, 1844), i. 356)

60. Henry Hallam changes his mind about Rochester

1839, 1864

From the *Introduction to the Literature of Europe in the 15th, 16th and 17th Centuries*.

Henry Hallam (1777–1859), was one of the most distinguished historians of the nineteenth century.

---

a) From the first edition, 1839:

We read with nothing but disgust the satirical poetry of Cleveland, Butler, Oldham and Marvell, or even of men whose high rank did not soften their style, Rochester, Dorset, Mulgrave.

(iv. 433)

b) From the seventh edition, 1864:

We cannot say of Dryden, that 'he bears no traces of those sable streams;'[1] they sully too much the plumage of that stately swan, but his indomitable genius carries him upwards to a purer empyrean. The rest are just distinguishable from one another, not by any high gifts of the muse, but by degrees of spirit, of ease, of poignancy, of skill and harmony in versification, of good sense and acuteness. They may be easily disposed of. Cleveland is sometimes humourous, but succeeds only in the lightest kinds of poetry. Marvell wrote sometimes with more taste and feeling than was usual, but his satires are gross and stupid. Oldham,

[1] A version of Pope's *Dunciad* (1743), ii. 293.

far superior in this respect, ranks perhaps next to Dryden; he is spirited and pointed, but his versification is too negligent, and his subjects temporary. [Discussion of Roscommon and Mulgrave omitted.] Rochester, endowed by nature with more considerable and varied genius, might have raised himself to a higher place than he holds. Of Otway, Duke and several more, it is not worth while to give any character. The Revolution did nothing for poetry; William's reign, always excepting Dryden, is our *nadir* in works of imagination. [Discussion of Blackmore omitted.] The lighter poetry, meantime, of song and epigram did not sink along with the serious; the state of society was much less adverse to it. Rochester, Dorset, and some more whose names are unknown, or not easily traced, do credit to the Caroline period.

(iv. 250–1)

61. An anonymous religious tract on Rochester

1840

The Conversion of the Earl of Rochester (1840), pp. 12, 14.

This booklet, issued by the British Tract Society, is a good example of the use of Rochester as a prodigal son figure. Its facts are drawn from Burnet's *Life*, and its chief interest is in its distortions of Burnet's account. This passage should be compared with the extract from Burnet (No. 10).

Sometimes he [Rochester] retired into the country and exercised his malice and his wit in writing libels and satires, in which he did not pretend to confine himself to truth: and so established was his reputation for this style of writing, that most productions of the kind were attributed to him. This wicked practice, the lies he invented, and the revengeful spirit in which he indulged, he was so daring as to defend.

His falsehoods he sometimes affirmed to be the greatest ornaments of his poems, which could not be omitted without spoiling their beauty;[1] and as to resentment, he considered it impossible for a man to write with life unless he was the subject of it . . . In short he was the English Voltaire.

62. G. L. Craik on Rochester

1845

Sketches of the History of Literature and Learning in England (1845), iii. 130–1.

G. L. Craik (1798–1866), friend of Carlyle and Leigh Hunt, became Professor of English Literature and History at the Queen's University (then College) of Belfast in 1849.

Sedley's fellow debauchee, the celebrated Earl of Rochester (Wilmot)—although the brutal grossness of the greater part of his verse made it and its author infamous—was perhaps a still greater genius. There is immense strength and pregnancy of expression in some of the best of his compositions, careless and unfinished as they are.

[1] It is interesting to compare this with D'Israeli's treatment of the same passage from Burnet (No. 53).

THE BEGINNINGS OF REASSESSMENT

1850–1903

63. 'S. H.', Rochester's truthfulness

1851

From an article signed 'S.H.', 'Information about Nell Gwyn from Lord Rochester's Poems etc.', the *Gentleman's Magazine* (October 1851), N.S. 36, 469–70.

I admit the objections which may be urged against the character of the witness I adduce. The acknowledged depravity of Lord Rochester, the scurrility and obscenity of much of his poetry, and the fickleness of his judgment, cause whatever he narrates, or whatever he describes, to be received with suspicion, if not with disgust. Yet so long as the works of an age are the witnesses of the moral standard of that age, it is only by their perusal that this knowledge can be acquired. So also as regards the lives of public characters. The sketch from the hand of a contemporary, with adequate means of information, is of far greater value than the more finished portrait drawn from the traditional or scattered records of later periods. It is in this respect that the poetry of the Restoration and that of Lord Rochester is valuable. The indecency of Lord Rochester I shall pass without comment. To him may be applied what Mr. Macaulay has written of Wycherley: 'His indecency is protected against the critics as a skunk is protected against the hunters. It is safe, because it is too filthy to handle, and too noisome even to touch'.[1] But to his poetical criticisms more lenity may be shown; his correctness in this respect argues favourably for the admission of his evidence on matters of fact, the truth of which more than most men of his day he was able to

[1] Macaulay, 'Comic Dramatists of the Restoration' *Works* (1866), vi. 515.

ascertain. In illustration of this, let us consider the description he has given of Dryden's facility of versification,—

> —his loose slattern Muse
> Five hundred verses every morning writ,
> Prove him no more a Poet than a Wit.
> Such scribbling authors have been seen before;
> 'Mustapha', the 'Island Princess', forty more,
> Were things perhaps composed in half an hour.[1]

Now these lines may be received as the mere workings of an inimical spirit. He had quarrelled with Dryden. [A brief account of Rochester's quarrel with Dryden omitted.] Yet notwithstanding this, notwithstanding Rochester had been described in the *Essay on Satire* (in which his poetry was also bitterly ridiculed) as:

> Mean in each action, lewd in every limb,
> Manners themselves are mischievous in him,

his truthful sketch of Dryden's fatal facility has been confirmed. The cause was shown by Sir Walter Scott, and the carelessness of the 'loose slattern Muse' has been admitted by Johnson, Hallam, and Macaulay.

Again; all biographers, even his contemporaries, admit the felicity with which he defines in one line Buckhurst Earl of Dorset and his poetry, as—

> The best good man with the worst-natured Muse;[2]

and it is still from Rochester's sketches of Charles that his character is presented to us on the stage, or drawn, with the aid of the acuter observations of Lord Halifax, by the historian.

[1] *An Allusion to Horace*, ll. 92–7 (Pinto, lv).
[2] *An Allusion to Horace*, l.60.

64. An anonymous comment on Rochester

1855

Extract from an unsigned review of *Bell's Works of Dryden* (1854) and *Scott's Life and Works of Dryden* (1854), *Edinburgh Review* (July 1855), cii. 15.

These poems and a few plays were all that Dryden had accomplished at the age of thirty-six. But thirty-six years comprehended the whole life of Byron, Burns, Rochester, and the younger Lyttleton. Shelley, at his death, was little more than thirty: his mind, indeed, had scarcely attained its full vigour. If the *Annus Mirabilis* had been the last work of Dryden, its author would have left a reputation by far inferior to that of Burns, and scarcely equal to the fame of Rochester.

65. A French view of Rochester

1857

Emile Daurand Forgues: 'John Wilmot, Count of Rochester'. *Revue des Deux Mondes* (August 1857), x. 822–62.

Emile Daurand Forgues was born in Paris in 1813. He contributed to many French periodicals, sometimes under the English pseudonym of 'Old Nick', generally on English literature. He translated many English literary works into French including *Jane Eyre*, *Shirley*, Macaulay's *Essays*, several novels of Wilkie Collins, *Uncle Tom's Cabin*, etc. etc.

Part 1. A Satirist at the Court of Charles II.

[The essay opens (pp. 822–25) with an account of the part played by Henry Wilmot, Rochester's father, in defence of Charles II during the Commonwealth period until his death in 1657.]

Here, at the moment of beginning on our subject proper, let me give a few words of explanation. However brilliant the role of Rochester was for his contemporaries, if he appeared to us only as a fashionable hero, aiming by extravagance to achieve literary glory, a witty debauchee, famous for his conquests and his *bons mots*, mixed up in quarrels with contemporary writers because of a few epigrams thrown out or received, he would not attract our attention for a moment: he would have been for us one of those damned souls of the second rank—a confused and abject mob on whom Dante has thrown, like an eternal veil, one of his disdainful and ferocious lines:

Non ragioniam di lor, ma guarda e passa.[1]

No, Rochester was something more than a vicious courtier and a poet here and there of genuine inspiration. His obscene and stinging sarcasms, his virulent and shocking satires depict the history of his age and make of this court favourite on the one hand a bold and successful

[1] Let us not discuss them, but look and pass on (*Inferno*, iii. 51).

competitor of his master, and on the other the faithful and inexorable recorder of a reign shameful to everyone. In this way his character is explained and his poems are of interest and justify our retrieving them from oblivion. He grovelled in the mud with which the second to last of the Stuarts had filled Whitehall and under which all trace of the blood of Charles I seems to have disappeared; but he did not, like a vulgar debauchee, succumb to the brutalising influence of drink, to the pressure of sensuality. By nature he had courage enough and a sensibility fine enough to be only half dominated by the enervating influences to which his youth was exposed. A secret resiliance, even in his worst days, made him re-act against these. Rather than assimilate the poison, he spewed it out in the face of his poisoners. He is certainly not a debased sceptic who doubts and dispises everything, even virtue and justice; rather I like to see in him the despairing believer who, surrounded by universal corruption and, by a caprice of fate, gathered up in a celebratory march of triumphant evil, throws from time to time, a sort of involuntary imprecation, a spontaneous curse in the midst of the celebratory chants, the bacchic refrains, the servile hymns. Such is the originality of Rochester, such the lesson that we can, in my opinion, learn from his life and works.

His life is not very well known. His works, proscribed, with a few exceptions, from all the collections, are hard to come upon in the less exclusive libraries, even in their inmost recesses. In commenting on them with some care, in letting ourselves be guided by contemporary witnesses, who confirm the violent censures of Rochester and make excusable the excess of his angry pen in so far as it can be excused, we aim to place in relief one of the most terrible and most salutary lessons that history can give. Everyone knows, thank God, that anarchy engenders slavery: fewer seem to consider that the exercise of an absolute authority by its intolerable abuses, leads to these same revolutions against which the establishment of this authority has often appeared as the best guarantee.

It was during the year 1664 that Rochester, scarcely eighteen years of age, appeared in Charles II's Court. It was still at the beginning, I would almost say the Spring, of the Restoration. The peculiar enthusiasm of 1660—so singular that it surprised even the man who was the object of it—had not suffered the grave set-backs which made way later for the resentments of 1688. Charles II was in all the flower of his youth and his popularity. There were certainly scandals, and on all sides; but these were tolerated in expiation of the exile whose bitterness the young king had so long savoured, an exile, however, well-enough spent, for during it one can count up to seventeen love affairs of various kinds and of various qualities. He was regarded as a young spark of a king, sowing his wild oats. His sceptical indifference re-assured the bulk of the nation, who, seeing him so bad a Protestant didn't think that he would ever become a zealous Catholic, and that was always an advantage. The servile poets, Dryden at their head, were still singing *Astraea redux*[1] with a quite mythic enthusiasm, sacrificing bulls to the god Portunus and sheep on the altar of tempestuous Oceanus,[2] who had brought to them with the exiled princes an era of eternal peace and fabulous prosperity. Scarcely 14 years of age Rochester—perfectly excusably—had mingled his voice with this formidable explosion of secular chants, monodies, threnodies, hymns, royalist cantatas, and earnt some university distinction or other which was awarded by the austere Clarendon, then Chancellor of Oxford. He arrived then with the triple distinction of his name, dear to all good royalists, his handsome looks, a virtue that did not go unregarded among the distinguished ladies of the day, and his precocious talents, which placed him among the very elite of the nobility, which prided itself, the fashion being such, on its poetry and learning.[3]

[The rest of the essay is largely biographical but the final paragraph sums up Forgues' over-all view of Rochester and prepares us for the second essay.]

We have occupied ourselves with these exuberant and passionate eccentricities enough—perhaps too much. It is time to consider the complex reputation which concerns us under a different aspect and follow Rochester in his relations with the literature of his country and his times. We shall gain from this an exact knowledge of a state of affairs which political liberty has gradually caused to disappear. We shall also gain in this a profound knowledge of Rochester's bizarre individuality, the contradictions of his character, the caprices of his vanity, his mixture of scepticism and indignation, of insolence and cowardice, whose incoherence seems at times systematic and as if premeditated. We shall see there finally how Rochester owes to his faults,

[1] 'The Return of Astraea' a poem of Dryden's welcoming Charles II back from exile in 1660. Astraea the daughter of Zeus and Themis symbolizes civilization.

[2] A bull to thee, Portunus shall be slain,
A lamb to you, the tempests of the Main (*Astraea Redux*, 121–2).

[3] pp. 825–7.

quite as much as to his qualities, the incontestable influence which he exerted for several years on literary trends.[1]

Part 2. English Poetry under Charles II[2]

[Opening section, pp. 144–60 deals with general conditions in the Restoration period and Dryden's career, giving Dryden-Rochester quarrel.]

Under Charles II [unlike the régimes of the eighteenth century] and up to Queen Anne literature was solemnly gagged for the more or less convincing purpose of 'preventing the publication of books maintaining opinions contrary to the Christian faith, to the doctrine or discipline of the Church of England, or tending to the deffamation of the Church or State or the governments thereof or of any other person.' I purposely quote here the actual terms of the statutes enacted against the liberty of the press by Parliament from the first years of the restoration of the Stuarts.[3] In reality these laws protected the profligacies of the king, the scandals of the court, the corruption of the statesmen and the extravagant impudence of the titled courtesans against a publicity which might have made these things impossible.

In the presence of such abuses and under the threat of the pillory, prison and even death there remained only one way open for the protests of outraged consciences, for the decency set openly at defiance; the unhappy method of the pamphlet, the anonymous lampoon, which, rarely printed—most often in their original form of widely circulating manuscript—gave the most direct and energetic expression to everyone's anger and indignation. And who began this most treacherous kind of attack that was in the long run the most dangerous kind ever hit on? The establishment itself. Their rivalries and intrigues soon broke the ties of political solidarity. Sometimes, even, we must believe they obeyed the revulsion of their good sense and the promptings of their alarmed consciences. And while on their part the austere Puritans watched in enforced silence, amassing treasures of bitter resentment and awaiting,

[1] p. 862.

[2] *Revue des Deux Mondes*, xi (1857), 144–87.

[3] This is presumably a reference to the Licensing Act of 1662 (*Statutes of the Realm*, 1819, 14 Car. II, c.33) though Forgues has not translated the actual terms, which read 'no person or persons whatsoever shall presume to print or cause to be printed either within this Realm of England or any other of His Majesties Dominions or in the parts beyond the Seas any heretical seditious schismatical or offensive Bookes or Pamphlets wherein any Doctrine or Opinion shall be asserted or maintained which is contrary to Christian Faith or the Doctrine or Discipline of the Church of England or which shall or may tend or be to the scandall of Religion or the Church or the Government' etc.

motionless and silent, the time of vengeful retribution, it was the courtiers, less respectful of a power whose internal weaknesses they recognised, better protected also against the severity of their indolent sovereign, who assumed the right of censure and added to the priveleges of rank and wealth this alluring monopoly of the liberty to pen unvarnished truth and merciless attack.

Unhappily, instead of a Juvenal or a Persius, only satirists of an inferior order can be found among them. Rochester, the best—much superior to Buckhurst and Savile—is of no higher status than Petronius.[1] And we must not be supposed to have the intention of straining the comparison. Charles II is no more Nero, than Buckingham is Tigellinus[2] or Rochester Petronius. However, allowing some differences, we recognise these two last as kindred spirits, as debunkers of a similar kind. Their two names are equally despised because of a special aptitude of the human spirit for repressing too bright a light and too naked a truth, a disposition in our days in the process of increasing rather than decreasing. However, let us face the possibility; perhaps there is more morality than we quite like to admit in the vengeful sallies hazarded by debauchees of a certain kind in their moments of revulsion. And if we must pass sentence against this or that poem—*Don Juan* for example, which seems at first inexcusable—we would be tempted to reconsider our verdict, remembering that Lord Byron found his most implacable adversaries among the least disinterested, the dandies and the 'stars' of Almack. His most severe judges were just those in whose secret misconduct he had shared and of whom he said, years afterwards, to his most intimate friends 'that there was nothing more corrupt in Europe.' In the light of this terrible accusation *Don Juan* is no longer altogether the audacious, corrupt jocularity so energetically repudiated in the name of public morality. It takes on the character of a witty and courageous protest opposed, by the spirit of the century to disorders revived from another age. Let us try if we cannot see the free satires of Rochester in a similar light.

Let us consider his youth. When at the age of twelve he entered as a nobleman among the students of Wadham College, Oxford, the Restoration had not yet arrived; when two years later in 1661 Lord Clarendon presented him with the degree of M.A. he was still, to say the truth, a child. He left for the Continent, visiting France and Italy

[1] Author of the *Satyricon*.
[2] A chief minister of Nero.

under the tutorship of a Scottish scholar who for a time was able to hold in check the passionate instincts aroused in his young pupil upon leaving the University. Dr. Balfour employed every device on this educational journey to awaken a taste for study and a sense of moral duty in this richly gifted adolescent. Perhaps if he had been able to watch over him a bit longer he would have been able to settle him permanently on this new road, but in 1665 master and pupil returned to England. Rochester was eighteen. He appeared at court. The spirit of the times, the cavalier spirit, took possession of him. This spirit involved at one and the same time the tendencies towards deistic misanthropy of Hobbes, towards the epicurism of Saint-Evremond and towards the bigotted Catholicism of James II—this last dogma thought of as an antidote to those protestant beliefs that were hostile to the principle of absolute monarchy. Under Charles II you could be an atheist or deist, indifferent or catholic, but you could not be at any price any kind of Puritan.

However the unpopularity that Macaulay has so well described in his fine introduction to the reign of James II[1] began to reveal itself. The royalists had in a way begun it by their noisy complaints, their demands and violent recriminations: they had an echo in the first satires of Rochester, who attacks the Restoration directly. Of what does he accuse the prince whose restoration it is? Of tolerance: 'this tolerance', he says 'is as accommodating to the Jews as to the Catholics and even the Mohammedan religion doesn't displease him'.[2] Rochester ought to have asked the two thousand presbyterian ministers who were expelled from their churches in 1661 alone, for their views on Charles II's tolerance, but we shall forget about that. The true grievance of the Royalists will not be long in making itself heard: the King rewards his father's enemies, saving those who caused the head of the martyr king to roll. He refuses bread to the old cavaliers, faithful guardians of the crown.[3] Nevertheless

[1] Macaulay, *History of England from the accession of James II*, ii. 75.

[2] A paraphrase of *The History of Insipids*, st. 4 (Pinto, lviii). Rochester's authorship of this poem has recently been called in question by George Lord and F. H. Ellis, who attribute it to John Freke. Vieth excludes it from his edition of the poems. In a recent article, however, (M.L.R. 65 (1970), pp. 11–15) Pinto convincingly defends the attribution to Rochester.

[3] *Insipids* 37–42

His Father's Foes he doth reward,
Preserving those that cut off's Head.
Old cavaliers the Crown's best Guard,
He lets them starve for want of Bread,
Never was any King endow'd
With so much Grace and Gratitude.

this solitary complaint would affect very few. The poet also addresses himself straightway to what today we would call the protestant interest, to anti-Catholic and anti-French sentiment. Beneath the ramparts of Maestricht a troop of English soldiers commanded by Monmouth had been seen giving aid to Louis XIV in one of his boldest undertakings. 'And for all that' cries the satire 'the rapacious wolf of France, the scourge and curse of Europe has spilt a sea of Christian blood'.[1] We must not deceive ourselves, however, it is not a question of the edict of Nantes and the tyrannical violence that followed its repeal.[2] The curses are directed at the soldier king, not at the persecutor. The revocation of the edict of Nantes happened five years after Rochester's death.

Inconsistencies abound, it is as well to recognise, in these sometimes eloquent imprecations. Charles II had accepted from the Lord Mayor (1674) the freedom of the burgesses of London. The aristocratic poet makes fun of him for becoming 'the premier shop-keeper'. But suddenly and without transition he attacks these shop-keepers themselves, discredited by their fawning before the throne.

> Go then, no more cringing, don't rumage in your purses any longer, opulent city fools. Enough of fetes and flowery speechifying! Beat the drum, close your shops, and the proud courtiers will come to lick the dust off your feet! Once armed tell this Papist Duke (evidently the Duke of York) who is now in charge that you are free-born subjects and not French Mules.[3]

Still better. Once onto this bent the Royalist Satire gradually changes: it has cursed Charles II and Louis XIV, now, drunk with its own audacity, it takes on all kings and every kingdom. It is a *Marseillaise*.

> To say such kings govern by Thee, Lord God, is the most tremendous blasphemy. . . . Cursed for ever be their Power and Name!
>
> May the execration of the universe fall on these monsters, described as sacred

[1] *Insipids*, st. 24, 25.

[2] The Edict of Nantes decreed that Protestants in France should be unmolested. It was revoked in 1685.

[3] *Ibid.* st. 21.

Cringe, scrape no more ye City Fopps,
Leave off your Feasting and fine Speeches,
Beat up your Drums, shut up your Shops,
The Courtiers then will kiss your Breeches,
Arm'd, tell the Popish Duke that Rules,
You'r Free-born Subjects, not French Mules.

by the vile knaves who want to bow before them! What is there then divine in all these princes? Most of them are wolves or sheep, goats or pigs.[1]

We don't add or manipulate anything, on the contrary we abridge, and the proprieties force us to water down. We don't however hide the strangeness of what is quoted.

It will be said no doubt that we are the dupe of some blundering editor, that the satire in question (*The Restoration or the History of Insipids, a lampoon*) is probably apocryphal, that no favourite of Charles II could so have anticipated the invectives of Camille Desmoulins or Danton. To this objection here is our reply: if there is an authentic satire among all the satires of Rochester it is certainly the one that caused him to be banished from court a second time. What will be said if exactly the same idea, the same profession of faith, is to be found there? Actually, in this very curious fragment[2], which defies textual quotation, it is at first sight only a question of Charles II's laziness, his taste for easy pleasures, and this latter point is treated with a freedom of language that is quite latin. Two lines that are reasonably chaste however are mixed up with these derisive obscenities, and these are:

> I hate all monarchs and the thrones they sit on
> From the Hector of France, to the Cully of Briton.

This is the true son of Henry Wilmot after seven or eight years of royal favour: a fascinating contrast and not the only one that can be offered to the attentive readers of Rochester's satires.

In effect we've just found him contradicting—and in what strange fashion!—the royalism that is expected of him; we go on to catch him (that is the right word) in the very act of strict virtue, moral chastity, refined delicacy. To be surprised at it as we are you must have read those foul pages where an unbridled licence has created scenes which

[1] *Ibid.* 148–50, 157–62.

> To say such kings, Lord, rule by Thee,
> Were most prodigious Blasphemy . . .
> Such Kings curst be the Power and Name,
> Let all the World henceforth abhor 'um;
> Monsters which Knaves Sacred proclaim,
> And then like Slaves fall down before 'um.
> What can there in Kings Divine?
> The most are Wolves, Goats, Sheep or Swine.

[2] 'On King Charles by the Earl of Rochester, for which he was banished the Court and turn'd Mountebank', Pinto, lxxii.

recall the most scandalous enormities of Aristophanes. Almost on every page you find words which the printed characters, those compliant letters, seem to refuse to reproduce, words which make publishers afraid, obliging then to conceal them under an initial, or to replace them with a gap which the wisdom of the saintly reader will have to supply. To sum up, here can be found a collection before which our *Cabinets Satiriques* of earlier times pale. The poets of the school of gluttons[1]—the Regniers, the Théophiles, even their coarsest disciples, Frénide and Colletet, Maynard, Motin, Berthelot and Sigogne would have disavowed such a truly frightening paternity. There are some pieces here which, to use an expression of the unfortunate historian of Louis XIII M. Bazin 'would get a man thrown out of the guard-room by his shoulders'. Once this has been said and established you can judge our astonishment at the sight of a true pearl of feeling lost in this vile dung. Let us gather it up, preciously, as we go.

[The next passage deals with the King's mistresses and the spurious piece 'The Royal Angler', pp. 165–7.]

We have wanted to show in this English Petronius a vein of almost democratic independence for which we give him credit. We have also wanted to note in him, in a circumstance we mentioned, a flame of delicate sensibility which makes us believe he had underneath a natural sense of moral rectitude. Strict critical honesty will not allow us to state the case more strongly. Without further rehabilitation—he ought not to be rehabilitated—it will have been sufficient to point out the force of his epigrammatic satire and to have provided the necessary light—in our opinion—for the dispassionate interpretation of the terrible sarcasms that he hurled at a corrupt court. We cannot forget that after being corrupted by it, he became one of the most active sources of corruption in it.

[Forgues continues now to discuss Rochester's attitudes towards the king's mistresses, and Nell Gwyn and the Duchess of Portsmouth in particular, again using texts that modern scholarship has rejected from the Rochester canon.]

We have had to point out the inconsequences, the inconsistencies of Rochester and hesitatingly to demonstrate the disagreement between

[1] 'L'école des goinfres'. Mathurin Regnier, 1578–1613, and Théophile de Viau, 1590–1626, were libertine poets whose example gave rise to a 'school' of free-thinking and often salacious poetry in the first half of the seventeenth century in France.

his life and his writings. Altogether, however, and in spite of everything, he still remains in our view the satirist *par excellence* of Charles II's reign. Dryden was only a marvellously gifted pamphleteer, but in whose writing the period is not made to come alive as it is in those of Hamilton, Rochester, Butler and Marvell. Pepys and Evelyn, naive chroniclers of the curiosities that passed before them can be left out of account. They were satirists without knowing it.

In the work of Rochester two kinds of composition are still to be discussed. In the first he makes use of the philosophical epistle, in the second of non-political satire, the depiction and criticism of social aberrations. This libertine of the streets and the alley-ways had his serious moments, his classical instincts; he imitated Boileau. Why not? Lord Byron admired Pope. In those innocent collections of samples of master pieces and of elegant extracts that is offered for the admiration of school boys you find this frightful name. Like this it passes under the eyes of the demure 'Miss', with white pinafore and rosy cheeks, who will grow old without ever suspecting that a creature like Nell Gwyn or a corrupter like John Wilmot could ever have existed. *The Discourse upon Nothing*, the *Satyr against Mankind* by means of some preliminary bowdlerization, have this strange fortune of being included as university exercises, of penetrating inside boarding schools, of being known equally alongside a homily of Paley or an elegy by Gray. In reading them one is surprised, for they are two pieces which, in my opinion, are of secondary importance.

To establish formally the inferiority of man compared with animals whose existence has always been accepted as inferior to his, to inveigh in turn against the passions which reason controls and against the reason which holds them in check, to seek in almost all human actions the least honourable motives, in prefering to attack those men whose mission it is to lead their fellow men—the leaders of church and state—such is the hackneyed enough basic purpose of these declamations, which the author himself calls paradoxes. A few energetic lines, a few antitheses, do not conceal the emptiness of these sallies of a misanthropy which has since found far more eloquent poetic expression. Five or six stanzas of the *Discourse upon Nothing*—those at the beginning—are ingeniously poetic all right, the others truly ought to be classed among the most vulgar of epigrams. One expects a metaphysical definition, but one is painfully disappointed in seeing it shortly change in order to give way to an equivocal satire directed against the emptiness of certain minds, of certain dogmas, the emptiness of royal promises and also the emptiness of the royal treasury; this last item however perfectly applicable to the ruined finances of Charles II who, bled white by his voracious favourites, did not always have enough in hand to pay his tavern reckoning.

We find more interest in humbler pieces where, without having such high pretentions, Rochester sketches from the life what we would today call *tableaux de mœurs*. These tracts of a pen nothing could stop and, appropriately enough, for very unscrupulous tastes, abound with scabrous details, with exposures and crudities inadmissable now, in this form at least and with this point-blank cynicism; but they reflect a precise moment in time and aside from certain exaggerations, must have been very accurate pictures.

The numerous readers of the *Memoirs of Grammont* should certainly not have forgotten a charming little spot, brought to life by the hand of a master, in the manner of Meissonnier, with a feeling for nature that one does not expect to encounter in a mocking and disillusioned courtier. It is the description of Tunbridge Wells.[1] Placed as it is there among two or three stories of the court, it gives the effect of one of those pretty parks that they nurture in London among the sombre palaces, the smoky colonnades, the heavy porticos overloaded with sculptures. Hamilton in a few lines makes us savour the freshness of 'this great avenue of leafy trees under which you walk when taking the waters,' the comfort of 'these little, neat and commodious dwellings spread over half a mile of lawn, finer and more tightly woven than the most beautiful carpet in the world.' Among these cottages, inhabited by the most exalted nobility of England, on these velvety bowling greens, along this walk, bordered with market stalls, and where an elegant fair is held, you see the fair and fresh village girls walking about, whom he depicts 'with very white linen, little straw hats and neatly shod,' offering their vegetables, fruit and flowers here and there. This delightful place 'as far from London as Fontainbleau from Paris' Rochester has also described,[2] with less sympathetic goodwill and certainly less grace, but with a satirical realism which has merit enough of its own, although some of the malicious allusions he allows himself—to personalities at that time well known—are lost to us today. On the other hand this variegated crowd, different groups of which he sketches in turn, attracts and holds the attention. We follow the poet successively as he records his meeting with a would-be wit, a kind of bourgeois

[1] See Anthony Hamilton's *Memoirs of Grammont*, 1811, ii. 208–9.

[2] The following passage discusses *Tunbridge Wells* (Pinto, liii).

nobleman, as thick in intelligence as in stature,[1] then a sententious and dogmatic fop, got up like a Spaniard, who buys eggs with a solemnity suitable to a member of Parliament,[2] then a group of ecclesiastical dignitaries each discussing his own sickness at the top of his voice,[3] further on, a group of noisy Irishmen, 'wretches below scorn'.[4] However at the end of the lower walk, waiting for her gallant, who is late, a young girl waits, 'leaning on cane and muffl'd up in Hood'.[5]

A pretentious person, hat doffed, approaches her with a deep bow, solemnly clicking his heels:

> Bowing advanc'd, then he gently shrugs,
> And ruffled Foretop, he in order tugs.

The compliment will accord with the pompous preliminaries:

> . . . Madam, methinks the Weather,
> Is grown much more serene since you came hither;
> You influence the Heavens. . . .

and

> With mouth screw'd up, conceited winking eyes,
> And breast thrust forward. . . .[6]

The beauty replies to these artificial conceits like Cathos-Polixene to the Marquis de Mascarille, like Madelon-Aminte to the Viconte de Jodelet.[7] After which he:

> . . . bites his Nails, both to display
> The Sparkling Ring, and think what's next to say.

This gallant, this Amilcar, is then reduced to lament with his amiable conversationalist the bad luck at cribbage the night before which caused her to lose a large sum of money. After this engaging conversation he takes her to the market stalls where he decorates the white breast she exposes to view with valueless trinkets.

No doubt the misadventures of Mrs. Muskerry, which also took place at Tunbridge Wells and which Hamilton recounts so pleasantly,[8] have a superior piquancy to this insignificant chatter, taken in passing, reproduced from the life; but Rochester's satire happily augments for the curious the anecdotes of the *Memoirs*. It furnishes the substratum,

[1] *Ibid.* II. 11–29. [2] *Ibid.* II. 35–45. [3] *Ibid.* II. 47–74.
[4] *Ibid.* II. 75–80. [5] *Ibid.* II. 91–118.
[6] Forgues takes his quotations in English from the 1739 edition of Rochester's *Works*.
[7] Characters from Molière's *Les Précieuses Ridicules*.
[8] *Memoirs* (1811), ii. 213–18.

the episodic figures, the background personalities. Should there now come a Walter Scott he would re-compose from the one and the other a whole day in the life of England in 1667. There is the value, there is the service of these documents that have been collected together from all sides with such care. Scholarship digs them up, genius re-animates them.

Rochester has not translated but imitated the *Repas Ridicule* of Boileau.[1] He made it one of those adaptations, in the English sense of the word, our *vaudevilles* undergo when crossing the Channel. As in the original a short dialogue begins the account that the poet 'Timon' gives us of his dissatisfactions. A fool meets him in Pall Mall and willy-nilly invites him home to dinner. Some wits he says, of his acquaintance will be there, but instead of Buckhurst, Sedley and Savile (taking the place of Lambert and Molière) he meets a frightful trio of bullies inappropriately pretending to wit. To crown the misfortune the host is married to a fading beauty who, regretfully remembering her past triumphs, always finds means to lead the conversation back—however far it has strayed—to the shores of the river of love.

'We got round' says the unhappy guest, 'to speaking of the conquests of the King of France. My lady was very surprised how heaven could allow such success to a man capable of carrying on two love affairs at once. She also wondered how his Majesty justified himself to each of his mistresses. Then she took it into her head to ask her brutal neighbour if he himself had ever felt the ardours of an amorous flame. Eh?' he replied brusquely, 'what do you take me for then, thank you very much?'[2]

We give the sense, not the words, of this impertinent reply. So much for the general tone of the conversation. The manner is entirely English. Timon's host professes a patriotic disdain of foreign cooking:

Our own plain Fare, and the best Terse *the* Bull
Affords, I'll give you, *and your* Bellies *full:*
As for French *Kickshaws, Cellery* and *Champoon,*
Ragous *and* Fricasses, introth we 'ave none.

[1] *Satyr, commonly called* '*Timon, A Satyr*' (Pinto, lvi).
[2] Timon, II. 55–60.

We chanc'd to speak of the *French Kings* success;
My *Lady* wonder'd much how Heav'n cou'd bless
A *Man* that lov'd Two *Women* at one time;
But more how he to them excus'd his Crime.
She askt Huffe, if Loves flame he never felt?
He answer'd bluntly—do you think I'm gelt?

There arrives, accordingly, a piece of beef which would weigh down a horse's back, a plate of long carrots, a joint of pork, a goose, a capon:

> Serv'd up with Sauces all of *Eighty, Eight,*
> When our tough Youth, wrestled, and threw the Weight.

The bottle circulated—not iced, but simply wrapped in a damp rag. Within three forkfulls they have to empty their glasses. The table is besides desperately large. At length the wine begins to take effect, hearts dilate, tongues loosen. The host, formerly a colonel of some malitia, speaks vaguely of 'a fortune consumed in the service of his prince' and of secret service rendered the 'good cause' in Cromwell's time. My lady complains of the degeneracy of modern love and the unqualified licence poets now allow themselves. Youth, if we are to believe her, has nothing in its heart but prostitutes and players. Talking of Falkland and Suckling 'they had fine pens'. With these words literary affairs were taken up. Lord Orrery's *Mustapha and Zeanger*, Etherege's comedies, Settle's *Empress of Morocco*, Crowne's *Charles VII* and Dryden's *Indian Emperor* are considered one by one. From these we go back to the year's military operations. Souches and Turenne are face to face. Who will beat the other? Who will prevail, the Germans or the French? 'The French are cowards' cries one of the guests. 'They pay but that is all. The English, the Scots, the Swiss, they are true soldiers, the others good on parade. Think of Crécy, Agincourt and Poitiers'. But here the insolent harangue is rudely interrupted:

> What they were then I know not, now th'are brave,
> He than denyes it—lyes, and is a *Slave*
> (Says *Huffe* and frown'd). . . .[1]

On that, in honour of France and of its warriors, the two bullies take each other by the hair. In the imitation, as in the original, this grotesque struggle brings the dinner and the satire to an end.

We have dwelt enough on these poems, whose value and importance exist only for literary history and for studious explorers of former times, of forgotten customs, of scenes of private life from this or that epoch and this or that country. Let us now pass on to the last days of this agitated existence, adventurous, full of noise, of excitement; splendid, devouring, devoured.

Rochester had given full rein to his youth. It had dragged him beyond vulgar dissipation to audacities of all kinds. An eloquent and active

[1] II. 163–5.

apostle, he had made conversions to immorality: his debauchery, which he had erected into a system—not without himself laughing at his strange maxims—counted a certain number of disciples. He had at times preached atheism with a success that astonished him, for which we are told he was almost afraid of himself. Whatever might happen to this remorse it produced no effect, it is said that later when all kinds of excess had brought him to the edge of the grave, he had a more serious return of conscience; this found access to an imagination ardent rather than systematic, in a reason which at no time, it seems to me, had mastered its contradictory impulses. The church then was able to announce triumphantly that all the sarcasm he had thrown out, the noisy denials he had offered to its dogmas, the demented behaviour he had shown in his intrepid sensualism, erected into a philosophical system, ended conclusively in the most humble and sincere repentance. The church didn't miss its opportunity.

[Forgues ends his article, pp. 178–87, with an account of Burnet's *Life of Rochester* and a summary view of the Restoration period as a whole.]

66. George Gilfillan: Rochester as wicked moralist

1860

Specimens with Memoirs of the Less-known British Poets, 3 vols. (Edinburgh, 1860), ii. 189.

George Gilfillan (1813–78), a Scottish minister, was a prolific editor and literary historian. Two of Rochester's songs are represented in the *Specimens*, a version of 'At last you'l force mee to confess' (Pinto, xxx) and 'My dear Mistress has a heart' (Pinto, xxvi).

We hear of the Spirit of Evil on one occasion entering into swine, but, if possible, a stranger sight is that of the Spirit of Poetry finding a similar incarnation. Certainly the connexion of genius in the Earl of Rochester with a life of the most degrading and desperate debauchery is one of the chief marvels of this marvellous world. [Provides biographical information.] With [his] early courage some of his biographers have contrasted his subsequent reputation for cowardice, his slinking away out of street-quarrels, his refusing to fight the Duke of Buckingham, etc. This diversity at different periods may perhaps be accounted for on the ground of the nervousness which continued dissipation produces, and perhaps from his poetical temperament. A poet, we are persuaded, is often the bravest, and often the most pusillanimous of men. Byron was unquestionably in general a brave, almost a pugnacious man; and yet he confesses that at certain times, had one proceeded to horsewhip him, he would not have had the hardihood to resist. Shelley, who, in a tremendous storm, behaved with dauntless heroism, and who would at any time have acted on the example of his own character in *Prometheus*, who, in a shipwreck,

gave an enemy
His plank, then plunged aside to die,

was yet subject to paroxysms of nervous horror, which made him perspire and tremble like a spirit-seeing steed. Rochester had the same temperament, and a similar creed, with these men, although inferior to them both in *morale* and in genius. . . .

[Provides biographical information.]

. . . His poems appeared in the year of his death, professing on the title page to be printed at Antwerp. They contain much that is spurious, but some productions that are undoubtedly Rochester's. They are at the best, poor fragmentary exhibitions of a vigorous, but undisciplined mind. His songs are rather easy than lively. His imitations are distinguished by grace and spirit. His *Nothing* is a tissue of clever conceits, like gaudy weeds growing on a sterile soil, but here and there contains a grand and gloomy image, such as—

> And rebel Light obscured thy reverend dusty face.

His *Satire against Man* might be praised for its vigorous misanthropy, but is chiefly copied from Boileau.

Rochester may be signalised as the first thoroughly depraved and vicious person, so far as we remember, who assumed the office of the Satirist,—the first, although not, alas! the last human imitator of 'Satan accusing Sin'. Some satirists before him had been faulty characters, while rather inconsistently assailing the faults of others; but here, for the first time, was a man of no virtue, or belief in virtue whatever, (his tenderness to his family, revealed in his letters, is just that of the tiger fondling his cubs, and seeming, perhaps, to *them* a 'much misrepresented character',) and whose life was one mass of wounds, bruises, and putrefying sores,—a naked satyr who gloried in his shame,—becoming a severe castigator of public morals and of private character. Surely there was a gross anomaly implied in this, which far greater genius than Rochester's could never have redeemed.

67. Hippolyte Taine on Rochester

1863

History of English Literature (1863), translated by H. van Laun (1878), i. 469–70.

Hippolyte Taine (1828–93), French historian and critic, perhaps the most distinguished foreign commentator in the nineteenth century on English life and letters. His *History of English Literature*, published in four volumes in 1864, is regarded as one of his most important works.

From carnage they thew themselves into debauchery. You should read the life of the Earl of Rochester, a courtier and a poet, who was the hero of the time. His manners were those of a lawless and wretched mountebank; his delight was to haunt the stews, to debauch women, to write filthy songs and lewd pamphlets; he spent his time between scandal with the maids of honour, broils with men of letters, the receiving of insults, the giving of blows. By way of playing the gallant, he eloped with his wife before he married her. To make a display of scepticism, he ended by declining a duel, and gained the name of a coward. For five years together he was said to be drunk. The spirit within him failing of a worthy outlet, plunged him into adventures more befitting a clown. Once with the Duke of Buckingham he rented an inn on the Newmarket road, and turned innkeeper, supplying the husbands with drink and defiling their wives. He introduced himself, disguised as an old woman, into the house of a miser, robbed him of his wife, and passed her on to Buckingham. The husband hanged himself; they made very merry over the affair. At another time he disguised himself as a chairman, then as a beggar, and paid court to the gutter-girls. He ended by turning charlatan, astrologer, and vendor of drugs for procuring abortion, in the suburbs. It was the licentiousness of a fervid imagination, which fouled itself as another would have adorned it, which forced its way into lewdness and folly as another would have done into sense and beauty. What can come of love in hands like these? One cannot copy even the titles of his poems; they were written only for the haunts of vice. Stendhal said that love is like a dried up bough cast into a mine; the crystals cover it, spread out into filagree work, and end by converting the worthless stick into a sparkling tuft of the purest diamonds. Rochester begins by depriving love of all its adornment, and to make sure of grasping it, converts it into a stick. Every refined sentiment, every fancy; the enchantment, the serene, sublime glow which transforms in a moment this wretched world of ours; the illusion which, uniting all the powers of our being, shows us perfection in a finite creature, and eternal bliss in a transient emotion,—all has vanished; there remain but satiated appetites and palled senses. The worst of it is, that he writes without spirit, and methodically enough. He has no natural ardour, no picturesque sensuality; his satires prove him a disciple of Boileau. Nothing is more disgusting than obscenity in cold blood. One can endure the obscene works of Giulio Romano, and his Venetian voluptuousness, because in them genius sets off sensuality, and the loveliness of the splendid coloured draperies transforms an orgie into a work of art. We pardon Rabelais, when we have entered into the deep current of manly joy and vigour, with which his feasts abound. We can hold our nose and have done with it, while we follow with admiration, and even sympathy, the torrent of ideas and fancies which flows through his mire. But to see a man trying to be elegant and remaining coarse, endeavouring to paint the sentiments of a navvy in the language of a man of the world, who tries to find a suitable metaphor for every kind of obscenity, who plays the blackguard studiously and deliberately, who, excused neither by character, nor the glow of fancy, nor science, nor genius, degrades a good style of writing to such a work, —it is like a rascal who sets himself to sully a set of gems in a gutter. The end of all is but disgust and sickness. While La Fontaine continues to the last day capable of tenderness and happiness, this man at the age of thirty insults the weaker sex with spiteful malignity:

> When she is young, she whores herself for sport;
> And when she's old, she bawds for her support. . . .
> She is a snare, a shamble, and a stews;
> Her meat and sauce she does for lechery chuse,
> And does in laziness delight the more,
> Because by that she is provoked to whore.
> Ungrateful, treacherous, enviously inclined,
> Wild beasts are tamed, floods easier far confined,
> Than is her stubborn and rebellious mind. . . .

Her temper so extravagant we find,
She hates or is impertinently kind.
Would she be grave, she then looks like a devil,
And like a fool or whore, when she be civil. . . .
Contentious, wicked, and not fit to trust,
And covetous to spend it on her lust.[1]

What a confession is such a judgment! what an abstract of life! You see the roisterer dulled at the end of his career, dried up like a mummy, eaten away by ulcers. Amid the choruses, the crude satires, the remembrance of abortive plans, the sullied enjoyments which are heaped up in his wearied brain as in a sink, the fear of damnation is fermenting; he dies a devotee at the age of thirty-three years.

68. *A Satire against Mankind* quoted

1872–80

---

a) By Benjamin Jowett, 1872:

Some eighteenth-century [*sic*] verses, which he was very fond of, and often repeated, I have forgotten; but perhaps you can recover them. All I remember of them is:

Thus age and sad experience, hand in hand,
Led him to God, and made him understand
That all his life he had been in the wrong.[2]

(A letter from Edwin Harrison to the authors, 12 July 1872, E. Abbott and L. Campbell, *The Life and Letters of Benjamin Jowett* (1897), ii. 38)

[1] It is doubtful if these lines are Rochester's, at least I have not been able to find them in any edition of his works. (tr.). Hayward prints these lines, under the title 'The Nature of Women', *Works*, p. 111. Subsequent editors have omitted the poem as spurious. Its first attribution to Rochester is not until Bragge's not very reliable edition of the *Works*, 1707.

[2] An ironically garbled version of lines 25–8 of *A Satire against Mankind*. Jowett's biographers give a more accurate version and add 'I owe the identification to the Rev. H. E. D. Blakiston of Trinity College, Oxford.'

b) By Alfred, Lord Tennyson, *c.* 1874–80:

His taste lay chiefly in sixteenth and seventeenth century poetry, in which he was widely read, and which he used to quote with admirable power. I can still remember the almost terrible force he threw into the noble lines of Rochester on the 'Vanity of Human Reason'.

'Reason an *ignis fatuus* of the mind . . .'[1]

('The Reminiscencies of the Right Honourable W. E. H. Lecky 1874–80', Hallam, Lord Tennyson, *Tennyson, a Memoir*, ii. 201)

69. Charles Cowden Clarke on Rochester

1871

Extract from 'On the Comic Writers of England', the *Gentleman's Magazine* (November 1871), N.S. vii. 693–5.

Charles Cowden Clarke 1787–1877 was a friend of Keats, Lamb, Leigh Hunt, Hazlitt and, later, Dickens. He was a prolific writer and is perhaps best remembered now for his contribution to Shakespeare scholarship.

One essay in this series having been devoted to the illustrious author of *Hudibras*, I pass (with this simple reference) to his eminent contemporary, the witty Lord Rochester.

When some miserable wretch lies charged with an atrocious crime, there is no lack of daily agents to supply the gaping multitude with tales of enormity imputed to his charge, the greater part being pure fictions. This was the fortune of Lord Rochester, who was by nature one of the most brilliant, as he was by practice the most perilously licentious, wit

[1] Lines 12–28 of *A Satire against Mankind* are quoted here.

of his age. In the collected editions of his poems—or poems attributed to him—a large proportion of them are so unworthy of his talent that it were unbelievable he could have so written below himself. The man had quite enough to answer for on the score of moral delinquency without having stupidity as well as indecency heaped upon his memory. But, indeed, the amount of natural ability that he possessed, and the proofs of it adduced by the testimony of the best judges (his contemporaries), justified his candidature to a niche with the satirists. He was evidently a spoiled child of the Court at the Restoration; for upon his early introduction to that world of ribaldry, he is said to have been remarkable for the modesty of his demeanour, even to a tendency to *blush*, when distinguished in company. His 'virgin modesty', however, soon became case-hardened in the Court furnace, and strange indeed was the course he ran.

With an inborn talent for shedding a lustre over the horizon of the gayest and most intellectual circles, he did not decline hazarding his person in the rudest warfare. He was a volunteer in the great Dutch fight under Albemarle; and was afterwards in the desperate affair at Berghem. Nothing but excess of excitement, and of triumph in everything he undertook, seemed to content him.

Rochester also inherited from nature a noble generosity of disposition, an invariable affability of demeanour, and a repugnance to all meanness in whatever station he found it; which he vented upon prince or commoner in a strain of invective as surprising for its intrepidity as in its diction it was copious and forcible. Marvell, who was no feeble or partial judge, and was himself a keen satirist, used to say that 'Rochester was the only man in England who had the true vein of satire.'[1] It is to be presumed that Marvell would consider Butler as a 'star dwelling so far apart' that with him no comparison could be instituted. Bishop Burnett also, when speaking of Rochester, says that he defended his personal sallies against public characters by saying that 'there were some people who could not be kept in order, or admonished, but in that way.' It has been said that 'some brains will yield to an appeal, others only to a *crow-bar*.'

Before his last illness Rochester began to alter his way of life, and to inform himself of public business, and especially of the constitution of his country. He spoke at times in the House of Peers with general approbation; and there is little doubt that, with his uncommon powers of understanding, he would have become as celebrated for his acuteness

[1] Quoted by John Aubrey (No. 29).

in civil policy as he had already been the admiration of the literary community for the remarkable fluency as well as versatility of his wit and fancy. His reform, however, commenced too late; and, like other wits of the same era, he seemed to have lived, as it were, in an atmosphere of hydro-oxygen, kindling the vital spark to an intensity of splendour, and thereby anticipating its natural resources. Worn out with intemperance, he died in the bosom of Mother Church, at the early age of thirty-three.

One branch of Rochester's talent consisted in the most successful mimicry. When he was banished from the Court, for some personal libel on the Duke of York (James II), whom he pursued with implacable hatred, and when he was, in fact, playing at hide-and-seek with the civil powers, he upon one occasion turned mountebank, and harangued the populace upon Tower Hill in a strain of extraordinary cleverness, acting his part of the quack with such truth that even those who were in his secret could perceive nothing by which he might be betrayed.

Rochester's satires are by no means to be indiscriminately instanced; and the keenest are the least tolerable anywhere. Here are four lines from his *Satire on the Times*,[1] quoted solely to give an idea of the rough and bold speaking of that age, when even the highest persons in the State became the objects of a lynch-law vituperation. In the reign of Charles II licence of speech and licentiousness of morals appear to have struggled for a bad pre-eminence—each a natural consequence of the other; and the consequence was as fortunate as natural; for, like the Kilkenny cats, they devoured each other. This is the passage of personality alluded to; it is an attack upon the same Duke of York, who was Lord High Admiral. Its coarse insolence forms its distinguishing feature:—

> This is the man whose vice each satire feeds;
> And for whom no one virtue intercedes:
> Destin'd for England's plague from infant time;
> Curs'd with a person fouler than his crime.

Rochester's poem on *Nothing* has been justly celebrated for its wit and originality; indeed, it comprises more novelty of thought and satirical point than any of his poems. Every stanza contains an epigram; and each is relieved by a grave or playful allusion to the subject, and its term, *Nothing*. Here is a grave stanza, which seems almost like irony as coming from so ribald a pen: but Rochester was a ribald from example

[1] Now rejected from the Rochester canon.

and contamination, not from nature and principle. He thus writes on *Nothing*:—

> Yet this of thee the wise may truly say:
> Thou from the virtuous Nothing tak'st away;
> And to be part of thee the wicked wisely pray.

The next stanza contains a playful sarcasm:—

> Whilst weighty Something modestly abstains
> From princes' coffers, and from statesmen's brains;
> And Nothing there like stately Nothing reigns.

And here is the summary and conclusion of the poem:—

> French truth, Dutch prowess, British policy,
> Hibernian learning, Scotch civility,
> Spaniards' despatch, Danes' wit, are mainly seen in thee!

As an instance that Rochester knew the better course of religious principles, although he was swayed by the evil, an anecdote is told of one of the Bishops at Court relating, in his hearing, to King Charles, the increase and popularity of Baxter the Nonconformist divine's preaching; adding, 'I went down, your Majesty, into his neighbourhood, and preached myself; and yet, my congregation was very small, while Baxter's was too numerous for the church.' Rochester quickly replied, 'Your Majesty can be at no loss to recognise the cause of my lord Bishop's non-success in his mission; since his lordship confesses to your Majesty that he went to "*preach himself*;" now Baxter preached no one but his Master.' The playfulness of the retort harmonises with the feeling which dictated it.

70. Henry Morley is contemptuous

1873

A First Sketch of English Literature (1873), p. 667.

This 'sketch of English Literature' by the Professor of English at London University went through numerous editions and reprints between the first edition in 1873 and the end of the century.

In 1680 Burnet wrote an account of the penitent close of the dissolute life of John Wilmot, Earl of Rochester, one of the court wits who trifled in verse, and whose best piece of verse is upon *Nothing*.

A courtier and poet of much higher mark was Wentworth Dillon, Earl of Roscommon.

71. Edmund Gosse on Rochester

1880

From the introduction to a selection of Rochester's poems in *The Seventeenth Century* (1880), pp. 424–5. This is a volume in the collection *The English Poets*, ed. T. H. Ward.

Sir Edmund Gosse (1849–1928), was a distinguished scholar and critic. The selection of Rochester's poetry in the anthology consists of six of the songs (including the spurious 'I cannot change as others do'—probably by Carr Scroope) and an epigram on Charles II.

By a strange and melancholy paradox the finest lyrical poet of the Restoration was also its worst-natured man. Infamous in a lax age for his debaucheries, the Earl of Rochester was unfaithful as a subject, shifting and treacherous as a friend, and untrustworthy as a man of honour. His habitual drunkenness may be taken perhaps as an excuse for the physical cowardice for which he was notorious, and his early decline in bodily strength as the cause of his extreme bitterness of tongue and savage malice. So sullen was his humour, so cruel his pursuit of sensual pleasure, that this figure seems to pass through the social history of his time, like that of a veritable devil. Yet there were points at which the character of this unfortunate and abandoned person was not wholly vile. Within our own age his letters to his wife have surprised the world by their tenderness and quiet domestic humour, and, above all, the finest of his songs reveal a sweetness and purity of feeling for which the legends of his life are very far from preparing us.

The volumes which continued to be reprinted for nearly a century under the title of Rochester's Poems form a kind of 'Parnasse Satyrique' into which a modern reader can scarcely venture to dip. Of this notorious collection a large part was spurious; the offensive matter that had to be removed from the writings of Dorset, Buckinghamshire, Butler, and other less famous profligate poets, found an asylum under the infamy of the name of Rochester. But readers who are fortunate enough to secure the volume edited by the dead poet's friends in 1691 will find no more indiscretions than are familiar in all poetry of the Restoration, and will discover, what they will not find elsewhere, the exquisite lyrics on which the fame of Rochester should rest. His satires, as trenchant and vigorous as they are foul, are not included in this edition; he uses the English language in them as Poggio and Filelfo[1] had used Latin. As a dramatist he is only known by his adaptation, or travesty, of Fletcher's tragedy of *Valentinian*; of which the sole point of interest is that he omitted all Fletcher's exquisite songs, including the unequalled 'Hear ye ladies that despise,' and introduced a very good song of his own, the latter as characteristically of the Restoration as the former were Elizabethan.

With Rochester the power of writing songs died in England until the age of Blake and Burns. He was the last of the cavalier lyrists, and in some respects the best. In the qualities that a song demands, simplicity, brevity, pathos and tenderness, he arrives nearer to pure excellence than any one between Carew and Burns. His style is without adornment, and, save in this one matter of song-writing, he is weighed down by the dryness and inefficiency of his age. But by the side of Sedley or of

[1] Two early fifteenth-century Italian humanist poets.

Congreve he seems as fresh as by the side of Dryden he seems light and flowing, turning his trill of song brightly and sweetly, with the consummate artlessness of true art. Occasionally, as in the piece, not quoted here, called *The Mistress*, he is surprisingly like Donne in the quaint force and ingenuity of his images. But the fact is that the muse of Rochester resembles nothing so much as a beautiful child which has wantonly rolled itself in the mud, and which has grown so dirty that the ordinary wayfarer would rather pass it hurriedly by, than do justice to its native charms.

72. Article in the *Encyclopaedia Britannica*

1886

The first edition of the *Encyclopaedia Britannica* (Edinburgh, 1771) has no entry on Rochester. Thereafter notices are largely biographical. The comments on the poetry in the third and fourth editions (1797, 1810), for instance, are confined to quoting Walpole's disapproval. The extract from the ninth edition is exceptional. Later editions revert to a largely biographical interest.

Extract from the ninth edition:

Rochester was one of the unworthies of the 'merry monarch, scandalous and poor'

> Who never said a foolish thing
> Nor ever did a wise one.

Rochester is the author of both of these imperishable descriptions of Charles II, and by them and his poem *Upon Nothing* and his death bed conversation with Bishop Burnet is now chiefly known. His poetry has hardly had a fair chance against that of his contemporaries, for owing to his scandalous character, which was probably worse than the time only in respect of his ostentatious defiance of proprieties, all kinds of indecencies were fathered upon him and inserted in unauthorized editions of his works. This has ensured his exclusion from decent libraries, an edition issued in 1691 by friends careful of his memory having been pushed out of sight by the more piquant publications. [Comment on his character omitted.] Some of his lyrics are very pretty, full of ingenious fancy and musical rhythm, but wit and intellect are more marked in his writing than the free flow of lyrical sentiment. For wit, versatility and intense vitality of intellect this strangely wasted life stood high above the level of the age.

73. W. H. Dircks: Rochester as lyric poet

1891

Cavalier and Courtier Lyrists (1891), pp. xxi–xxii.

The small anthology of minor seventeenth-century verse from the introduction of which this extract is taken includes twelve lyrics under Rochester's name, two of which are spurious.

To Rochester, the most pernicious of scamps, and perhaps the most exquisite lyrist of his day, it is left to set forth with fine conviction and exquisite sweetness of measure, the ideal of the constant lover:

> I cannot change as others do
> Though you unjustly scorn . . .[1]

Rochester may almost be regarded as the Verlaine of his period,—a singer of such truth and melody; who, while he did not neglect to prostitute his verse shamelessly enough, can contrive at times to give poetic effect even to a philosophy of easy depravity; and whose legacy is a few careless perfect songs.

[1] The whole of the first stanza of this lyric is quoted and the complete poem is included among the twelve selected for the anthology. David Vieth has recently demonstrated, however, that the poem is probably by Sir Carr Scroope.

74. G. S. Street, 'Rochester'

1892

Article in the *National Observer* (5 March 1892)

This article was republished in book form in *Miniatures and Moods* (1893). Its use of sources is completely uncritical but there are some valid critical judgments.

To a certain order of mind the contemplation of a laborious and useful life, ending full of years and deserved honours, though that life be coloured by commanding abilities, has less of attraction in it than the memory of a genius on whom, after a brief period of fitful dazzling, the gods have put the seal of their love. It is odd, then, that Rochester, who died in his thirty-fourth year, confessed pre-eminent in wit by the universal judgment of his time, and eulogised for it by a critic so antipathetic to his failings as Dr. Johnson—Rochester, the hero of so many adventures desperately wicked—should be known to most readers to-day only for a couple of moderate epigrams on Charles the Second. His coarseness occurs at once to your mind; but that can be matched in many a well-known author—in Catullus, for example, read in schools and furnished with one of the most elaborate and learned commentaries in the record of English scholarship. In the matter of circumstantial excursions on forbidden ground Rabelais beats him to nothingness. Not mere coarseness is the reason, but the fact that Rochester chooses almost invariably as his material subjects whose mention is offensive to our manners. Had he but smeared a page with ribaldry here and there, a common pair of scissors had secured him permanence. But in truth—be it that an obsession of such things was the cause, or an enjoyment of amused deprecation, or (but this is not likely) a lower pride in his daring—effects and motives on which we have agreed to silence are his usual themes; so that if you remove the coarseness you leave nothing behind—or rather his poem upon Nothing (and one or two more), which Johnson calls his strongest effort. There one may suppose with deference that the Doctor was misled by his chaste mind; for, in spite of some well-sounding lines, the thing is but a frigid result of easy ingenuity. It is rather in some of his least fastidious attempts that you find exceeding good wit, sense, and pungency; and should there come a time when all natural things shall be free of mysterious evil and reproach, so that pruriency shall be impossible and coarseness motiveless, a time when—most like it will never be—all fields shall be playgrounds for art without exception, then the dog will have his day. For 'in all his works,' says Johnson, 'there is spriteliness and vigour, and everywhere may be found tokens of a mind which study might have carried to excellence.' It is not, of course, merely a tolerance which will allow any subject to be mentioned that is required of him who would read this author, but one which will grant any subject to laughter and gibes; an absolute equality of subjects must be premised. Now and again there is a note of self-mocking pathos, and sometimes of a *sæva indignatio* that reads curiously real, as in the Satire on Charles, 'for which he was banished the Court.' And in some of his attacks on his enemies there is a quite refreshing power of abuse. But do not run to read Rochester, for he is beyond all conception ribald. By the way, he is hard to get at, and the authenticity of some of the poems even in the early editions is doubtful. Even in his own day, says Bishop Burnet, anything extraordinary in the way of satire was laid at his door.

The man's life is of more interest than his writings. Even his friends in those merry times deplored his excesses. In preaching his funeral sermon, a sort of composition not over exact as a rule, the worthy clergyman remarks: 'From the breasts of his Mother, the University, he first sucked those Perfections of Wit, Eloquence, and Poetry, which afterwards by his own corrupt Stomach or some ill Juices after, were turned into Poison, to himself and others.' St-Evremond in that letter to the Duchess of Mazarine in which he places Rochester above Boileau as 'nearest the ancients in Satire,' yet, remarking that he was born in the year of Charles the First's martyrdom, adds the unkind reflection: 'The King was fitter for the world to which he went from the Scaffold than his Lordship for that he entered into from his Mother's Womb.' As for our friends Evelyn and Pepys, the one calls him 'a very prophane wit,' the other 'an idle rogue.' (You may dig out of the last-named gossip a story of how my lord ran away with and married Mistress Mallet, 'the great beauty and fortune of the North.' 'A melancholy heiress,' Grammont calls her, but says nothing of the elopement.) And Johnson finishes him with customary thunder: 'Thus in a course of drunken gaiety and gross sensuality, with intervals of study perhaps yet more criminal'—surely that is passing hard—'with an avowed contempt of all decency and order, a total disregard to every moral and a resolute denial of every religious obligation, he lived worthless and useless, and blazed out his youth and his health in lavish voluptuousness.' In truth he was a mass of contradictories. Distinguished for personal bravery in the Dutch war—at Bergen he took a message from one ship to another in an open boat, hotly fired on the while—he lived to gain a reputation for cowardice in private quarrels. It is just possible that a life to undermine the nerves may not have been the reason for this so much as a contempt for public opinion pushed to an extreme; in the spirit of his own saying that 'every man would be a coward if he durst.' Again, he was often indifferent to the advances of Court beauties, but he would go to an infinity of trouble (as in the famous Newmarket story) for a low amourette. And—one is almost sorry for it—he affords the common spectacle of the rake repentant on his death-bed, if one may trust Dr. Burnet, who to be sure had something to gain by the conversion of so notorious a sinner. He showed then that moral weakness which attributes vices to unhappy opinions: declaring, according to Parsons, that he owed his undoing to Hobbes' philosophy!

But neither these deploring clergymen nor his eulogistic friends appear to have found the secret of his life. It was the passion for acting. The stories of his strange disguises, his habit of going among all classes, speaking their language and adopting their manners, and above all his grand *coup* of setting up as a quack-doctor—('Alexander Bendo's speech' is excellent reading)—show the histrionic instinct. Now he would be a brave soldier, and now the sturdy patriot, lashing the vices of the Court and hurling his satires and epigrams at the King's mistresses —at Portsmouth and Cleveland who deserved them, at Mrs. Gwynn who did not. And, by the way, he was generally, says St-Evremond, 'in contradiction to the Town' in his dramatic judgment; 'and in that, perhaps, he was generally in the right, for of all audiences in polite nations perhaps there is not one that judges so very falsely of the Drama as the English.' Good St-Evremond, had you but lived to-day!

No, you can hardly tell the secret of this complex life. Perhaps it was an insatiable curiosity: the man, for no earthly reason you can think of, set detectives to note him the indiscretions of the Court. Perhaps—perhaps the artificial elegy on him of Mistress Behn was all he deserved:

> Mourn, mourn ye Muses all; your loss deplore:
> The young, the noble Strephon is no more;

and so forth. But Rochester was a man of genius, was (he said) drunk for years together, and died of old age at thirty-three. And yet there is no cult of his memory.

75. Richard Garnett, Rochester as satirist

1895

The Age of Dryden, London (1895), pp. 46–7.

The volume from which this extract is taken forms part of a series on English literature under the general editorship of J. W. Hales. Richard Garnett (1835–1906) was a distinguished man of letters, whose works include poetry, biography, criticism and a history of Italian literature. He was the keeper of printed books at the British Museum, 1890–99.

Chapter 2, 'Poets Contemporary with Dryden'.

John Wilmot, Earl of Rochester (1647–80), is principally known to posterity by his vices and his repentance. The latter has helped to preserve the memory of the former, which have also left abiding traces in a number of poems not included in his works, and some of which, it may be hoped, are wrongly attributed to him. For a number of years Rochester obtained notoriety as, after Buckingham, the most dissolute character of a dissolute age; but at the same time a critic and a wit, potent to make or mar the fortunes of men of letters. 'Sure', says Mr. Saintsbury 'to play some monkey trick or other on those who were unfortunate enough to be his intimates'.[1] Many a literary cabal was instigated by him, many a libel and lampoon flowed from his pen, among others, *The Session of the Poets*,[2] correctly characterized by

[1] Saintsbury; *Dryden* (1881), p. 68.

[2] There is some disagreement among Rochester scholars over the authorship of *The Session of the Poets*. J. H. Wilson's view that it was probably composed as a communal effort by a group of court wits, including Rochester, seems the most plausable conjecture.

Johnson as 'merciless insolence'. Worn out by a life of excess, he died at thirty-three, and his penitence, largely due to the arguments and exhortations of Burnet, afforded the latter material for a narrative which Johnson, entirely opposed as he was to the author's political and ecclesiastical principles, declares that 'the critic ought to read for its elegance, the philosopher for its arguments, and the saint for its piety'.

Rochester's acknowledged poems fall into two divisions of unequal merit. The lyrical and amatory are in general very insipid. The more serious pieces, especially when expressing the discomfort of a sated votary of pleasure, frequently want neither force nor weight. Four particularly fine lines, quoted without indication of authorship in Goethe's *Wahrheit und Dichtung*,[1] have frequently occasioned speculation as to their origin. They come from Rochester's Satyr against Mankind, and read.

> Then Old Age and Experience, hand in hand,
> Lead him to Death, and make him understand,
> After a search so painful and so long,
> That all his life he has been in the wrong![2]

Goldsmith's 'best-natured man, with the worst-natured muse', is purloined from Rochester, who is also the propounder of the paradox, 'All men would be cowards if they durst'.[3] Some of his songs are not devoid of merit. After all, however, nothing of his is so well known as the anticipatory epitaph on Charles II, ascribed sometimes to him, sometimes to Buckingham, and very likely due to neither:

> Here lies our mutton-eating King,
> Whose word no man relies on;
> Who never said a foolish thing,
> And never did a wise one.[4]

[1] Goethe's *Autobiography* (see No. 54).

[2] *Satire against Mankind* (Pinto, lxiv) II. 25–8.

[3] *Satire against Mankind*, I. 158.

[4] The ascription to Rochester is certainly reliable. See Vieth, *Complete Poems of Rochester*, pp. 209–10.

76. Oliver Elton, Rochester as lyric poet again

1899

Oliver Elton, *The Augustan Ages* (1899), pp. 233–6.

Oliver Elton (1861–1945), was a scholar whose range of interests extended from medieval Icelandic literature to modern Russian.

The treachery or cruelty of the clearest-cut figure amongst all these, John Wilmot, second Earl of Rochester (1647–80), were tasted by Dryden, Settle, Crowne, and Otway, his literary clients; and his expertness in self-destruction, which took premature effect, cannot be said to be unrecorded in his writings. These become harder to authenticate when upon Rochester is liable to be fathered every obscene application of wit and finish; but much of his genuine work is to be read in the collection of 1714 (such, liberally remarks his editor Rymer, 'as may not unbecome the Cabinet of the severest Matron').[1] Nothing is incorruptible in Rochester but his sarcastic insight and his sense of style. He has the soul of song, not only in measure but in kind, very far beyond his companions. Against the low spite of the *Session of the Poets*,[2] in anapaests, may be set the Horatian *Allusion* already named, where, apart from his abuse of Dryden ('poet Squab'), he shows sound literary judgment. His *Satire against Mankind* is deeper than its original in Boileau, and his cynicism draws blood. He knew the sting and vanity of luxury, and in the midst of his Satanic reminiscences he expresses them: his mind, as his deathbed talks with Burnet show, wore no blinkers; and his finish, if not (owing to his lack of Dryden's skill with the couplet) all that his age believed, becomes perfect as his tone approaches the lyrical. The ditty 'Tis not that I am weary grown' has little like it for a pungency that is *malin*, yet for once not rancorous. His true songs, 'An age in her embraces past', 'Absent from Thee', 'All my past life', 'I cannot change as others do', have not only the fine chasing

[1] This is a reprint of Tonson's edition of 1691. Rymer wrote the Preface, but was almost certainly not the editor (see Zimansky's edition of Rymer's Criticism).

[2] See No. 75, n.2.

possessed by his school in their record of a love fleeting as the clouds, but the solemnity of a compunction certain that itself is fleeting also. 'Faithless to thee, false, unforgiven, I lose my everlasting rest'. Hence he has depth, and more of the incommunicable than any maker of songs between Herrick and Burns. An unfinished blackguard after all, he was tantalised by his higher moments. The philosophy of the verses *On Nothing* (which are perhaps touched by Buckingham) is sincere: they are not caprice or trick; some of their cadence, which Pope in his parody *On Silence* missed, may even have been with the translator of Omar Khayyam:—

> But Turn-Coat Time assists the Foe in vain,
> And, bribed by thee, assists thy short-lived reign,
> And to thy hungry Womb drives back thy slaves again . . .[1]
>
> Whilst weighty Something modestly abstains
> From Princes' Coffers, and from Statesmen's Brains[2]

The Restauration, or the History of Insipids ('Chaste, pious, prudent Charles The Second'), is but the sprightly application of this temper to the time.

The costume of Horace and Boileau, as worn by these persons of rank and condition, was but a half-success, instructive to Pope; but their lyrical gift, which perished with them, was inherited in their blood. On the best lyric of the time, however, classicism tells. The escape from conceits and the greater instinctiveness of finish accompany the muffling of the higher and more passionate notes. A mood prevails of gallant and mundane sentiment, derived from the school of 'natural, easy Suckling' and of Ben Jonson, and if it sinks often into a too palpable snigger, it can rise into a ritual courtliness. What dies hardest is the old science of splendid rhythm, this outlasts the passions that gave it birth; and in Dryden, in Rochester, nor least in Aphra Behn and even in D'Urfey, is heard the earlier Caroline cadence.

[1] *Upon Nothing* (Pinto, li) ll. 19–21.
[2] *Ibid.* ll. 40–1.

77. Walter Raleigh on Rochester and Milton

1900

Milton (1900), pp. 259–63.

Sir Walter Raleigh (1861–1922), an academic with a wide ranging interest in literature and history.

And if we wish to find Love enjoying his just supremacy in poetry, we cannot do better than seek him among the lyrists of the Court of Charles II. Milton, self-sufficient and censorious, denies the name of love to these songs of the sons of Belial. Love he says, reigns and revels in Eden, not

in court amours,
Mixed dance, or wanton mask, or midnight ball,
Or serenate, which the starved lover sings
To his proud fair, best quitted with disdain.[1]

Yet for the quick and fresh spirit of love in the poetry of that time we must go to the sons of Belial. . . . Roystering libertines like Sir Charles Sedley were more edifying lovers than the austere husbands of Mary Powell and of Eve . . . Then there was John Wilmot, Earl of Rochester. He was drunk for five years on end,—so his biographer, who had it from his own lips, alleges[2]—and he died at the age of thirty-two. Like Sedley, he professes no virtues, and holds no far-reaching views. But what a delicate turn of personal affection he gives to the expression of his careless creed:—

The time that is to come is not . . .

[Quotes stanzas 2 and 3 'All my past life is mine no more', Pinto, xv.]

[1] *Paradise Lost*, iv. 767–70. The passage on the sons of Belial *P.L.* i. 497–502, has often been taken to be a reference to the rakes of Charles II's court.

[2] Burnet (see No. 10).

Rochester's best love-poetry reaches the top-most pinnacle of achievement in that kind. None has ever been written more movingly beautiful than this:—

When, wearied with a world of woe,

[Quotes stanzas 3 and 4 'Absent from thee I languish still', Pinto ix.]

Or than that other piece (too beautiful and too intense to be cited as a sudden illustration of a thesis) beginning—

Why dost thou shade thy lovely face? O why . . .

[Quotes the first stanza of 'To his Mistress', Pinto, lxix.]

The wind bloweth where it listeth; the wandering fire of song touches the hearts and lips of whom it will. Milton built an altar in the name of the Lord, and he put the wood in order, and loaded the altar with rich exotic offerings, cassia and nard, odorous gums and balm, and fruit burnished with golden rind. But the fire from Heaven descended on the hastily piled altars of the sons of Belial, and left Milton's gorgeous altar cold.[1]

[1] Raleigh seems to be suggesting that Rochester is the better poet, if so it is a surprising judgment at this date.

78. Thomas Longueville has little good to say about Rochester

1903

[Thomas Longueville], *Rochester and other Literary Rakes of the Court of Charles II* (1903), pp. 287, 290–4.

Thomas Longueville (1844–1922), published several books on seventeenth-century subjects; including a *Life of James II.* He contributed frequently to the *Saturday Review*. In the book from which this extract is taken he is most interested in Restoration gossip, on which he is a mine of information. His attitudes to Rochester's poetry are less than critical.

As to these best known works of Rochester *Upon Nothing* and *A Satire upon Mankind*, one cannot but ask one's self, when reading *Don Juan*, whether Byron may not have had both of them in his mind when he wrote:—

> Must I restrain me, through the fear of strife,
> From holding up the nothingness of life?
> Dogs or Men! (for I flatter you in saying
> That ye are dogs—your betters far) ye may
> Read, or read not, what I a now essaying
> To show ye what ye are in every way.[1]

Regrets have been expressed at most of Rochester's poems being too broad to be read by modern ladies. Have ladies much loss? His verses unquestionably have their merits. Here and there, in not a few of them, is a brilliant spark of wit: many of them are full of keen satire; they are mostly and not ineptly devoted to the exposition of the vices, and still more of the follies and feeblenesses of mankind. But they deride things evil without condemning them; and occasionally they tolerate vice, while in more than one instance they extol it, even at the expense of

[1] *Don Juan*, Canto vii, st. 6–7.

virtue. Good and noble actions are scarcely mentioned: perhaps Rochester may not have believed in their existence. [Provides biographical information.]

If the poems of Rochester excite the passions, they never stir the emotions. No line written by his hand could produce a tear. There are many jarring notes in his verses; there are few of music. He laughs at the fallen, without ever offering a hand to raise them. His effusions are as devoid of hope as they are devoid of faith and of charity. He had a keen sense of the ludicrous, but none of pathos; and his frequent and dazzling displays of virulent antipathies are untempered and untoned by any relieving evidences of kindly sympathy for man, woman, child or beast.

Rochester's poetry is realistic to an extreme, and it is quite as extreme in its want of imagination; while even in his realism there is little true power of description. He rarely brings a scene vividly before the eyes of his readers, and both his lyric and his dramatic abilities were very limited. The only natural objects in which he took any interest were men and women; and they only interested him with their vices and failings. For their virtues he cared nothing. Scenery did not appeal to his feelings; nor is there any evidence of his having appreciated music.

It might be expected that there would be too great, rather than too slight, an exhibition of poetic energy in Rochester's amatory verses. Any such expectation would be grievously disappointed. It would be scarcely too much to say that there is no love in his love-songs. As has already been shown, they breathe the spirit of inconstancy, in himself as well as in the objects of his amours:—

Then talk not of inconstancy,
False hearts and broken vows;
If I by miracle can be
This live-long moment true to thee,
'Tis all that heaven allows.

Nor did he expect constancy from the objects of his affections. What can be said of the romantic emotions of the singer who could exclaim to his lady-love:—

'Tis not that I am weary grown
Of being yours, and yours alone;
But with what face can I incline
To damn you to be only mine?

The chances are that had it not been for Rochester's position as a peer and a courtier, his verses would neither have attracted much attention during his life nor have survived his death. Their popularity when first written is chiefly to be attributed to their scandalous attacks upon living people, and especially upon living women.[1] Such unsavoury squibs, or libels as they were then not inaptly called, he constantly produced and handed about in manuscript. Happily, only a limited number—and yet too many—of these found their way into print.

To the student of human nature, and of characters which, if not in themselves historical, have attracted notice from having been the friends or companions of historical characters, Rochester's rhymes have a considerable interest, as illustrating their author, and through their author, the period in which he lived; but intrinsically, as verses, they are of little value; and a large proportion of them are worse than valueless.

On their worst and most flagrant features, the features for which they are unfortunately best known, it is not intended to dwell here, but in judging of them, due allowance must be made for the tastes and the tone of the period in which they were written. [Provides information on Restoration society.]

In censuring the indecency of Rochester's writings, it should not be forgotten that there are a few passages little, if at all, less indecent in the celebrated *Colloquies* of the pious Erasmus; and, if we may be allowed to use such a term, for verbal uncleanliness Erasmus, when at his worst, equals Rochester.

[1] Few of Rochester's poems are specific attacks on women and his poetry is sympathetic towards women in general.

79. W. J. Courthorpe: The influence of Hobbes on Rochester

1903

A History of English Poetry (1903), iii. 464–6.

W. J. Courthorpe (1842–1917), had a distinguished literary career in which his edition of Pope's Works (1871–89) and the *History of English Poetry* (1895–1910) were highlights.

Rochester tried several styles of poetical composition, and up to the point at which he aimed, proved himself a master in each. From very early days he had shown that he possessed the power of writing well in verse. Like Buckingham, he was an excellent critic. Some of his verdicts on the writers of the time became proverbial, and his *Allusion to the Tenth Satire of the First Book of Horace* shows penetrating judgment. The frankness with which he expressed his opinions in this poem led him into a dispute with Sir Carr Scroop, who, imagining that he was the person sneered at in the allusion to the 'purblind knight', replied with an ironical panegyric, *In Praise of Satire*, containing some reflections on Rochester's cowardly conduct in a midnight brawl. Stung by the retort, the Earl turned upon his assailant with a furious libel, the point of which lay in its descriptions of Scroop's personal ugliness. Unfortunately for him, he forgot that to be a coward is a worse disgrace to a man than to be ugly, and Scroop contented himself with the pungent couplet:—

> Thou canst hurt no man's fame with thy ill Word:
> Thy pen is full as harmless as thy sword.

The epigram is remembered, while the lampoon has been forgotten.

His best literary work is to be found in his more general satires. Andrew Marvell, a good judge, thought him the greatest master of satirical style in his day, and with the exception of Dryden, Pope and Byron, no man, perhaps, has possessed an equal command over that peculiar English metrical idiom which is 'fittest for discourse and nearest prose'. He puts forward his principles, moral and religious, such as they are, with living force and pungency, showing in every line how eagerly he has imbibed the opinions of Hobbes. His study of the *Leviathan* gave him a taste for the kindred philosophy of Lucretius, and there is something very characteristic in his choice of a passage from that poet for translating into English verse:—

The gods by right of nature must possess
An everlasting age of perfect peace,
Far off removed from us and our affairs,
Neither approached by dangers or by fears,
Rich in themselves, to whom we cannot add,
Not pleased by good deeds, nor provoked by bad.

Hobbes is the source where Rochester, in his *Satire on Man*, derives his contempt for those who strive by metaphysical reason to transcend the bounds of sense:—

The senses are too gross, and he'll contrive
A sixth, to contradict the other five, etc.

[Quotes lines 8–24 of the *Satire against Mankind*.]

The following passage from the same poem, comparing men unfavourably with beasts, and drawing a logical conclusion from the comparison, may be cited as containing the essence of philosophy in the Court of Charles II, ultimately traceable to the *Leviathan*:—

For hunger or for love they bite or tear
Whilst wretched man is still in arms for fear, etc.

[Quotes lines 139–73 of the *Satire against Mankind*.]

From the philosophy of the *Leviathan* to the abyss of Nihilism was only a step. Rochester, in his imaginative address to *Nothing*, did not fear to take it:—

Great Negative, how vainly would the wise
Enquire, define, distinguish, teach devise,
Didst thou not stand to point their dull philosophies!

Is or *is not*, the two great ends of fate,
And true or false, the subject of debate,
That perfect or destroy the vast designs of Fate[1] . . . Etc.

[Quotes altogether lines 28–51 of *Upon Nothing*.]

[1] The negligence of the rhymes in this stanza is characteristic of the writer. (Author's note.)

When he chose to be decent, Rochester could write with elegance in the lyric style. Amid floods of indescribable filth, assigned to him in a volume of his collected poems (for much of which he may not be really responsible), there are to be found songs like the following on *Love and Life*, in which, whatever is to be said of the sentiment, the form is above criticism:—

All my past life is mine no more
  The flying hours are gone . . . etc.

[Quotes whole poem.]

Bibliography

This short bibliography records those works that contain lists of books and articles on and references to Rochester's writings.

HORNE, C. J., Appendix to *Pelican Guide to English Literature 4: From Dryden to Johnson* (1957), contains short list of works on Rochester.

PINTO, V. DE S., *The English Renaissance 1510–1688*, London (1938), pp. 351–2, contains short bibliography of Rochester's work and Rochester criticism.

PINTO, V. DE S., *The Restoration Court Poets*, London (1965) (Writers and their Works No. 186), pp. 41–4, gives a short list of works on Rochester.

PRINZ, J., *John Wilmot, Earl of Rochester*, Leipzig (1927), pp. 309–443, contain a fairly thorough, but by no means complete, list of editions of Rochester's writings as well as lists of works on Rochester and his poetry.

SUTHERLAND, J., *English Literature of the Late Seventeenth Century*, Oxford (1969), pp. 561–3.

VIETH, D. M., *Attribution in Restoration Poetry*, Yale Studies in English No. 153 (1963), gives lists of manuscript and printed sources of poems by and attributed to Rochester as well as a check list (Appendix B) of manuscripts, early editions and anthologies where Rochester's poetry is to be found.

VIETH, D. M., *Complete Poems of John Wilmot*, London (1968). The introduction includes a list of editions, biographies and critical works on Rochester written between 1925–67, bringing Prinz's bibliography up to date.

WILSON, J. H., *The Court Wits of the Restoration*, London (1948), pp. 218–22, contain a short list of works on Rochester.

Index

The Index is divided into three sections: I. Works attributed to John Wilmot, Second Earl of Rochester; II. Rochester's life and personality, characteristics of his works and their reception; III. General (including authors, contemporaries, periodicals, etc.). Rochester is abbreviated to 'R.' in Section III.

I. WORKS ATTRIBUTED TO JOHN WILMOT, SECOND EARL OF ROCHESTER

II. ROCHESTER'S LIFE AND CHARACTERISTICS

III. GENERAL

INDEX